DEATH OF THE
TERRITORIES

EXPANSION, BETRAYAL AND THE WAR THAT CHANGED PRO WRESTLING FOREVER

TIM HORNBAKER

Published by ECW Press
665 Gerrard Street East
Toronto, Ontario, Canada M4M 1Y2
416-694-3348 / info@ecwpress.com

Editor for the press: Michael Holmes
Cover design: David A. Gee

Library and Archives Canada
Cataloguing in Publication

Hornbaker, Tim, author
Death of the territories : expansion, betrayal and
the war that changed pro wrestling forever /
Tim Hornbaker.

Issued in print and electronic formats.
ISBN 978-1-77041-384-9 (softcover).
ALSO ISSUED AS: 978-1-77305-232-8 (EPUB),
978-1-77305-233-5 (PDF)

1. Wrestling—United States—History—20th
century. 2. World Wrestling Entertainment,
Inc.—History. 3. WrestleMania—History.
I. Title.

GV1198.12.H676 2018   796.8120973
C2018-902528-X   C2018-902529-8

PRINTING: MARQUIS   5   4   3   2   1
PRINTED AND BOUND IN CANADA

FSC
www.fsc.org
RECYCLED
Paper made from
recycled material
FSC® C103567

Get the
eBook free!*
*proof of purchase
required

At ECW Press, we want you to enjoy this book in whatever format
you like, whenever you like. Leave your print book at home and take
the eBook to go! Purchase the print edition and receive the eBook free.
Just send an email to ebook@ecwpress.com and include:

• the book title
• the name of the store where you purchased it
• your receipt number
• your preference of file type: PDF or ePub

A real person will respond to your email with your eBook attached.
And thanks for supporting an independently owned Canadian publisher with
your purchase!

For always being there,
this book is dedicated to:

Lola
Wilson

ACKNOWLEDGMENTS

For their eternal support and encouragement, I'd like to thank my family, Jodi Hornbaker, L.W. Hornbaker, Timothy and Barbara Hornbaker, Melissa Hornbaker, Virginia Hall, Sheila Babaganov, Frances Miller, and John and Christine Hopkins.

Additional gratitude goes to my editor Michael Holmes for his tireless efforts and superb advice, and to everyone at ECW Press. Many thanks go out to Amy Miller and the amazing Interlibrary Loan team at the Broward County Main Library in Fort Lauderdale, FL.

A big thank you goes out to wrestling historian Steve Yohe for his unflinching assistance in the creation of this book. For their help in answering my questions, providing documentation, and sharing their memories, I'd like to extend my warmest gratitude to the following: J Michael Kenyon, Don Luce, Jeff Walton, Steve Dini, Gary Juster, Dave

Meltzer, Jim Zordani, Graham Cawthon, Steve Johnson, Libnan Ayoub, Greg Oliver, Daniel Chernau, Gene Bowman, Dr. Mike Lano, Scott Teal, Rich Tate, Dick Bourne, Matt Farmer, Kit Bauman, Brian Bukantis, Glenn Mon, Arnie Weintraub, Noah Warren of the Minneapolis Central Library, Randy Thompson of the National Archives and Record Administration at Riverside, Betty Furimsky of the National Archives and Record Administration at Chicago, and Tracy L. Goss of the Michigan Corporations Division.

CHAPTER ONE

THE ESTABLISHED SYSTEM

From makeshift mats in barns to the largest arenas in the world, professional wrestling has really come a long way to become an international phenomenon. Though its evolution has been gradual, it received significant help from innovative promoters looking to change the core aspects of the business. For example, the matches themselves needed to be improved. Instead of developing at a snail's pace with protracted rest holds, bouts became more action-packed and exciting with aggressive competitors using a whole host of newfangled moves. The introduction of the flying tackle and the dropkick in the late 1920s and early '30s was revolutionary, and promoters wisely built upon their popularity.[1] Around the same time, wrestlers were testing the waters with character-based gimmicks, and good versus evil feuds were born, invoking incredible audience reactions.

This is all old hat in today's marketplace, but in the early days, everything was remarkably unsophisticated. With no clear-cut and defined wrestling organizations to manage the day-to-day operations of the industry, the sport was completely devoid of orderliness. It wasn't until the 1920s and '30s that circuits were fashioned and shows were offered on a more regular basis in specific regions. Wars between grappling syndicates were legendary, akin to those between crime organizations erupting across the United States. But in place of bootlegging and prostitution, promoters were at odds over high-value attractions and territorial control, and money was the bottom line. Those who had it wanted more, and small-timers just wanted to make a living.

On September 16, 1930, the sport's first major three-letter acronym to be used with any consistency made its debut with the advent of the National Wrestling Association. An outgrowth of the National Boxing Association, the NWA was administered by state athletic commissioners, and its mandate was to keep pro wrestling on the level. In truth, those involved were often more interested in the political ramifications and profit margins of the sport than anything else. They monitored the business, stepped in when convenient, but mostly collected money for little in return. The promoters who dealt with the NWA were protected to a certain extent, and if they kept their noses clean, they were allowed to run their operations unhindered.

Rather than be pushed around by political appointees, promoter Paul Bowser in Boston struck back at the NWA concept by creating his own private group, the American Wrestling Association, in 1931. He occasionally worked with local bureaucrats for photo opportunities to garner publicity, but he had the first and last say in whatever happened in his rings. Columbus, Ohio, promoter Al Haft followed with the Midwest Wrestling Association that same year, and, like Bowser, Haft crowned his own regional "world" heavyweight champion, the first of whom was John Pesek. Haft was fully autonomous in his leadership, unlike those in NWA states who were bogged down by hierarchy and regulations.

Bowser and Haft created a local circuit for their wrestlers and champions, and by the mid-1930s, most major promoters had done the same. On a national level, promotional alliances such as "The Trust" were organized and thrived until being destroyed by greed.[2] Wrestling was plagued by a general lack of integrity among promoters, and partnerships were almost always on shaky ground. For that reason, the sport entered a never-ending cycle of conflict. Within the chaos were innumerable heavyweight title claimants, and conniving promoters were doing everything in their power to tear down their rivals. Wrestlers jumped sides with impunity, seeking the best financial deal they could make, and again, an overall lack of integrity left everything fair game.

Yet, some promotional alliances survived. In 1948, Paul "Pinkie" George of Des Moines, Iowa, aligned with affiliates in several neighboring states and expanded his localized "National Wrestling Alliance" into a budding cooperative. This new NWA was completely independent of all established organizations, including the still-active National Wrestling Association. Unlike the Bowser and Haft groups, the Alliance wasn't structured with one man at the top of the pyramid, but allowed each and every man to have an equal membership. And since the body was founded and run by the promoters themselves, they implemented a crafty set of bylaws that protected their interests. Pro wrestling had never seen anything like it.

Of the many statutes written into the new organization's bylaws, the acknowledgment of specific territories was among the most consequential.[3] In common wrestling lingo, a "territory" was defined as a region in which a promoter operated, from one city to multiple states. The NWA supported territory ownership, meaning that once an Alliance-affiliated promoter laid claim to an area, he was untouchable. If an outsider attempted to run a competing promotion, the full power of the NWA would be turned against them. Alliance members would also respect the boundaries of their brethren, allowing all members to book matches and promote events without fear of interference. Member-promoters structured their enterprises as they saw fit, and each office had its own flavor. As a whole, the Alliance acted as an umbrella entity that united the various promotions and sponsored the recognition of a single world heavyweight champion. This sanctioned titleholder traversed the entire NWA map, appearing for promoters in cities large and small across dozens of states. His task was to demonstrate night after night that he was the best in the world, proving to fans that the Alliance was the most important organization in wrestling. Lou Thesz, who was given NWA support as heavyweight kingpin in 1949, took up that extraordinary challenge and succeeded in every regard.[4] His clean-cut, no-frills style was crucial as promoters pushed wrestling's legitimacy. In this kayfabe era, it all worked beautifully. Focusing on bringing in the best big-named talent and fostering a long-term relationship with the wrestling public in their areas, promoters used television to welcome a new generation of enthusiasts to the sport. Must-see performers like Gorgeous George and Antonino "Argentina" Rocca lit up arenas from coast to coast. Within its first year, the Alliance had spread from its humble beginnings in the Midwest to include Los Angeles, Toronto, Honolulu, and New York and all points in between. Membership was attractive to promoters because the NWA's wide-ranging influence all but guaranteed success.

But the NWA didn't eradicate the competitiveness of wrestling promoters and, in some cases, might have heightened the drama. For example, in 1950, Chicago's Fred Kohler, a bespectacled entrepreneur with an enormous sense of humor, found no comedic value in the help his cross-town rival, and non-NWA member, Leonard Schwartz was receiving from Al Haft, his supposed Alliance brother. To Kohler, it was an egregious violation of organization rules. He pleaded his case to Alliance members to have Haft immediately cease his incursion into the Windy City.[5] Haft believed he had a right to book his wrestlers to Schwartz, and the situation escalated into a full-fledged feud. Adding the importance of television to the fray, and with great sums of money involved, neither side wanted to back down. Kohler, in a fit of anger, resigned from the NWA, only to be coaxed back a short time later. Finally, after painstaking negotiations, the conflict was resolved with both operations running peacefully in Chicago.

Under the watchful eye of the National Wrestling Alliance, the esteemed territorial system was born. The map of North America was effectively partitioned and boundaries were set. For the most part, every city on the continent was assigned to one territory or another, and when questions arose about the status of any particular town, the democratically voted administrators of the group worked to iron out the problems, often with special committees appointed to mediate. While the NWA operated with surprising functionality, big personalities were involved, and the men in the Alliance were known for their loud and sometimes obnoxious behavior. They epitomized a boys' club mentality — smoking, drinking, and swearing freely — and when things got contentious, anything was possible.

In some cases, egos were exceptionally fragile, as shown by the ill-fated 1957 plot to split the NWA world heavyweight championship. The idea was to give a recognized claim to French tumbler Edouard Carpentier, while lineal champion Lou Thesz ventured overseas. The sneaky deal was snapped in two after Carpentier's manager Eddie Quinn of Montreal protested independent promoter Jack Pfefer's attendance at the NWA's annual convention.[6] His hatred of Pfefer was so strong that he stormed out of the convention and quit the NWA, bringing an end to the dual championship ploy. A few years later, Quinn rejoined the Alliance, but he never made peace with Pfefer.

Quinn was one of many colorful members involved in the NWA during the 1950s and '60s. Johnny Doyle in Hollywood was a lavish spender who loved airplanes and the ritzy nightclub life. Toots Mondt of New York was a sizable man with an impressive background on the mat. He knew how to create superstars and turned ex–boxing champion Primo Carnera and the Argentinean high-flyer Antonino Rocca into box-office sensations. When he wasn't backstage at a wrestling event, he was usually at the nearest gambling venue, amassing substantial debts. His self-destructive personality hurt a number of once-thriving promotions, and business at Madison Square Garden dwindled in the early to mid-1950s because of his lackluster management. But regardless of his vices, he was still considered a member of wrestling royalty.

Frank Tunney in Toronto was the opposite of Mondt, and was as straightlaced as could be. Don Owen in Portland was similarly respected. Down in Texas, the Houston booking office of Morris Sigel controlled much of the state, and aside from a major blowout with Dallas operator Ed McLemore in 1953, things ran smoothly.[7] Wrestler Dory Funk Sr. and Dory Detton were connected in West Texas prior to the latter bowing out in 1955. Funk then realigned with Dr. Karl Sarpolis, a former grappler himself. Since he was the central star in the territory, Funk's ownership stake was kept out of the press, but insiders knew how much power he wielded. In Kansas City, Orville Brown, the initial NWA heavyweight champion whose career was cut short by a car accident in 1949, was the man in charge. He retired in the early 1960s, and the region was taken over by well-known wrestlers Bob Geigel and Pat O'Connor.[8]

The Southeast was ruled by several different men during the 1950s and '60s. Paul Jones, a smart ex-wrestler and businessman, built a fortune in Atlanta, Georgia. Another former grappler, Cowboy Luttrall was successful in Florida, while "Big" Jim Crockett Sr. controlled the Carolinas and parts of Virginia. Nick Gulas and Roy Welch ran an impressive circuit across the rugged regions of Tennessee and Kentucky, and Harry Light was the man in Detroit. In San Francisco, Joe Malcewicz was known for his generosity to wrestlers, especially those in need. After "Wild" Bill Longson was injured during a bout in 1937, Malcewicz stepped up to pay his medical bills. In a time of greed, it was a righteous move by one of pro wrestling's genuine good guys.

Of them all, Sam Muchnick in St. Louis, who served 22 years as the president of the NWA, was undoubtedly the spirit behind the coalition from 1950 until his retirement in 1982. He was the guy who saw the good in Toots Mondt and Jack Pfefer, while still trying to appease fiery tempers like Eddie Quinn's. Short in stature with a contagious smile, Muchnick was known for his easygoing nature, and he negotiated amicable resolutions to an untold number of Alliance problems. He was so important to the everyday management of the union that without his otherworldly efforts, the NWA probably wouldn't have survived the 1950s intact. In fact, the odds were in favor of the coalition being derailed by the U.S. government in 1956 as a result of an investigation into the NWA's so-called monopoly. Muchnick went well beyond the call of duty to see that the NWA lived another day. He went to Washington, D.C., to speak at length with officials and pulled strings through his political friends. In the end, the membership of the NWA signed a Consent Decree agreeing to halt its restraint of trade. In return, the group would be allowed to continue operating, and Muchnick retained a frequent correspondence with investigators in the years that followed. He wanted to make sure the Alliance was living up to its promises. Despite various complaints that the NWA wasn't truly changing its monopolistic ways, the government never again chose to prosecute. The Alliance, and wrestling itself, had dodged a major bullet.

Muchnick's executive management skills were unequaled. He spent most of his days on the phone coordinating between the various offices to ensure everything was running smoothly. On top of that, he booked the heavyweight champion. It wouldn't be a stretch to say that his own promotion in St. Louis was the third most time-consuming thing he managed during any given week or month, but that didn't stop him from running an exceptional town. His professionalism was lauded by wrestlers and his peers alike. There was a reason why he was the go-to voice in the National Wrestling Alliance for three decades.

Keeping the peace in pro wrestling was a big part of his job, and Muchnick tackled his duties with an even hand. In 1960, superstar grappler Verne Gagne made it clear that he wanted to split from the NWA and form his own sanctioning organization based in Minneapolis, and Muchnick had no problem with the idea. His only goal was to ensure that Gagne and the wrestlers he used in his American Wrestling Association (AWA) remained on good terms with NWA members, keeping all lines of communication open. Muchnick wanted Gagne to attend Alliance meetings as well, and although it appeared to the public that the AWA was a competitor to the NWA, there was no real competition between the two groups.

Three years later, Vincent J. McMahon of Washington, D.C., also decided to break from the NWA and create an independent promotion. Associated with the Alliance since the early 1950s, McMahon became an official member in 1960 and, thanks to his sound business ideas, experienced tremendous growth. His locally produced television show became the most popular program in the northeastern territory and pushed him into a leadership position in New York City, the number-one market in the United States. As McMahon spent time with the Alliance membership, it was hard for his colleagues to not be impressed with his ingenuity and innovation. He was a natural in a social environment, and when he was pushing a concept, people listened intently.

In late 1960 and into '61, McMahon sold the idea of giving "Nature Boy" Buddy Rogers the NWA world heavyweight title. Considering the union's history, bestowing the coveted championship upon a heel performer was far from the ordinary. The arrogant blond grappler was the antithesis of Lou Thesz, a man who had represented the Alliance for years and symbolized the honorable titleholder. Putting the belt on Rogers was a dramatic shift, but, to McMahon, it was a smart move for him and the rest of the organization. Rogers was a box-office attraction like no other, and he delivered high-quality matches against both fan favorites and heels. This gave regional promoters the opportunity to book their top grapplers against the champ, regardless of their in-ring gimmick.

Muchnick and other influential NWA members jumped on board, and the title shift was authorized. On June 30, 1961, Rogers defeated New Zealander Pat O'Connor in a two-of-three-falls bout before a whopping crowd of 38,000 at Comiskey Park in Chicago. Everyone was thrilled by the box-office numbers — the gate was estimated at $125,000 — and great things were expected throughout the NWA. But it quickly became apparent that McMahon and a select group of Alliance members were the only beneficiaries of Rogers's reign. In many ways, the skewed booking of Rogers as titleholder drove a wedge between a number of dues-paying NWA affiliates and what was seen as the establishment of the organization — McMahon, Sam Muchnick, Fred Kohler, and several other high-profile members. Those promoters representing smaller circuits were routinely ignored, and the notion that Rogers would benefit the entire union was incorrect. In the Northeast, though, McMahon and Rogers did exceptionally well. While wrestling championships weren't officially recognized in New York, fans knew from the national publications that Rogers wore the NWA belt. It was win-win for McMahon, and he let Muchnick deal with any disgruntled NWA members.

However, McMahon had a bigger plan for his territory, and ultimately decided to follow Verne Gagne's footsteps and withdraw from the Alliance. His decision was coordinated with Rogers's loss of the championship to Lou Thesz on January 24, 1963, at Maple Leaf Gardens in Toronto. But instead of acknowledging the title change, McMahon claimed Rogers was still world champion. He formed the World Wide Wrestling Federation (WWWF) and initiated a complete change of course from the NWA.

It was already well known that the northeastern circuit, from Virginia to Maine, was big enough to support a champion all its own. No one man could fulfill all the obligations of the region plus maintain a national touring schedule. Rogers did the best he could in that regard, but after months of grueling travel, he was beginning to fall apart. He suffered several injuries, and by early 1963, he was displaying signs of heart trouble.[9] The stress had gotten to him. With Buddy in need of rest, McMahon needed a new champion who could represent his new WWWF with credibility and zeal. Lucky for him, he had a young man in the wings ready for the job. On May 17, 1963, the championship was moved from Rogers to Italian powerhouse Bruno Sammartino in a 48-second match at New York's Madison Square Garden.

The territory was primed for a hero to take the reins, and Sammartino was the perfect antidote for spectators weary of Rogers and his antics. He was a hulking strongman, larger than life, and brought amazing charisma to the ring. In the months and years that followed, McMahon utilized a genius booking scheme for his champion, one that kept fans returning to the arena with gusto. The central idea was to build up a succession of threatening challengers for Sammartino, and Bruno would show his vulnerability in near defeats only to rise up in the end to conquer his opponents. His performance never failed to capture the imagination of audiences. Among his villainous rivals were the 350-pound Gorilla Monsoon, the 6-foot-5 Bill Miller, and the 6-foot-3, 275-pound Bill Watts. As Sammartino worked through one feud, McMahon pushed several other prominent challengers at the same time to keep the cycle continuing all over the circuit.

Appreciated for his babyface qualities, Sammartino was a dominant wrestler and exceptionally tough. He didn't need a gimmick to get over with crowds. Off the mat, he appeared genuine and as a man of integrity. The New York fanbase didn't just buy into any wrestler pushed by promoters, and it took a special breed of grappler to become a cultural icon in that territory. Sammartino's first reign as champion lasted from 1963 to 1971. Few people in history can claim such a prolonged and successful run, especially in a promotion the size of the WWWF. His durability was a testament to his drawing power and physical conditioning.

One of the strengths of the territorial system was the clear-cut avenues for trading talent. Promoters within the NWA, including the AWA and WWWF, loved to send away burned-out workers from their region and receive fresh faces from cohorts elsewhere. This custom kept their shows from getting stale and allowed for new feuds on a regular basis. Sometimes, a big name from another region was enough to spark attendance all over a territory, and promoters relied on imported talent. The appearance of a special attraction was also a big boon to attendance. Women wrestlers, the troupe of little people, and other fascinating performers bounced from region to region, and fans responded in droves.

Even to this day, much about professional wrestling is cyclical, and the popularity of the sport has fluctuated countless times. During the late 1950s, the end of the TV explosion created a sizable economic downturn for the industry, corresponding with the U.S. government's antitrust investigation into the NWA. These factors put a strain on the Alliance, and membership declined from 39 in 1955 to a dozen in 1961.[10] The union managed to endure the hardship and soon regained much of its lost momentum. Notably, Vince McMahon rejoined the Alliance in 1971, and his heavyweight crown lost its "world" title status. Membership did have its privileges, and it was hard to dismiss the benefits of being affiliated to the worldwide contingent. Over previous years, NWA champions Lou Thesz, Gene Kiniski, and Dory Funk Jr. — all effective scientific competitors with their own styles — had given the Alliance enormous international credibility. In comparison, McMahon placed an emphasis on towering, muscular brawlers. The WWWF was seen as a completely different product than the NWA, and the northeastern approach, while popular in that territory, wasn't altogether appreciated elsewhere. And vice versa.

Syndicated television provided many fans with exposure to outside territories for the first time. People in WWWF regions received telecasts from Los Angeles, Florida, and other locales, and their interest in Alliance wrestling spiked. To meet the growing curiosity, McMahon filled his Madison Square Garden shows with grapplers from the WWWF, the AWA, and the NWA, and Verne Gagne joined the Funks, the Grahams, and Dusty Rhodes for appearances. Cooperation between booking offices was never greater.

In 1975, Sam Muchnick stepped down as president of the NWA, an inevitable move he'd been contemplating for years. The loss of his esteemed leadership was a blow, but others lent their experience to the role, starting with Jack Adkisson (Fritz Von Erich) and Eddie Graham.

As for the WWWF, it faced several choppy years and brushed back a handful of coordinated invasions by independent promoters. Bruno Sammartino dropped his heavyweight crown to the "Russian Bear" Ivan Koloff on January 18, 1971, at Madison Square Garden, but Pedro Morales picked up the mantle as the promotion's top fan favorite and titleholder less than a month later, on February 8, 1971. A popular wrestler from Puerto Rico, Morales retained the belt for well over two years, until being upset by Stan Stasiak, a veteran grappler from Canada, on December 1, 1973. Sammartino returned to the throne nine days later, much to the delight of his supporters. He remained WWWF champion until April 30, 1977, when "Superstar" Billy Graham beat him in Baltimore and captured the belt.

Graham had the longest championship reign for a heel since Buddy Rogers and was an astronomical draw. On February 20, 1978, at Madison Square Garden, McMahon went in a different direction, though, and put his faith behind a former collegiate champion, the type of wrestler more likely to star in the NWA. Bob Backlund, a native Minnesotan, was his choice, and his wholesome personality was a stark change from his predecessor. What he lacked in charisma, he made up for in athletic ability, and crowds appreciated his virtuous in-ring methods.

Over in the NWA, the world title passed through the capable hands of Terry Funk, Harley Race, and Dusty Rhodes between 1975 and '79, and Giant Baba of Japan received a week long reign in late 1979. The business, at that point, was being inundated by a classy crop of new blood, and guys like Ric Flair, Ted DiBiase, and Ricky Steamboat were leading the charge.

As the 1970s came to a close, the territories retained their exceptional individualism, but promoters were coming to grips with a variety of new challenges. Cable TV was the biggest quandary. The medium made it possible for a regional operator to broadcast his show not only in neighboring regions but nationally. It was a pathway to immediate expansion, and every established promoter had cause for concern. In fact, the potential of cable made the already suspicious members of the NWA even more paranoid. However, the territorial system, defined over decades, was still in place and safe, and there was no way for an outsider to change that — at least, that's what the old-time promoters believed. But, as time would tell, they couldn't have been more wrong.

CHAPTER TWO

TITAN SPORTS

In a boom period of professional wrestling, promoters easily maximized the weekly box office from live events throughout their regions. A promotion's top priority was strengthening an "A" circuit featuring its top stars in its biggest-market cities. In many cases, promoters also fostered a secondary circuit composed of smaller towns using lesser talent. Spot shows were another important cog in a promoter's repertoire, as these programs serviced locations outside of the regular circuits where fans watched the weekly program on TV but seldom saw the sport live. High school gymnasiums were routinely booked for these events, and in the case of the World Wide Wrestling Federation, spot shows were an essential element of its business. Imagine the WWE today running regular shows at high schools around the country. Just an inconceivable thought, but back in the 1970s and into the '80s, it was a regular thing.

The WWWF's territory consisted of 11 states: New York, Pennsylvania, Massachusetts, Maryland, Connecticut, New Jersey, New Hampshire, Rhode Island, Vermont, Delaware, and Maine. Additionally, the promotion operated in parts of Virginia, West Virginia, and Ohio. In terms of geographic area, it was far larger than any single promotion in the United States with the exception of the AWA, which ran from Minnesota to California and encompassed nine states (and parts of three others). The NWA — a union of promotional offices and not owned by a single entity like the AWA or WWWF — operated in at least 25 states, sharing Virginia, West Virginia, and Ohio with the WWWF and Colorado, California, and New Mexico with the AWA.

Considering the heavy population centers such as Philadelphia, Baltimore, Boston, and, of course, New York City, it is not surprising that the WWWF possessed the most lucrative territory in the business. It received significant mainstream press from New York–based wrestling magazines and had a widespread influence. Monthly programs at Madison Square Garden, the "World's Most Famous Arena," were monetary windfalls for WWWF management, and Vincent J. McMahon carefully booked his events to maintain their sense of importance to area enthusiasts. For that reason, tickets for wrestling at the Garden were a hot commodity, and events were frequently sold out. By September 1980, McMahon's company was in a much better financial position than it had been only a year before, and after taking in more than $4.1 million in total box-office receipts, it had $330,000 more in its coffers than it had at that point in 1979, with $639,000 in assets.[11]

The cordiality between the WWWF, NWA, and AWA — known as the "Big Three" — grew immensely during the 1970s, and McMahon wasn't the only promoter to feature wrestlers from all three groups. Frank Tunney in Toronto, a roundish, amiable fellow with a perpetual smile, also benefited from the cooperation. Tunney, who turned 65 in 1977, began his career as an understudy to Jack Corcoran of the old Queensbury Athletic Club in 1931 and assumed a leadership role of the territory nine years later. With an outstanding cast of wrestlers, led by the ultra-popular "Whipper" Billy Watson, Tunney built Toronto into one of the most successful and reliable wrestling cities in the world.[12] Fans packed Maple Leaf Gardens, drawing immense gates, and the biggest names in the business made

Tunney's city a must for shows. And because Tunney was so well liked by fellow promoters, he received unparalleled assistance when it came to booking his events.

The WWWF was intrinsically linked to Toronto from its earliest days as a promotion, mostly because of the widespread local popularity of its champion, Bruno Sammartino, north of the border. Between February 1964 and July 1969, Sammartino headlined the Gardens many times, earning a good payday for both himself and his handlers. Toronto was an easy flight from New York City, less than two hours, but after the Sheik took over as booker and began a lengthy reign of dominance beginning in 1969, the WWWF pulled back from its active working relationship. In 1976, Tunney renewed things with McMahon, and Sammartino made a triumphant return, followed by his title successors "Superstar" Billy Graham and Bob Backlund. Tunney also broke off with the Sheik, turning to the AWA for steady talent in October 1977, including appearances by world champion Nick Bockwinkel. A year later, Tunney locked in a new arrangement with Jim Crockett Promotions, a Mid-Atlantic-based operation. Tunney's membership in the NWA never abated either, leaving him in the best possible position to bring quality wrestlers to Toronto.

St. Louis was in a similar situation. Sam Muchnick was the godfather of the Alliance, and he was celebrated for the elegant way he managed the union. He was also respected for the above board way he administered the St. Louis promotion, both behind the scenes and in the ring. Muchnick fostered the belief that pro wrestling was a legitimate sport, to be covered with dignity in newspapers, and he banned gimmicky grapplers from appearing in his shows. St. Louis was always considered the headquarters of the NWA, and for talented up-and-comers to be considered for a run with the world heavyweight title, they had to perform well in Muchnick's proving grounds. That's where the Funks, Jack Brisco, the Von Erichs, and many others were assessed by Muchnick for their potential to be the traveling titleholder.

For most wrestlers, St. Louis was a pleasure to work, and Muchnick brought in talent from across the NWA. In 1976, AWA owner Verne Gagne and Pat O'Connor, part owner of the Kansas City promotion, bought into Muchnick's company, adding to the dynamics in the city. Shows often highlighted wrestlers from the AWA, Kansas City, the WWA in Indianapolis, and a number of NWA offices, demonstrating that St. Louis was one of wrestling's most unique melting pots. Greg Gagne, Jim Brunzell, and Baron von Raschke were among the contingent imported from the AWA, while Bob Brown and Mike George were brought over from Kansas City. Dick the Bruiser, co-owner of the WWA, was routinely featured in St. Louis, and Andre the Giant was an occasional special attraction, booked from Vincent J. McMahon. Ric Flair, a skilled youngster, was introduced to St. Louis audiences in 1978, and, needless to say, he was more than impressive.

The one other major city in North America to feature talent from each of the Big Three organizations with any consistency was Houston. Under the watchful eye of Paul Boesch, an ex-wrestler who had competed for more than three decades, Houston was a haven for superstar grapplers, big matches, and extraordinary super shows.[13] Talent from throughout Texas, plus appearances by AWA champion Nick Bockwinkel, who had secretly purchased 11 percent of the office, gave the city tremendous depth. And although Boesch was never an official member of the NWA, he received regular appearances by the Alliance world champion as well.

It is not surprising that McMahon, Tunney, Muchnick, and Boesch were on a different level than the average promoter: each was a forward-thinker and remarkably honest, bringing great credibility to their region. These promoters were beloved by their audiences for the exceptional shows they offered and by the wrestlers themselves, who were respected and paid fairly.

McMahon booked his most valuable star, Andre the Giant, with promoters across the world, regardless of their affiliation. Standing nearly 7 feet tall and weighing more than 450 pounds, he was an unbelievable sight to behold, and in a world of behemoths, he was far and away the most extraordinary. Andre was a force of nature with stunning agility and strength, and throughout the 1970s, he toured relentlessly. "I don't think there is [a] man in America who puts together the air miles this man does," McMahon said about Andre in 1983. "He's traveling every day. Two weeks ago, he was in Japan. He's everywhere. Lucky for us, his IQ is as large as his body. He travels most of the time on his own, does everything for himself. There are guys who have to have someone with them all the time — I don't think any general manager in any sport can say he has a larger collection of eccentrics than we do — but not Andre. He'll always be there where you need him."[14]

Known as the "Boss" by his contemporaries in the locker room, Andre was a commanding personality with a sarcastic wit. He was ever-giving to fans, but the burden of always being the center of attention was taxing. It didn't matter if he was in the middle of the ring, walking through an airport, or strolling down the street: all eyes were fixed on him. Andre carried himself well in spite of the fact that he had almost no privacy. His ability to consume massive amounts of food and drink was legendary, and one reporter claimed he usually spent four hours eating dinner, while drinking 7,000 calories of beer or wine a day. Verne Gagne remembered a story of a famous beer-drinking contest between Andre and former Olympian Chris Taylor, claiming Andre passed Taylor at 126 bottles and was still going at 147.[15] To meet all of his commitments, Andre traveled in as many as 300 airplanes a year and humbly admitted, "You forget where you are sometimes."[16]

Without question, Andre was immensely important to wrestling's resurgence from the mid- to late 1970s, and he was a crucial weapon in McMahon's arsenal. The WWWF, which shortened its promotional name to the World Wrestling Federation (WWF) in 1979, was riding a nice high as the decade came to a close. Attendance remained consistent at Madison Square Garden, and McMahon wasn't relying only on babyface champion Bob Backlund to pull in crowds. He padded events with Dusty Rhodes, Pat Patterson, and even Bruno Sammartino, along with a deep roster of up-and-comers. Future legends Ted DiBiase, Tito Santana, Roddy Piper, and Larry Zbyszko were given opportunities to shine on wrestling's biggest stage. On November 19, 1979, David Von Erich made his Garden debut, defeating Davey O'Hannon in 8:47. The next month, on December 17, McMahon ran the Garden with nine matches, five of which were title affairs. NWA world champion Harley Race beat Dusty Rhodes and NWF champion Antonio Inoki was victorious over Hussein Arab. In another bout, Bob Backlund went over Bobby Duncum to capture the vacant WWF heavyweight championship.

Also on the show was the Incredible Hulk Hogan, a 26-year-old Florida native in only his second year of pro wrestling. At 6-foot-8, Hogan was a true standout, beating Ted DiBiase with a bearhug in his Garden debut. He had superstar written all over him, and promoters could see the dollar signs. Competing in other regions as Terry "The Hulk" Boulder, he adopted the Hulk Hogan gimmick upon his arrival in the WWF in

November 1979, where he worked as a heel with ultra-talented mouth-piece Fred Blassie as his manager. With his enormous strength and arrogance, Hogan proved his supremacy in TV handicap squash matches and remained undefeated on the circuit for months. His unconquerable persona worked well, and before departing the WWF in April 1981, only two wrestlers had gotten clean pinfall victories over him: Tony Atlas and Andre the Giant. The latter took a number of wins from Hogan, the most famous being their Shea Stadium battle on the undercard of the big Bruno Sammartino–Larry Zbyszko showdown on August 9, 1980, in front of 36,295 spectators.

Under the leadership of McMahon, the WWF maintained a high level of professionalism, and its success can be traced back to his excellent management style. In many respects, business was formulaic and, from a fan perspective, the booking was often predictable, but that didn't mean it was any less exciting. McMahon loved to push larger-than-life heels, and as with Hogan, nearly every rulebreaker had a manager. Blassie, the Grand Wizard, and Captain Lou Albano were legendary as the vocal emissaries for growling roughnecks. The role of manager was crucial in the development of feuds, and their colorful antics were endlessly entertaining.

Sometimes just the astonished look on the face of the television host was enough to tell the story as Blassie or Albano ranted and raved. The use of a straight-laced interviewer and commentator was also mandatory for WWF broadcasts. In addition to showing a rational fear and shock when faced with the everyday outrageousness, the commentators were hyping the feuds, building up the wrestlers, and laying the groundwork for live events. During ordinary TV bouts, when a superstar faced off against an enhancement worker, the commentators usually gave a few compliments to the "jobber" early in the match, which served to further boost the superstar as they went on to an easy victory. On occasion, the enhancement talent would get in a little offense, and the commentators would light up with surprise, only to see the superstar quickly regain control of the match, hammer home his finisher, and end the bout.

The commentators, essentially, were storytellers as they described the action. They explained the observable and unobservable facets of the matches and displayed reverence to the extraordinary athletes. WWF telecasters spoke as if everything related to the promotion was bigger than life. Everything was a "spectacular," crowds were always in a state of "pandemonium," and arenas were constantly filled to "capacity." The organization's lead commentator, Vincent Kennedy McMahon, the son of the owner, was the undisputed champion of such declarations.

Noted for his "ultra-serious" TV presence by *New Orleans Times-Picayune* critic Bob Wisehart, McMahon was diametrically opposite to the character he would make famous on WWE television decades later.[17] Profoundly knowledgeable and an expert at generating excitement, McMahon first joined his father's WWWF (and its parent company, the Capitol Wrestling Corporation) in 1969, a year after graduating from East Carolina University with a business degree. He was eager to become a pro wrestler himself until his father steered him away from the idea.[18] McMahon Sr. wanted his son to study accounting, but young Vincent jumped at the chance to help the promotion in any way he could.

Even though they had different middle names (the elder McMahon's middle name was James), they were known as "Senior" and "Junior" in wrestling circles, and it was easy to differentiate the two that way.[19] McMahon Jr. was hired as a WWF TV commentator in 1972, replacing Ray Morgan, and he also had a run as a promoter in Bangor, Maine. As a third-generation wrestling impresario, he had a lot to live up to, but he proved himself in his early endeavors. With his wife, Linda, as his most trusted partner and his father teaching him from the ground up, he was in an incredible position to establish a long-term career in pro wrestling.

As fans at the time could see, McMahon's work as host and commentator of WWF's *Championship Wrestling* TV program was instrumental in the advancement of many memorable angles and feuds. Originating from Philadelphia, and later Allentown beginning in 1978, *Championship Wrestling* was syndicated throughout the Northeast, including on the WWF flagship station, WOR-TV (channel 9) in New York City. WOR was an ideal outlet for the promotion, as it was also the home of the New York Mets, Rangers, and Knicks, opening the door for potential crossover sports fans. Ratings were strong on the network, even at the midnight hour on Sunday mornings, and both WWF officials and station management were pleased with the mutually beneficial relationship.

WOR executives followed in the footsteps of Atlanta's Superstation WTBS and began transmitting its broadcast feed nationally via satellite.

By the end of the decade, WOR was featured on several hundred cable systems. In one flip of a switch, the WWF was being showcased all over the United States, reaching an entirely new audience and creating limitless possibilities for Vincent J. McMahon's company. But for the National Wrestling Alliance, the advances in cable and satellite distribution were worrisome. Programs on WOR and WTBS, which broadcast Georgia Championship Wrestling, crossed territorial boundaries and heightened tensions not seen in wrestling circles since the 1950s.

Back then, the major networks, DuMont among them, created all manner of difficulty in professional wrestling when they telecast centrally based shows into out-of-town cities. Chicago, Dallas, and Hollywood were the main offenders, and it took a long time for paranoid promoters to settle their nerves. Agreements were made to highlight the stars of various territories on the network channels, and it was believed similar deals would be made with WWF and Georgia officials to pacify nervous NWA affiliates. The other concern of the Alliance, of course, was the threat of radical expansion, but since the WWF and Georgia were members of the union, it seemed unlikely. But things needed to be hashed out, and the annual NWA convention was the perfect place to address such grievances.

Taking cable television out of the equation for a moment, the wrestling world was already peacefully dealing with some overlap in local broadcasting in some parts of the country. For instance, Little Rock, a stronghold firmly in the grasp of promoter Leroy McGuirk of Tulsa, received telecasts from two outside territories, Memphis and Dallas. Caused by the natural reach of frequency waves and captured by fans with antennas, there was nothing McGuirk could do to block the programs in his region. And if local fans decided that World Class had a more entertaining product than he did, they could choose to watch the Dallas show instead of his. In effect, wrestling fans were better off because they had more options, but promoters were being thrust into a situation in which they had to strengthen their TV to remain competitive. By the end of 1981, McGuirk was also dealing with the arrival of Georgia and the WWF on cable.

As for the happenings in the ring, the NWA saw the world championship change hands four times in 1981. Harley Race, who was in the midst of his fifth reign, dropped the belt to popular Southern hero Tommy Rich in a shocker on April 27, 1981. A few days later, on May 1, Race regained the title, only to lose it again the following month to Dusty Rhodes. Finally, the strap went to the arrogant heel, "Nature Boy" Ric Flair, on September 17, 1981, in Kansas City. Flair, a protégé of Verne Gagne, became a star in the Mid-Atlantic region and bowled over the NWA board of directors with his combination of in-ring science and verbal skill. He was the total package, just the kind of guy the Alliance needed. As for the WWF, Bob Backlund continued his reign on top. Andre the Giant suffered a broken ankle during the spring, and promoters creatively blamed the injury on Killer Khan.[20] Their feud lasted months, drawing well across the circuit, including a sellout at Madison Square Garden in August 1981.

WWF legend Bruno Sammartino wrestled what was billed as his "farewell appearance" on October 4, 1981. He defeated his old foe George "The Animal" Steele in less than seven minutes. Prior to the event, sportswriter Jerry Izenberg called Sammartino, "The Captain Marvel and the Cyrano de Bergerac of all that is pure in that peculiar world of good and evil." Vincent J. McMahon added, "There has never been a greater fighter on the side of good."[21] The show also marked the organization's debut at the Byrne Meadowlands Arena in East Rutherford, New Jersey, about a half-hour drive from New York City. It should be noted that Sammartino didn't retire for good that night, and officially wrestled his final match six years later in 1987.

Vincent Kennedy McMahon, the voice of the WWF, was known for his enthusiasm and had proven his value as a commentator. But McMahon was an entrepreneur at heart, willing to take risks, and saw the wrestling landscape a lot differently than his father, his father's peers, and the majority of fans. His experiences since moving up from North Carolina in 1969 encompassed everything from selling tickets to handling ring-announcing duties for his father's telecasts. The lessons he learned were priceless, especially those in and around Capitol Wrestling's home office, watching McMahon Sr. manage the day-to-day operations.

Even though he was still relatively young, McMahon Jr. was a visionary when it came to professional wrestling. He shared that trait with his father to a certain degree, although their mental images of the business couldn't have been more different. The elder McMahon used his great intellect to unify the entire northeastern territory under his WWWF banner, a tremendous achievement. But he refused to consider further expansion because it was against the gentleman's agreement binding the sport's promoters. The territories were set in stone, and there was no room for anyone to expand. McMahon didn't want to rock the boat and sought to make the most of the region he controlled. His son was uniquely different in that respect.

McMahon Jr. saw the wrestling landscape as full of opportunity. Everything was ripe for the taking, including territories and talent. The Sherman Antitrust Act prevented any exclusivity, and the National Wrestling Alliance was bound to U.S. laws stemming from the 1956 Consent Decree. McMahon, who turned 36 in 1981, understood the bigger picture and the established protocols of the business. He knew his father respected the relationships between the WWF, NWA, and AWA, and, for the time being, he had to keep his dreams to himself.

Naturally, McMahon Jr. was also keen on the prospects of closed-circuit and cable television. During the 1970s, he worked behind the scenes on two high-profile events: Evel Knievel's Snake River Canyon jump in 1974, and Muhammad Ali's boxer-versus-wrestler bout against Antonio Inoki in 1976. McMahon coordinated closed-circuit venues for both occasions, learning a great deal about this additional source of revenue. And the exciting possibilities offered by cable TV were not lost on McMahon either. He could see how a far-reaching broadcast would give the WWF the opening it needed to broaden its promotional scope.

Sometime in 1982, McMahon Sr. broached the idea of selling the Capitol Wrestling Corporation and getting out of pro wrestling. His reasons are unknown, but it's possible he wanted to live a quieter life with his wife, Juanita, far from the arenas he'd worked in for three decades. At 67 years old, he was a veteran of the squared circle. By selling off his shares, he could live the rest of his life free from wrestling's everyday stresses. But the sale of Capitol Wrestling to an outsider potentially put McMahon Jr. out of a job, and ruined his grand plans for expansion. If his father was serious about selling, McMahon Jr. would be the man buying.

In addition to his responsibilities as the WWF's lead commentator, McMahon had been proactive on his own. In 1979, his family moved to South Yarmouth, Massachusetts, approximately 75 miles from Boston, and he assumed the mortgage for the struggling Cape Cod Coliseum.[22] He arranged a slew of events at the Coliseum, from hockey games to concerts. A few months later, on February 21, 1980, he incorporated his new company, Titan Sports, Inc., a domestic profit corporation, in Massachusetts with McMahon serving as president and treasurer.[23] Titan Sports would remain a small outfit, made up of a handful of people, and Vince's wife, Linda, was a significant factor in the company's early success. Around the time McMahon Sr. brought up his possible retirement, McMahon Jr. and his wife began considering a buyout, and realized it was the gamble of a lifetime. For a visionary like McMahon, it was an opportunity he couldn't pass up.

But, despite 10 years in the business, owning an arena, and having national name recognition, McMahon Jr. was not a rich man in 1982. In fact, he was scraping by, though in a better position than he had been six years earlier when he'd declared bankruptcy. It wasn't like he could dip into his deep pockets and easily buy out the four shareholders of Capitol Wrestling. However, McMahon Jr. was determined to make the purchase a reality.

Of the four men holding interest in Capitol, Robert Marella, better known as wrestler Gorilla Monsoon, was the youngest at 45. Arnold Skaaland, another retired grappler, was 57, and longtime company secretary-treasurer Phil Zacko was in his 70s. Along with McMahon Sr., this quartet agreed to sell the company outright to Titan Sports, and a contract was drawn up by attorneys. The stipulations called for an initial liquidation of all of Capitol's surplus funds.[24] That meant Capitol would pay more than $640,000 to Marella, Zacko, and Skaaland for a combined 385 shares of their common stock, which would be turned over to Titan at the completion of the sale. Titan would pay $1 million to all four stockholders for the remaining 615 shares.

The initial payment was for $230,736, while $769,264 was broken into three parts, paid on October 1, 1982, February 1, 1983, and June 1, 1983. Of that $1 million, $822,132 was going to McMahon Sr. himself, the company's largest stockholder with 500 shares. Imbedded within the contract were a number of conditions, including specific items protecting Capitol's outgoing shareholders. If Titan defaulted on any payment, all shares would return to McMahon, Marella, Zacko, and Skaaland, and the group would keep any money paid to date. Gathered together for a secret meeting on June 5, 1982, these individuals shook hands and affixed their signatures to the contract. Capitol Wrestling was now the property of Titan Sports, and Vincent Kennedy McMahon was the new head of the World Wrestling Federation.

Without kayfabe-defying websites to break the news, the sale, essentially, went unreported, and it was business as usual across the board. For McMahon Jr., there was a new burden, and that was coming up with a significant amount of cash before June 1983. The entire deal hinged on his ability to make good. At the same time, he was considering bringing in outside talent and the feasibility of expansion. The ball was rolling, and McMahon was looking at an uphill fight. The WWF was charted on a new course, and its future was in the hands of an enthusiastic and enterprising new skipper.

CHAPTER THREE

THE BEGINNING
OF THE END

In the two decades following the establishment of the National Wrestling Alliance, the territorial map cordoning off specific regions for promoters didn't change all that much. If there was a modification, it tended to be more of a reorganization stemming from a change in ownership, which happened from time to time. Some promoters dropped out of the picture because of old age and retirement, while others passed away, leaving their heirs with the burden of selling out or trying to sustain business without them. Hugh Nichols, an ex–wrestling champion and NWA representative in Hollywood and San Diego, California, was one of the first major affiliates to meet a sudden demise. On December 15, 1956, he committed suicide at age 58 in his Southern California home, reportedly despondent about declining business. The following year, on July 1, veteran Max

Clayton of Omaha died at age 61, and another big hole in the wrestling world was created.

Both Hollywood and San Diego were quickly absorbed by Cal Eaton, who already operated a territory in Los Angeles. Clayton's promotion was annexed by his protégé, Joe Dusek, a native Omahan, and it became a valuable stop for the AWA. During the 1960s, Paul Bowser of Boston, Bill Lewis of Richmond, Morris Sigel in Houston, and Karl Sarpolis of Amarillo each passed away while still in charge of their respective locales and were succeeded by competent replacements, keeping the territorial system within balance. Eaton himself died on January 10, 1966, at age 57, and his promotion was taken over by his wife, Aileen Eaton, and his stepson, Mike LeBell. Seven years later, on April 1, 1973, "Big" Jim Crockett Sr., the beloved promoter of the Mid-Atlantic states, died of a heart attack. His wife, Elizabeth, and four children continued the business and the territory was never in real danger of failing.

The same was true following a host of retirements. Cowboy Luttrall, manager of the Tampa franchise and ruler of most of the Sunshine State since 1949, walked away from the business in 1970. His interest was sold to his right-hand man Eddie Graham, another top-notch leader. Things were handled in much the same way in Tulsa and Buffalo. However, Pinkie George in Des Moines, Orville Brown in Kansas City, and Harry Light in Detroit suffered a different fate. These men were among the earliest members of the NWA, but were supplanted by aggressive, politically strong opponents.[25] Unable to fend off their rivals, they quietly retired, but the territories themselves remained unfazed by the changes.

Interestingly, as various promotions were changing management during this time frame, a number of former grapplers stepped up to become regional administrators. As mentioned, Joe Dusek and Eddie Graham took hold of Omaha and Tampa, respectively, and both had been mentored by the men previously in charge. Leroy McGuirk in Tulsa, Fritz Von Erich in Dallas, and Dory Funk Sr. in Amarillo were also students of both promotions and booking prior to owning their individual territories. The smart and indisputably tough Ray Gunkel had the privilege of working side by side with longtime promoter Paul Jones, another ex-wrestler, and the two combined their knowledge to create a top-notch product in Atlanta. Roy Shire enjoyed a lengthy pro career before settling in as a promoter in San Francisco. His efforts, though, were in direct opposition to the local veteran operator, Joe Malcewicz, and within a short time, Shire took over all of northern California.

As of 1976, there were 27 NWA offices, including three in Japan, three in Canada, one in Korea, one in Australia, and one in Mexico.[26] The 6-foot-10 Giant Baba was at the helm of All Japan Pro Wrestling, Antonio Inoki was leading New Japan Pro Wrestling, and, according to the NWA's official roster for the year, Junzo Sato was in charge of "Japan Pro Wrestling" out of Tokyo. Kim Il, former WWA world heavyweight champion, was the boss of Kim Il Pro-Wrestling Foundation in Seoul, Korea, and Salvador Lutteroth Jr. was in charge south of the U.S. border, running Arena Mexico. Up in Canada, Frank Tunney was still operating in Toronto and Stu Hart was promoting in the western part of the country, based in Calgary, Alberta. In the far eastern part of Canada, Leo Burke was holding court, headquartered in New Brunswick. Montreal, notably, did not have its own office at the time. In Australia, Ron Miller and Larry O'Day operated World Championship Wrestling.

Regardless of how popular pro wrestling was on an international scale, as years went by, some established territories began to fail. Detroit, Columbus, Cleveland, and Buffalo were no longer among the top wrestling cities, and by the late 1970s, they were either burned out or on very thin ice. The reason for this decline was complex, and caused by much more than a singular external factor. In the case of Detroit, the social climate and economy contributed to its demise. The "Motor City" was the hub for American auto manufacturing, and blue-collar workers had embraced the vibrancy of pro wrestling during the 1930s. At that time, Adam Weissmuller, the cousin of the famous *Tarzan* actor, Johnny Weissmuller, fashioned a reputable circuit featuring mostly nonheavyweights. Weissmuller allied himself with partners in surrounding states, particularly veteran promoter Al Haft of Columbus, and in 1936, he garnered national publicity by joining what journalists dubbed the "Little Trust," a secondary faction to wrestling's leading promotional syndicate. The members of the Little Trust were thrust into the headlines after German heavyweight Dick Shikat double-crossed Danno O'Mahoney on March 2, 1936, in New York, stealing the world championship and declaring his loyalty to their group.[27] By doing so, Shikat elevated the status of wrestling in Detroit and Columbus while simultaneously damaging major promotions elsewhere in North America. What Shikat and his cronies couldn't have known was that his unscheduled victory over O'Mahoney would have long-term detrimental effects on the sport. In essence, it is an actual moment in history that people can point to and say: "That event changed the course of pro wrestling forever." The ramifications were harsh. The public's trust in the sport was severely damaged in the resulting chaos caused by the in-ring betrayal. Greedy promoters created a slew of "world" title claimants exclusive to their own regions, and what was left of pro wrestling's credibility was quickly lost.

During the tumultuous 1930s and '40s, Al Haft displayed great resiliency in Columbus, and the location of his city was pivotal as wrestlers crisscrossed America. Workers venturing from points in the Northeast, headed to Chicago or St. Louis, could easily stop there for engagements. And for that reason, Haft was never without good talent. Grapplers also knew that Haft's promotion was an honest payday, whereas in some towns, promoters were hesitant to pay evenhanded wages. Haft's fairness was attributed to the fact that he was a former wrestler himself, and had traveled the same back country roads years earlier for scant sums. He wanted to ensure the wrestlers he promoted were taken care of.

Haft also loved the purity of wrestling and sought legitimate grapplers for his shows. John "Tigerman" Pesek, Ruffy Silverstein, and Dr. Bill Miller enjoyed lengthy stays in Columbus, and when it came to genuine mat knowledge, they were among the best in the business. To balance his programs, Haft utilized the likes of "Nature Boy" Buddy Rogers, a top-shelf performer and box-office sensation. Throughout it all, Haft was a shrewd promoter, knowledgeable about the mechanics of wrestling inside the ring and out, and was counted on by many of his peers for his wisdom. He overcame a number of hurdles in his administration of Columbus, and became one of the longest-enduring wrestling promoters of the 20th century.

The wrestling scene in Detroit was a bit more turbulent. After Weissmuller died, Eddie Lewis and Louis Markowitz took over, then Harry Light assumed the mantle in 1942. A product of France, Light was a smart entrepreneur and, with help from Bert Ruby and Jack Britton, rebuilt Detroit into a stable market. Notably, Ruby was known for his coaching abilities and taught many up-and-comers, including Killer Kowalski, and Britton managed the troupe of little people grapplers, who became a hot ticket on the global stage during the late 1940s. Like Haft, Light was an early member of the NWA and benefited from the national coalition's talent sharing. Things ran smoothly for him until 1959, when ex–Chicago booker Jim Barnett set his sights on Detroit and began running opposition.

Teamed with Johnny Doyle, Jim Barnett established studio wrestling in Windsor, Ontario, and Cincinnati, Ohio, and with a stunning cast of big-named talent, burst into Detroit on April 11, 1959.[28] The reported attendance for the show, headlined by Angelo Poffo and Wilbur Snyder, was 16,226 with a gate of $40,000. The Barnett–Doyle clique quickly nabbed a huge percentage of the local market with must-see talent such as Dick the Bruiser, Hans Schmidt, "Cowboy" Bob Ellis, and Verne Gagne, completely eclipsing Light's promotion. To stay afloat against that kind of competition, Light worked a deal with Vince McMahon's Capitol Wrestling in 1961, and began importing workers like Antonino Rocca and Bruno Sammartino. But it was too little too late for Light, and he retired the next year.

Barnett and Doyle made bundles of money in Detroit, and their outward expansion reached impressive distances during the early 1960s, fanning out to Denver and Los Angeles in the west and New Orleans in the south. By 1964, the duo shifted their attention to Australia and sold the Detroit territory to Edward Farhat for a cool $50,000. The name "Edward Farhat" might not be recognizable to many people, and in 1964, nobody outside the business knew it. But Farhat was none other than the Sheik, the epitome of an ultra-violent wrestling villain. For years, the Sheik had been a major figure on the Barnett–Doyle circuit and an international attraction. When his hometown of Detroit went on the market, he wanted the city for his own and soon made it the headquarters of his new promotion, Big Time Wrestling.

Not surprisingly, a few years before taking off for the Land Down Under, Barnett and Doyle also edged into Columbus against Haft, sponsoring Don Leo Jonathan as the American Wrestling Alliance World champion. But following the end of hostilities, and after the title moved over to shooter extraordinaire Karl Gotch in the fall of 1962, Haft actually started promoting him as titleholder. It was a unique turnabout and reflective of Haft's crumbling relations with both Buddy Rogers, the reigning NWA champion, and the NWA itself. Aided by his son, Al Jr., the 80-year-old Haft continued to promote into 1967, but was hindered by a lack of box-office drawing power. Wrestling historian Don Luce identified Haft's last show as occurring on February 25, 1967, at the Cooper Arena, just weeks after he celebrated his 50th anniversary as a promoter in Columbus.[29]

With Haft bowing out, Farhat quickly absorbed Columbus into his growing circuit beginning in February and March 1967, and acquired television outlets across Michigan and Ohio. Among them were WTVN in Columbus and WEWS in Cleveland. In the ring, the Sheik was unpredictable, but as a booker, he was all too conventional in the way he promoted himself as the center attraction. In time, staleness set in, as fans were overexposed to the Sheik's antics. This worn-out formula didn't decay overnight; in fact, Detroit and the surrounding area was hot well into the 1970s. Appearances by Bobo Brazil, whose feud with the Sheik was legendary, Ernie Ladd, Luis Martinez, Pampero Firpo, and the Fabulous Kangaroos were a key reason why Big Time Wrestling was consistently a draw. And for the longtime followers of Al Haft, who saw first-rate mat wrestling regularly, the Sheik was a dramatic change of pace.

Diehard fans in the region adjusted and embraced the Detroit methodology, and the Sheik perpetrated nearly every evil deed known to the squared circle. He was an innovator of ruthless aggression, and his tactics established a basic forerunner of the modern hardcore style. Over the lifespan of his Detroit promotion, the Sheik captured the United States heavyweight title a record 14 times and defeated a number of Hall of Famers, including Abdullah the Butcher, Terry Funk, and Bobo Brazil. But the promotion itself began to suffer due to Detroit's crippled economy, and attendance dwindled at downtown's Cobo Hall. A massive migration of people from the inner city to the suburbs forced Farhat into smaller venues with a toned-down crop of talent going into 1981.

Around that same time, Ohio was experiencing the rapid growth of cable television. In Columbus, 25 percent of households were receiving cable via Warner's QUBE system by 1980, while another 20 percent of homes in Dayton were receiving programming through Viacom Cablevision. Cleveland, too, had increased coverage with 16 percent, but, in contrast, only two percent of homes in Detroit were receiving the expanded pro-gramming. This was significant where pro wrestling was concerned because of the importance of WTBS on each cable system. WTBS out of Atlanta was a prime station in the budding cable universe and featured a strong combination of popular old sitcoms, family programming, and Braves Major League Baseball action. But its most-watched program was the exceptional Georgia Championship Wrestling broadcast on Saturday nights, and viewers from Florida to Alaska were entertained by the lively matches every week.

In the *Detroit Free Press*, TV critic Mike Duffy affectionately called the channel 17 offering "Redneck Rasslin'," and explained that it was "two hours of good old boys and bruiser brothers going at it."[30] The popu-larity of Georgia Championship Wrestling was infectious, and the wres-tling fans in Ohio were enraptured by the southern style of grappling. The chairman behind GCW was none other than Jim Barnett, who, in 1973, left Australia and paid six figures for 38 percent of the Atlanta-based company. In January 1980, Barnett hired well-known ex-wrestler "Cowboy" Bill Watts as his booker, and the latter was quick to see the value in WTBS's expansive reach.[31]

To gauge the popularity of GCW outside Georgia, Watts set up a stylish angle between NWA world heavyweight champion Harley Race and the ever-popular Mr. Wrestling II, a masked Johnny Walker. The scene unfolded as the competitors battled to a Broadway draw at the Omni in Atlanta on April 6, 1980, and a trio of judges —former NWA champions Lou Thesz, Dory Funk Jr., and Dusty Rhodes — split the votes to pick a winner. However, it was determined that Dory originally scored Mr. Wrestling II as the victor before changing his vote at the last minute. The decision created a wave of backlash and fans were furious with the result. GCW commentator Gordon Solie told fans they could send letters to the Atlanta office and voice their complaints, and the audience did — in tremendous numbers.

Thousands of letters from around the country were received by Georgia wrestling officials, and they were overwhelmingly in support of Mr. Wrestling II. But for Watts and Barnett, the letters were less important than their postmarks, which they used to determine where GCW's telecast was most popular. Thanks to the growing cable structure in Ohio, it wasn't surprising that the Buckeye State was at the heart of GCW's fanbase outside Georgia. The people of Columbus were particularly enthused by the show, and it didn't take Watts and Barnett long to consider an expansion into Ohio.

"Expansion" was like a four-letter word to the members of the National Wrestling Alliance. If someone was expanding, someone else was facing an invasion. Ohio was most recently the "property" of Ed Farhat, and in the summer of 1980, Big Time Wrestling was still somewhat afloat. For Georgia to attempt any kind of expansion, it needed to first consult Farhat to discuss territorial rights. Despite plummeting attendance in Detroit, Farhat wasn't keen on giving up Ohio in any shape or form. He turned down a mutually beneficial deal offered to him by GCW and expected his NWA membership rights to protect his territory.[32]

Georgia was determined to move on Columbus, deeming it an open city because of Farhat's limited promotions there. Utilizing an old contact from his previous dealings in the region, Barnett solidified a deal to bring Georgia wrestlers to Columbus's brand-new Ohio Center beginning in September 1980. With sizable help from his new booker, Ole Anderson, who replaced Watts in May, GCW marched into Columbus to considerable success. Houses were strong, and the amazing thing was, Georgia was doing it all based on the strength of its WTBS cable program. In the past, the development of a new city, especially one far from the regular circuit of a territory, needed months and months of targeted build-up and more importantly, a local television outlet to promote awareness. But Columbus fans were already champing at the bit to see Dusty Rhodes, Tommy Rich, and Mr. Wrestling II live.

Putting in overtime to work out the details, the always dignified Barnett obtained local TV outlets in Columbus, Dayton, Canton, Cincinnati, and Cleveland.[33] This only helped reinforce their Ohio incursion, and GCW made arrangements for Les Thatcher to become the promoter of record in Cincinnati, Dayton, and towns in Michigan. Veteran operator Vince Risko, the brother of former boxing champion Babe Risko, represented the company in Canton and, with Georgia stars, drew the largest crowds in 30 years. After the town drew a more than $20,000 gate, a reporter for the *Cleveland Plain Dealer* wondered if Canton was now "the pro wrestling capital of Ohio."[34]

From a distance, the NWA was watching the first coordinated expansion of one member into the backyard of another in years. Barnett, as booker for the NWA world heavyweight champion and longtime secretary for the organization, was considered Alliance royalty. He was highly influential, and if he was authorizing the invasion of another territory, he must have been on solid ground to do so. Farhat didn't think so. He was angry beyond belief and actually consented to appear for a non-NWA promoter in Atlanta on May 3, 1981, at GCW's main arena, the Omni Coliseum. The gig was for the International Wrestling League and saw him battle Thunderbolt Patterson in the main event.[35] Wrestling for an outlaw promotion was a big no-no, and the NWA voted to suspend Farhat's membership at the 1981 annual convention in Las Vegas.[36] On December 27, 1981, Farhat lost his TV on channel 62 in Detroit, and Big Time Wrestling was gone for good. The Detroit territory, as it was known, was officially dead.

Cleveland was on GCW's radar, but it was considered one of the weakest wrestling cities with a population greater than 500,000. In fact, when Ole Anderson asked Vince McMahon Sr. about the city, McMahon told him Cleveland was dead, killed off during the promotional run of Johnny Powers during the 1970s.[37] His comment referred to Powers's time at the helm of the National Wrestling Federation, an outlaw promotion operated in conjunction with Buffalo entrepreneur Pedro Martinez. The once-successful NWF was launched in 1970 and a number of top attractions were booked for high-profile shows in Cleveland and Buffalo. At the NWF's height, on August 12, 1972, the group drew 14,000 people to the outdoor stadium in Cleveland for the "Superbowl of Wrestling," and it was a defining moment in the promotion's history. The following year, Powers sold the rights to the NWF world title to Antonio Inoki of New Japan Pro Wrestling and kept Cleveland afloat going into 1975. However, Powers's overexposure, combined with the same economic downturn plaguing Detroit, ended up sinking Cleveland. Attendance dropped to nearly nothing, and instead of big shows at the Arena or Stadium, Powers ran the gymnasium at St. Joseph High School with a crew of mid-card performers. As for Martinez, he quietly closed up his Buffalo office and bowed out of wrestling around 1974, a very wealthy man.

Buffalo fell into the open, and the WWWF ran sporadic shows there during the mid-1970s, but gave up the town in 1976. Three years later,

Jim Crockett Promotions obtained a local TV spot for its *Mid-Atlantic Championship Wrestling* program on WUTV-29 on Saturday mornings at 11:00, debuting on December 1, 1979. To the uninformed observer, the sudden expansion of a Charlotte-based promotion into Buffalo, New York, was a little out of the ordinary. But Crockett was already established in the region, only 100 miles away, in Toronto, Ontario, where his heavyweight stars appeared at Maple Leaf Gardens on a regular basis. Since Buffalo was close enough to run semi-regular shows, it only made sense to exploit the opportunities there as well.

In late 1980, the network station WIVB (channel 4) acquired the rights to the Mid-Atlantic show in Buffalo and improved viewership.[38] But WIVB was a sports-heavy outlet, and wrestling was routinely preempted by football, basketball, and tennis on Saturday afternoons. A concerned wrestling fan inquired to the *Buffalo Courier-Express* about the show in the summer of 1981, wondering if the station had plans to offer alternate viewing times because of the upcoming college football schedule. A spokesman for WIVB replied simply: "I doubt if [Mid-Atlantic Wrestling] will be rescheduled if preempted."[39] The promotion plodded on, only to see channel 4 cancel the program outright in November 1981. They held three additional live events in Buffalo through May 1982 before finally giving up.

Buffalo enthusiasts were exposed to "Nature Boy" Ric Flair, Greg Valentine, Wahoo McDaniel, and Ray Stevens, among others, during Crockett's run in the city, and the respected NWA style of wrestling was preserved. On August 9, 1982, the WWF came to the city for the first time in more than six years, and planted its flag. The promotion was reclaiming the entirety of upstate New York, adding Buffalo to a circuit that already included Rochester and Syracuse. In addition to its program on the WOR cable network, the WWF had begun a local show on WUTV in March to prepare the town for its arrival. With a boom, the WWF made its debut, featuring heavyweight champion Bob Backlund and Jimmy Snuka, while former world champion (and future Hall of Famer) the Destroyer, born and raised in the region, wrestled on the undercard.

The WUTV (channel 29) program in Buffalo also broadcast across the Canadian border to Toronto. Local promoter Frank Tunney had worked with the McMahons for years, and the TV exposure gave the WWF heightened leverage. In 1982, Backlund was showcased in Toronto five times alongside Jim Crockett workers, and the bonds between the Tunney, Crockett, and McMahon offices were exceptionally robust. Toronto fans enjoyed the diversity of performers, and Tunney was coining his own mint. The WWF's reacquisition of Buffalo was a pivotal move, demonstrative of the younger McMahon's broad understanding of the wrestling scene.

His determination to expand was better defined by his next major move, and in 1982, he reached out to Mike LeBell in Los Angeles, one of his father's most trustworthy associates, and sought a meeting. The 52-year-old LeBell was more than willing to hear McMahon out. In recent years, his promotion had fallen on hard times, and was a far cry from Southern California's glory days. In 1952, Hollywood had been witness to a historic show headlined by Lou Thesz and Baron Michele Leone, drawing the sport's then-largest gate in history, a whopping $103,277. Fred Blassie and John Tolos topped that mark on August 27, 1971, at the Memorial Coliseum with $142,158 paid into the till. The NAWA and later the WWA had been the cornerstone of Los Angeles wrestling between 1958 and 1968, and the success continued under the NWA banner through the first half of the 1970s.

LeBell went into a funk after KCOP-13 canceled his TV program around 1974, and then he lost his outlet on KBSC-52 in 1980. A Spanish-speaking channel, KMEX (channel 34), became his only reliable means to reach a widespread TV audience, and although it was better than nothing, the UHF station wasn't available to all viewers. He tried to boost attendance by importing talent from Mexico, and the masked sensation Mil Mascaras was a frequent headliner at the Olympic Auditorium. But despite some spikes in crowd size, things were flat for the most part with wrestling-smart fans not buying LeBell's unenthusiastic efforts and new fans few and far between. He also faced a rent increase at the Olympic and eventually moved over to the Sports Arena.[40]

With McMahon trying to arrange a meeting, there were interesting prospects for an expanded relationship between the WWF and Los Angeles, a move that could seriously benefit both promotions. The WWF's glitzy performers were guaranteed to dazzle the region that once showcased the flamboyant Gorgeous George, and relished in his showmanship. Wrestling insiders might've figured a WWF takeover of Los Angeles was far-fetched, but looking at the modified status of Columbus, Buffalo, Cleveland, and

Detroit, each an individual territory at one point, demonstrated that anything was possible. And with cable television giving fans a view of outside promotions, beamed directly into their living rooms, in a weird way, it appeared that pro wrestling was shrinking and growing all at the same time.

CHAPTER FOUR

SOUTHERN CALIFORNIA

Across the wrestling world, promoters went to great lengths to insulate their territories from all types of adverse contingencies, and they were ever-creative in their manipulations. In dealing with talent, they often exercised pressure to maintain loyalty, and the notorious blacklist, however unfeasible it might have legitimately been, was considered an unspoken part of the business. NWA members benefited from the security of the union, and a fundamental component of the old territory system was the relationships between wrestling offices and local government. That included the state athletic commissions, which acted as a supervisory body for wrestling in those regions. The athletic commission authorized promotional licenses in most cases, and they could obstruct the licensing of any competitor the NWA member wanted, thereby preventing an invasion.

In Los Angeles, the Eaton-LeBell family was politically connected all the way up to the California governor in the 1950s, and they held a tight monopoly over heavyweight wrestling and boxing in southern California.[41] They were faced with a number of challengers at different times, only to stomp out their competition with help from the commission or by calling the NWA for reinforcements. By the early 1980s, Mike LeBell had more than 30 years' experience as a wrestling administrator at the Olympic Auditorium and had served as an officer in the NWA and as part of the group's board of directors. But his tenure in Los Angeles was losing a little more steam each year, and his own lack of motivation was partially to blame.

Despite solid talent-sharing agreements, LeBell was struggling to put his weekly lineups together. He'd imported some of the greatest names in the world for years, but between 1980 and 1982, he was failing to highlight talent worthy of the third-biggest U.S. market. Paying wrestlers poorly was part of it, as LeBell was known for giving talent a percentage of the gate, rather than guaranteed sums. With souring interest and weak houses, Los Angeles was anything but a lure for top-name grapplers. Only years before, LeBell had taken part in the behind-the-scenes wrangling of the infamous Muhammad Ali–Antonio Inoki contest in Tokyo, a multimillion-dollar affair, but now his wrestling operation was on its last legs.

LeBell knew Vince McMahon Jr. well. He'd been working with the McMahons for years, cycling wrestlers, and cooperating mostly because Los Angeles TV was being shown in New York on the local Spanish International Network (SIN) channel. That was essentially the reason the New York and Los Angeles offices first came together, and the benefits of a strong relationship far outweighed the negatives. In addition, they shared a connection to Inoki's New Japan, and their wrestlers went back and forth to Asia with regularity. Looking a little deeper into the business relations between McMahon Sr. and LeBell, it is clear they were much more than fleeting acquaintances.

LeBell and McMahon Sr. actually formed a joint company, the Atlantic and Pacific Wrestling Corporation, established in Washington, D.C., on May 5, 1976. Phil Zacko, a shareholder of Capitol Wrestling before it was sold to the younger McMahon, explained during a 1984 deposition that the Atlantic and Pacific Wrestling Corporation made $19,000 at one juncture from the distribution of tapes.[42] He added, though, that it was split between McMahon and LeBell, and as far as McMahon was concerned, it was absorbed by expenses, leaving no profit. The two promoters called each other multiple times a week, sharing stories and relaying gate numbers, and when McMahon was preparing to venture to Japan, he made arrangements through LeBell's office.[43] In 1982, LeBell got word that McMahon Jr. was taking over Capitol's territory, and with his own promotion's future in doubt, he consented to a meeting that would alter the destiny of pro wrestling in Los Angeles.

The conference between McMahon Jr. and LeBell occurred in the middle of the country, at a coffee shop at O'Hare International Airport in Chicago in October 1982. At that meeting, they discussed the current state of affairs, leading into a formal decision allowing McMahon's Titan Sports to purchase LeBell's interest in three separate entities.[44] The first was the latter's entire wrestling promotion, incorporated as Mike LeBell Sports, and the price tag was $520,000. This included all promotional rights to the Los Angeles territory, extending from the Olympic Auditorium to Hollywood and down to San Diego. For an additional $520,000, McMahon acquired full control of both the Atlantic and Pacific Wrestling Corporation and the LeBell–McMahon TV setup. The deal allowed McMahon to pay LeBell in weekly installments of $2,000 for 10 years.[45]

LeBell would remain employed as the WWF's official representative on the ground in southern California. He'd give interviews to promote shows, book undercard performers, and use his political contacts when needed. The agreement was huge for McMahon, but there was still one obstacle he needed to straighten out before the WWF could formally move into the territory. That hurdle was the acquisition of a local television station to bolster publicity in advance of live events. LeBell had struggled for years to attain a major English-speaking outlet for his programs, and although McMahon expressed a desire to land one, the veteran Los Angeles promoter felt it was impossible.[46]

But McMahon had two things going for him. For one, he was close with influential people at WOR-TV, and as luck would have it, WOR's parent company, RKO General, also owned a powerful independent station in Los Angeles, channel 9, KHJ-TV (now KCAL). It wasn't long before McMahon was on a plane to Los Angeles to take a meeting with

KHJ executives, where he promised to deliver a first-class wrestling production on a weekly basis. The other thing McMahon had up his sleeve was an incredible proposal, almost too good for any businessman to pass up. He offered to pay KHJ $2,500 a week for a Saturday morning timeslot, amounting to $130,000 annually.[47]

Wrestling promotions doling out money to stations for air time used to be a foreign concept. In fact, in the 1950s, promoters expected to be heavily compensated with advertising dollars, but when ratings went down, station managers didn't hesitate to eliminate wrestling from their schedules. To regain position on a popular channel, promoters had to pay the stations, and WOR was a perfect example. The WWF was paying WOR $1,750 a week to broadcast *Championship Wrestling* on Saturday nights, and had been doing so for years.[48] There is little doubt LeBell, like many of his old-school brethren, still expected to be paid for any kind of TV efforts. But McMahon didn't expect to make a dime. He saw TV as a promotional expense to boost the gates of live shows, and for that reason, his pitch to KHJ was successful. Beginning January 1, 1983, *Championship Wrestling* would be featured on Saturday mornings at 9:30 throughout southern California.

The acquisition of Los Angeles was McMahon's biggest expansion yet, and he was paying more for it than he had to purchase Capitol Wrestling. Looking back east, he was only holding part of the far eastern edge of Ohio in 1982, promoting sporadically in Steubenville and Hubbard. But the extensive viewing area reached by WOR on cable opened up the same opportunities for McMahon as TBS had for Georgia Championship Wrestling. McMahon was eyeing Akron, Cincinnati, and Dayton, in addition to several smaller towns. Notably, Jim Barnett, a shareholder of GCW and secretary of the NWA, addressed the potential dangers of cable "superstations" (which WOR and TBS both were) at the 1982 NWA convention in Puerto Rico.[49]

According to the meeting minutes, Barnett deflected criticism by stating that GCW had "nothing to do" with the decision to broadcast his promotion's show nationally. It was the station's prerogative, and he relayed the rumor that the AWA would soon be featured on WGN, out of Chicago, on a nationwide basis. He "announced his willingness to use good wrestlers then working for other promoters on his WTBS shows, either as live performers or through tapes." As a result, he could offer a grappler "broad exposure and effectively promote his appearance in any market where WTBS [had] a significant cable audience interested in wrestling. This [benefited] the promoter using the wrestler in that market."[50] The generous offer was seemingly a product of widespread NWA unity, and members saw the benefits of working with Barnett and GCW to feature their stars on WTBS.

Not everything was ironed out and Barnett scheduled a special television seminar for October 11, 1982, in Atlanta to bring everyone up to speed. He later canceled the meeting because the Atlanta Braves appeared to be headed to the World Series and the date conflicted.[51] The TV questions were sustained through the end of 1982, and Barnett, who was no stranger to making waves in the world of wrestling, was rumored to be organizing a wider expansion. But behind the scenes, Barnett and his booker, Ole Anderson, were realizing their promotion was overextended financially, and instead of rapid, dramatic growth, they needed to cut expenses. Nevertheless, the GCW show, which was renamed *World Championship Wrestling* in August 1982, remained one of the highest-rated programs on cable TV.

Another cable TV show with far-reaching influence was launched on the USA Network on December 5, 1982, run by ex-wrestler Joe Blanchard out of San Antonio. Blanchard, who began his career in 1953, was well liked by his peers for his kindly manner. He was a solid grappler on the mat with amateur knowledge, and at the height of his wrestling tenure, traveled upwards of 2,500 miles per week. He settled in San Antonio as an associate of longtime promoter Frank Brown in 1964 and took over the business during the mid-1970s.[52] In 1978, after things turned sour between Blanchard and Jack Adkisson (better known as Fritz Von Erich and the owner of Texas's largest booking office in Dallas), Blanchard formed his own independent promotion, Southwest Championship Wrestling.[53] He continued to show a high level of cooperation with friends across the wrestling landscape, and gave fans in his territory great shows thanks to his years of experience as a matchmaker.

Southwest Championship Wrestling was known for its violence and bloody battles. "We make money with chain matches and bullrope matches and cage matches and dog-collar matches," Blanchard told a reporter in

1982 after there was a complaint about the riotous nature of his live shows. "The wrestlers know what they are doing with those items. They know what the risks are. They're trained and they're strong and they're tough and it would cost us money to have these things taken away from us and it would cost the fans excitement."[54] Blanchard was never shy about waging war, and his hostilities with Adkisson were consistent. In late 1982, shortly before his USA program debut, his longtime alliance with Paul Boesch in Houston ended, giving him a second conflict in Texas.

Boesch and Adkisson shared concern about Blanchard's SCW cable program — and they were right to worry. The San Antonio promoter planned to expand, not only in Texas, but in several other states as well. In fact, he might've had coast-to-coast aspirations, but Blanchard was in a tough position from day one. His USA Network deal was reportedly $7,000 a week, and unless his investment began to pay serious dividends, his financial situation was slowly going to deteriorate. One of the first territories Blanchard considered for takeover was Tulsa, Oklahoma, a region with an exceptionally rich history in pro wrestling.

It was in the 1920s, during the heyday of Ed "Strangler" Lewis, that Tulsa became a major wrestling town. The incomparable Sam Avey, a banker by trade, established a professional outfit featuring the best in the business. By the 1930s, he shifted his focus to nonheavyweight competitors, building his promotion around a local grappler, Leroy McGuirk. A product of Oklahoma A&M, McGuirk won an NCAA championship in 1931 and had several reigns as world light heavyweight titleholder in the professional ranks. In 1939, he became world junior heavyweight champion, a title he held for more than 10 years until a car accident cost him his sight.[55] When Avey retired, McGuirk took over the Tulsa promotion and was a loyal NWA member for three decades.

Tulsa had been a symbol of stability for the NWA too, and the downward slide McGuirk faced in the late 1970s and early '80s was caused by several factors. As noted earlier, because of its location, Tulsa was being affected by several outside television programs, specifically those in Dallas (Adkisson) and Memphis (Jerry Jarrett). Cable TV added to the problem, bringing in the WWF, GCW/WCW, and, in 1982, SCW. McGuirk simply couldn't compete with the extraordinary talent, high production values, and creativity of those promotions. He tried to stay relevant by hiring

George Scott, recently of Mid-Atlantic and GCW fame, as his booker, and propped up well-known stars Jimmy Snuka and Paul Jones as headliners.[56] But problems with workers, and an assortment of varied challenges, including the loss of a key venue in Little Rock, slowly pushed McGuirk's business past the point of no return.[57]

The wolves were circling Tulsa, and Joe Blanchard was joined by both Jack Adkisson and "Cowboy" Bill Watts, waiting for McGuirk to go belly-up. Of the three, Watts was in the best position. He was an Oklahoma native, personally trained by McGuirk to turn professional in 1961, and was a headliner all over the country. Weighing more than 270 pounds, Watts had first made a name for himself on the football field, playing several years in the AFL and NFL. Around 1970, he settled in the Tulsa area and joined the promotional end of McGuirk's franchise, running shows in Oklahoma, Missouri, Arkansas, Louisiana, Mississippi, and parts of Texas. For the next nine years, Watts worked in conjunction with McGuirk, and bolstered wrestling in New Orleans to the point where it overtook Tulsa as the territory's main city.

Six extravaganzas at the Louisiana Superdome were enormously successful. His July 22, 1978, show drew one of the largest gates of the decade, over $142,000, and with popular attractions like Dusty Rhodes, Andre the Giant, and Mr. Wrestling II appearing regularly, fans were always eager for the next show. The following year, realizing the potential for his own territory, Watts broke from McGuirk's office and established Mid-South Sports Inc., retaining ties to the NWA but without formal membership in the Alliance. He continued promoting in Louisiana and Mississippi, leaving McGuirk with his original three states (Oklahoma, Missouri, and Arkansas). By 1982, with McGuirk fading, Watts wanted to annex Oklahoma. He landed a prime network timeslot in Tulsa on KJRH (channel 2) for Saturdays at noon and made his debut at the Assembly Center beginning in May 1982.

McGuirk's promotion couldn't compete against the Junkyard Dog, Ted DiBiase, Dick Murdock, Paul Orndorff, and the rest of Mid-South's extraordinary talent, and it went out of business. As tribute to his mentor, Watts scheduled a special gala event in honor of McGuirk on July 18, 1982, in Tulsa, and longtime supporters paid homage to the legendary promoter. But as much as Watts seemed to be the logical successor to McGuirk in Oklahoma, Jack Adkisson of the Dallas-based World Class Championship

Wrestling wanted his say in who ran the state. He'd been edging into Oklahoma on his own, and his prize crew of wrestlers headlined by his sons — David, Kevin, and Kerry Von Erich — were heavy favorites. Watts and Adkisson came to a peaceful resolution on July 21, 1982, and agreed to divide the profits on shows in Tulsa and Oklahoma City.[58]

Like Watts, Adkisson had an athletic background, having played college football at Southern Methodist University and briefly as a member of the AFL's Dallas Texans. In 1953, he turned to pro wrestling and a few years later adopted the "Fritz Von Erich" German heel gimmick. He was hated all over North America, but his box-office draw was unmistakable as people direly wanted to see him beaten. Von Erich rose to the heights of the industry, and held the AWA world heavyweight championship in 1963. He returned to Dallas three years later, and was taught the ins and outs of promotions by Ed McLemore. In 1969, after McLemore's death, he assumed sole control of the Dallas franchise, and his booking office sent wrestlers throughout Texas. His three eldest children, Kevin, David, and Kerry, followed his footsteps into the ring, and the youngsters became heroes in Dallas, drawing in bobbysoxers and screaming teenage fans to the Sportatorium.

Adkisson himself was no longer a diabolical heel in the ring, and the Von Erich family represented all that was good in the world of wrestling. On the business side of things, the Dallas territory made impressive strides in the early 1980s. The company signed a deal with local independent station KXTX (channel 39) in 1981, seeking an upgrade of its television product, and producer Mickey Grant was going to deliver in a big way.[59] Working with a budget of several thousand dollars per episode, Grant instituted a multi-camera system for matches, and viewers were provided with a more inclusive look at the action. The content appeared much crisper than most contemporary wrestling shows, and with popular music, vivid graphics, slow-motion, and instant replays worked into the weekly scheme, it was definitely an attention grabber.

Ratings skyrocketed, and the Christian Broadcasting Network, which owned KXTX, decided to syndicate the program across the country, allowing World Class to consider expansion. It was in this time frame that the promotion changed its name from Big Time Wrestling to World Class Championship Wrestling, and the alteration reflected an expanded view of its standing in the global marketplace. Adkisson saw the potential for cross-country promotions and international tours. In late 1982, the Von Erichs entered into a legendary war with the Fabulous Freebirds, and fans were captivated by the explosive feud. Crowds were popping and things couldn't have been better in the Big D.

Pro wrestling was a family business in Texas. Approximately 365 miles from Dallas, in Amarillo, another father had proudly supervised the grappling education of his sons. An accomplished grappler in his own right, Dory Funk Sr. won a plethora of regional championships in West Texas, part of an NWA territory that stretched to southeastern Colorado in the north, El Paso in the south, Abilene in the east, and into New Mexico in the west. On February 11, 1969, Funk Sr. saw his namesake, Dory Jr., achieve one of the sport's greatest honors when he captured the NWA world heavyweight title from Gene Kiniski in Tampa. Unfortunately, he didn't live to see his younger son, Terry, capture that same championship on December 10, 1975, as it was two years after his death. Without a doubt, the Funk brothers became the most successful siblings in wrestling history, and between them, they have been inducted into more than 19 Halls of Fame.

West Texas was known for its creative booking, innovative matches, and violence. There was a perfect blend of scientific and submission grappling with wild brawling. Funk Sr. was the backbone of the promotion from the 1950s to the early '70s, and the crowds at the Amarillo Sports Arena saw some of the most exciting bouts anywhere in the world. He faced off with nearly every big name in the industry and used his famous spinning toehold to put many of them away. When it was time for a straight-up fight, he set the standard for the wrestlers to emulate, and he drew the best from his opponents. Texas Death matches were commonplace in the territory, and buckets of blood were spilled on local mats.

The Funks were part owners of the West Texas territory as well. In 1967, after Funk Sr.'s partner Dr. Karl Sarpolis died, Dory Jr. and Terry Funk purchased his interest, while a smaller percentage was sold to Jerry Kozak, who replaced Sarpolis as the front for the outfit. Since the Funks were in-ring competitors, Kozak served as the official promoter throughout the 1970s. Dory Jr. and Terry were in high demand all over the world, and their reigns as NWA world champions only elevated their box-office draw. Extended tours of Alliance territories stateside and overseas in Japan limited their time in West Texas, and with the Funks missing from weekly bills, attendance plummeted. The Funks were ever committed to their hometown fans and traveled great distances to make important dates, but the territory was changing.

Finally, the Funks sold West Texas in October 1978 to Dick Murdoch and Blackjack Mulligan, two wrestlers with local roots. Murdoch grew up in Amarillo and Mulligan was from Sweetwater, and they were fully invested in keeping the great wrestling heritage of West Texas alive. Murdoch and Mulligan continued their active careers, and with wrestlers imported from Dallas (including the Von Erichs), plus youngsters like Ted DiBiase and Merced Solis (Tito Santana), Amarillo seemed to be in good shape. Not immediate members of the NWA, Murdoch and Mulligan were expected to submit an application prior to the 1979 convention. But their membership status was actually hurt by their maneuvering, especially after it was realized they had landed a timeslot on an indie TV station in San Jose, California, more than 1,300 miles from Amarillo.

If this had been as the result of normal cable TV expansion, such a thing might not have registered with many people, but that was not the case. Roy Shire, the NWA member in northern California, considered the arrival of Amarillo TV part of an invasion, plain and simple. The bold move was likely made as part of a greater plan to establish a coastal stop for grapplers en route to Japan. Murdoch, for one, was routinely traveling to All Japan Pro Wrestling, as were the Funks and many other American grapplers. A setup in California could have been beneficial in that regard. Between April and June 1979, the Amarillo group ran at least three shows in San Jose, Santa Rosa, and Salinas, but with low attendance and heat coming in from Shire and the NWA, it was a losing endeavor, and future shows were canceled.[60] The NWA, in turn, approved their membership at the 1979 annual meeting in Las Vegas.

Amarillo was a hot and cold territory under Murdoch and Mulligan, but things rapidly deteriorated toward the end of 1980. The promotion's working relationship with Dallas stopped on a dime in November, and management turned to Joe Blanchard's San Antonio office for wrestlers before Murdoch and Mulligan decided to cut their losses and bowed out of the region. Nick Kozak and Ricky Romero picked up the scraps and looked to Leroy McGuirk in Tulsa for help the following year, but

McGuirk's business wasn't healthy either. Amarillo was a shadow of its former self, and although programs were held, the glitz and glamour of big-time wrestling in West Texas had disappeared.

Albuquerque, New Mexico, was in the same boat. Once an independent NWA territory all its own, Albuquerque had been run by promoter Mike London since 1949. London, a former wrestler known for his trademark beard, was an intelligent booker for the region that ran northward along the future I-25 corridor, from Albuquerque to Cheyenne, Wyoming, and included Denver and Colorado Springs. With a solid talent-sharing agreement with Fred Kohler of Chicago, London was highly successful, turning mediocre-drawing towns into hotspots. In June 1974, a devastating fire at the McIntosh Building destroyed nearly all of his personal and business property. Despite the massive loss, he was determined to go on, telling a local newspaper that his television program would be taped that weekend "come hell or high water."[61]

By that time, London was relying exclusively on talent from West Texas, since a local booking office wasn't sustainable, and he coordinated through Nick Kozak in Amarillo. But the same problems affecting Amarillo hurt Albuquerque as well, and in mid-1975, London ceased running regular programs. Three years later, he was honored by the Albuquerque Sports Hall of Fame, and it was claimed he had been on television longer than anyone in U.S. history, consecutively since the late 1940s.[62] With London's quiet retirement from the wild world of pro wrestling, Albuquerque was void of pro grappling until November 1981, when an independent group operated by R. Dewain Miller tried its luck at the Civic Auditorium, billing Jackson Cromwell Brodie as champion. Among the other grapplers featured were Frederick "Nature Boy" Von Hess, Hillbilly, and Tommy Reynoso.

Toward the end of 1982, there were rumblings about a new promotion hitting the Southwest, and it had an interesting connection to two prime NWA territories in the Southeastern part of the United States. On September 24, 1982, a new entity called Global Wrestling Inc. was established in Georgia.[63] This organization was headed by Ann Gunkel, the widow of wrestling legend Ray Gunkel, and had ties to Eddie Graham in Florida. Gunkel, who was remembered by many wrestling fans for her war against Georgia Championship Wrestling and the NWA between 1972 and 1974, was ready to take the nation by storm, and with Graham, she had Florida and Georgia locked up. In addition, she was pursuing a syndicated television deal, looking to run live events in Los Angeles, Phoenix, Las Vegas, and Albuquerque.

The fact that another outfit had far-reaching expansion plans was astonishing. The WWF, GCW, SCW, World Class, and now Ann Gunkel's Global were all trying to increase their market share — and at the same time. North America was only so big, and, surprisingly, this list didn't include Jim Crockett Promotions, which, outside of a foray into Buffalo and Toronto, had yet to commit to a major outside expansion. The absorption of Southern California by the WWF and Oklahoma by Watts–Adkisson were major developments in the world of wrestling. With the collapse of West Texas and Albuquerque, the wrestling map looked much different in December 1982 than it had a decade earlier. Cable TV and syndication was the biggest threat to the territorial system, and emboldened promoters were investing big money to capitalize on the opportunities created. With that being said, and considering all the players now involved, the old territories didn't stand much of a chance of surviving the 1980s intact.

CHAPTER FIVE

THE SURVIVING TERRITORIES

The early 1980s was an incredibly fluid time for professional wrestling. Left and right, promoters were expanding and absorbing territories, while others were selling out and leaving the sport behind. One of the biggest changes to the business was actually a well-deserved retirement. On January 1, 1982, Sam Muchnick stepped down from his leadership role in St. Louis, and although he'd remain around the local office for another year as an adviser, his days running the day-to-day operations were finished.[64] His retirement was not only a loss to wrestling in St. Louis and to the National Wrestling Alliance, but to the business as a whole. He had been a wise advocate for peace, a sounding board for grievances, and the glue between various organizations. In an industry not always known for its integrity, Muchnick was trusted, and he was the shining star everyone looked to for guidance.

For 37 years, Muchnick ran St. Louis with professionalism and class.[65] The famous *Wrestling at the Chase* TV program was mandatory viewing for fans, and wrestlers who worked St. Louis always knew they were getting a fair shake. In terms of talent and booking angles, Muchnick was exceptionally conservative. Matches usually went to a conclusive finish, and he enjoyed promoting wrestlers of legitimate skill and strength. He wasn't thrilled by gimmicks, nor was he impressed by egomaniacal personalities behind the scenes. Muchnick didn't have time for games and he never wanted to risk disappointing his patrons. If someone wanted to no-show a booking in St. Louis without proper advance notice, that wrestler was likely not to be welcome again.

It was an admirable practice, and the St. Louis populace appreciated his extraordinary dedication. With heavy hearts, those same fans acknowledged and celebrated his great career upon his retirement. Wrestling went on, though, and the St. Louis Wrestling Club, under the ownership of Bob Geigel, Pat O'Connor, and Verne Gagne, kept the territory alive. Larry Matysik, Muchnick's longtime assistant, was retained to manage the office, and the transition of ownership appeared relatively painless. Of course, there was bound to be adjustments, mostly because of the new influence of Geigel in the territory. A former wrestler of note, Geigel was the head of the Central States region, headquartered in Kansas City, and in August 1982, he was elected to his third term as NWA president.[66]

The merging of ownership in St. Louis and Kansas City was going to streamline things a little too much for some tastes. Definite characteristics of Geigel's promotion were going to show up in St. Louis, and to purists like Matysik, the change would be difficult to accept.[67] Kansas City relied on more gimmickry than St. Louis had under Muchnick. They popped houses for immediate returns rather than considering long-term effects and used crooked finishes to incite crowd reaction. Matysik knew what made wrestling tick in his city and didn't understand changing a thriving system. Several times in 1982, he butted heads with Geigel and even resigned, only to return in the hopes of protecting the unique qualities of St. Louis. There was no city in wrestling like it.

Geigel possessed an entirely different mindset. Originally from Algona, Iowa, he served in World War II and enjoyed a successful run as a football player and wrestler at the University of Iowa. In 1948, his grappling skills earned him All-American honors, and two years later, he turned professional. Geigel toured the country but spent much of his time in his home territory of the Central States. He learned the promotional side of the business from George Simpson in Kansas City and Gust Karras in St. Joseph, and in 1963, he joined his mentors and Pat O'Connor to form Heart of America Sports Attractions Inc. The new company would become the principal entity behind wrestling in Iowa, Kansas, and western Missouri, a region with a tremendous history in wrestling. Iowa had been at the center of the sport's focus during the first quarter of the 20th century, with Frank Gotch and Earl Caddock ruling the roost.

Iowa was also the birthplace of the National Wrestling Alliance. Under the sensible leadership of Paul "Pinkie" George, the NWA was formed in 1948, initially as a Midwestern outgrowth of his Des Moines–based organization of the same name. But the NWA quickly grew beyond Pinkie's control, and by the early 1960s, George found himself at odds with the Alliance. Even though he was the father of the organization, he was essentially muscled out of the business by the politically strong Heart of America Sports Attractions. The company did the same to Orville Brown, the very first NWA world heavyweight champion, who owned a slice of the Kansas City office for years. As Geigel's group consolidated power, Brown was pushed into retirement.

Without competition, the Kansas City office controlled the territory, and Geigel strengthened his standing in the NWA, becoming a member of the board of directors in 1972, an officer in 1977, and president in 1978. There was little doubt Geigel was greatly respected by his peers and wrestlers alike. He was a college-educated guy and a veteran of thousands of matches. On extended tours of West Texas he picked up a lot of knowledge about booking and creativity from Dory Funk Sr. and implemented many of those tricks of the trade in the Central States. Having New Zealander Pat O'Connor around was a big help to him too. The former NWA world champion (from 1959 to '61) aided with booking, worked matches, and acted as the middleman between Kansas City and St. Louis, where he owned a percentage and also worked as a matchmaker.

There was another major player in the Central States, and he was arguably the most valuable: Harley Race, a brilliant grappler from Quitman,

Missouri. Race, by 1982, was already a six-time NWA world heavyweight titleholder and an important box-office attraction around the globe.[68] A product of the territory, he was celebrated in towns large and small, and both Geigel and Muchnick supported his numerous title reigns. He was a multifaceted performer, able to wrestle or fight at a moment's notice, and was the perfect opponent for any number of foes. It didn't matter if they were Andre the Giant or a scientific grappler like Jack Brisco, Race was an ideal ring rival. And beginning in 1982, he also owned stock in the St. Louis office. The combination of Geigel's position in the NWA and Race's value as a grappler gave the Central States–Missouri contingent enormous power.

Jim Crockett Jr., head of the Mid-Atlantic territory, was another well-situated member of the Alliance, and his star grappler, "Nature Boy" Ric Flair, was the organization's heavyweight champion. The Crocketts were part of wrestling tradition in the Carolinas and Virginia going back decades. Jim Sr. actually began in the promotional business in the 1930s and joined the NWA in 1951. He developed a thriving region, utilizing the best talent in the business, and earned the respect of both wrestlers and fans. Enthusiasts appreciated the consistency of his first-class presentations and grapplers were never cheated by his payoffs. He was sincere, loyal to the community, and widely appreciated in big cities and small. His death in 1973 was a stunning blow to the wrestling world at large, and his friends within the NWA mourned the loss of a veteran leader and colleague. The Mid-Atlantic promotion was inherited by his family with Jim Crockett Jr. taking a central role.

During the last half of the 1970s, under the watchful eye of booker George Scott, Jim Crockett Promotions (JCP) evolved as an organization, and really became one of the crown jewel territories for the NWA. Featuring outstanding talent like Flair, Ricky Steamboat, Roddy Piper, Greg Valentine, and Paul Jones, JCP was riding an impressive high, and Jim Crockett Jr. was lauded for his leadership. His political position inside the Alliance grew, first as a second vice president in 1976, and then as president beginning in 1980. The 37-year-old Crockett sponsored Flair for the NWA title, and on September 17, 1981, in Kansas City, the Nature Boy went over Dusty Rhodes for his first world championship. Crockett was reelected NWA president in 1981 but didn't seek the position the following year. In fact, he didn't attend the 1982 annual meeting in San Juan, Puerto Rico, and his brother David represented the promotion.[69] At that convention, Bob Geigel became president.

Within the political hierarchy of the NWA, egos ran rampant and volatility was often the norm. The loss of the even-tempered Sam Muchnick had hurt the coalition, but a new generation of leaders stepped up, and Crockett's voice at the table was vitally important. Another key leader was Eddie Graham of Tampa, Florida. Born Edward Gossett in Chattanooga, Tennessee, he became one-half of the renowned Graham Brothers tag team along with Dr. Jerry Graham. Their villainous act was a showstopper all over the wrestling map, and they turned crowds on their heads from the moment they stepped through the backstage curtain. In Florida, Eddie branched out on his own, wrestling for his original trainer, Clarence "Cowboy" Luttrall. Remembered for his ill-fated boxer versus wrestler bout against legendary fighter Jack Dempsey, which resulted in a knockout for the latter, Luttrall is credited with creating the first viable wrestling circuit in Florida.[70] His territory extended from Tallahassee to Key West, and Graham was a major box-office draw.

Surprisingly, Graham was a better fan favorite in Florida than a heel, and his ring wars with the Great Malenko and Johnny Valentine are still talked about today. Following Luttrall's retirement in 1970, Graham assumed control over the region and became a member of the NWA board of directors around 1971. Five years later, in August 1976, he was elected NWA president, replacing Jack Adkisson. Graham was an extraordinary promoter, and his love for the business was nearly unparalleled. He had a special affinity for pure wrestling, even in the worked professional environment. That meant he enjoyed booking shooters, and he had great respect for amateur grappling. Graham donated significant amounts of money to area wrestling institutions, including the University of Florida in Gainesville, and endlessly supported local charities and events.[71] He established a youth camp and was influential in the lives of thousands of boys.

Wrestler Steve Keirn told the *Lakeland Ledger* in 1976 that Graham was hugely important in his development. "Seeing that I never had a father around, Eddie sort of took over and straightened me out on things," Keirn explained. "[He] discouraged me against fighting and kept me out of a few fights. He basically showed me how to defend myself and how easily I could be hurt in a fight."[72] Graham was also a man of great principle, and after a newspaper heavily criticized a wrestling show in St. Petersburg in 1972, he swiftly pulled all future events from the city's Bayfront Auditorium. The reason, according to the *St. Petersburg Evening Independent*, was that he'd happily forfeit tens of thousands of dollars "rather than risk adverse publicity for wrestling."

"My files are full of letters from mayors and teachers and sheriffs asking us to help in putting on programs in schools," Graham said. "We want to keep doing that, but when things like that (article) come out, we may become ineffective because even the kids will start doubting us."[73] Florida wrestling epitomized action, and matches between Jack Brisco and Dory Funk Jr. established a high bar for scientific wrestling seen anywhere in the world. But that's the way Graham liked it. He featured top wrestlers, brawlers, and colorful performers, and the mixture gave the Sunshine State incredible in-ring flavor. And the warm weather made Florida a hotbed for big-name talent during the winter months. In March 1978, Graham resigned as president of the NWA due to health problems, but he retained his influence and was a vocal supporter behind the world title reigns of Dusty Rhodes in 1979 and 1981.

Another member of the NWA board of directors in 1981–82 was Ron Fuller, a man with wrestling deep in his blood. Standing 6-foot-9, he was a third-generation wrestler who followed in the footsteps of his grandfather, Roy Welch, and father, Buddy Fuller. He was a multiple-time regional champion, winning titles in Alabama, Tennessee, Georgia, and Florida, and he assumed control of the Knoxville promotion around 1974. In January 1978, it was announced that Fuller had acquired the Gulf Coast wrestling business from Lee Fields, effectively widening his scope of operations.[74] His Southeastern Wrestling promotion was responsible for Alabama and northwestern Florida and, after selling out of Knoxville, he moved his home office to Gulf Breeze, Florida. During the early 1980s, Fuller's company was on fire, and a combination of captivating angles, star wrestlers, and well-booked matches sparked attendance all over the territory.

Fuller's grandfather, Roy Welch, began his wrestling career around 1930 and was followed into the sport by three of his brothers, Herb, Jack, and Lester. He teamed with Nick Gulas and established a Nashville office during the 1940s. In 1949, they joined the NWA and franchised a territory that included parts of Tennessee, Kentucky, Alabama, and Mississippi, with further extensions into Arkansas, Missouri, and Indiana. For more than 30 years, Welch and Gulas worked in partnership, controlling the infamous "gasoline circuit" and exerting strong influence in the Alliance. But in 1977, after what *The Tennessean* called "internal management difficulties," the territory was fractured, with Welch and Jerry Jarrett on one side and Gulas on the other.[75] A handful of months later, in September 1977, Welch passed away.

At the time of the separation, the 34-year-old Jarrett took control of the predominant stars in the region and challenged Gulas head to head throughout the territory.[76] Memphis was ground zero for the war, and Gulas was handicapped from the beginning after losing his TV outlet. Jarrett capitalized with his own studio television program and seized the Mid-South Coliseum for his shows, establishing his local dominance. The war continued elsewhere, but in the eyes of the NWA, both Jarrett and Gulas were members and were accorded the rights of the organization. But Jarrett was exploring his options, and strengthened his ties to Verne Gagne's AWA. He also acknowledged the Continental Wrestling Association as a sanctioning body, and recognized a local world champion between 1979 and 1981. Billy Graham, Dory Funk Jr., and Billy Robinson were among those to hold the CWA world title during that time period.

Jerry Lawler, the "King" of wrestling in Memphis, was another CWA titleholder and, over the course of his career, held more than 160 championships. His legendary status in and around the Mid-Southern territory was undisputed. In 1982, he garnered national attention with a feud with comedian-actor Andy Kaufman, who played Latka Gravas on the hit sitcom *Taxi*. Kaufman was known for interjecting a large dose of psychology into his comedy, and was drawing the ire of fans by participating in intergender bouts. Lawler was not pleased by Kaufman's off-color shenanigans, and things took a serious turn in April 1982 when Lawler put Kaufman in the hospital with a neck injury after a bout in Memphis. A few months later, on July 28, the two appeared on *Late Night with David Letterman*, where Lawler slapped Kaufman, only to receive a cup of hot coffee to his face in return. The angle developed perfectly and had everyone talking.

All the way across the country, in Northern California, pro wrestling experienced a series of changes between 1979 and 1982. The established promoter, Roy Shire, an ex-grappler from Hammond, Indiana, first entered San Francisco in 1961 and quickly outperformed his competition to put the final nail in the coffin of Joe Malcewicz's promotion. He drove attendance upwards with solid booking and impeccable performers, and his annual battle royal at the Cow Palace was a must-see event in the late 1960s and 1970s. He joined the NWA in 1968 and was named to the board of directors the following year. In 1971, he also had a stint as second vice president, and with strong friendships, it was all but guaranteed that the Alliance would come to his aid if needed. And Shire did eventually need major support. In 1979, he collapsed his booking office and began relying on outside talent, pulling in grapplers from Mike LeBell, Bob Geigel, and later Eddie Graham in Florida.

But the out-of-town TV productions, specifically those provided by Geigel from Kansas City, were not in line with what San Francisco fans expected, and Shire's business further suffered. On January 24, 1981, Shire ran his final program at the Cow Palace with Dusty Rhodes, the Funk Brothers, and Pat Patterson on the bill, and his 20-year run in San Francisco came to an end. But the Bay Area was never void of big-time wrestling. Nine days before Shire boarded up his enterprise, Verne Gagne's AWA debuted at the Oakland Coliseum Arena with a stacked card. With local TV already in place, Gagne meant business, and by mid-1982, he'd moved into the Cow Palace and successfully absorbed the territory.

Up the coast in Portland, Don Owen was the boss of the Pacific Northwest territory, a prosperous area that encompassed most of Oregon and Washington. Having begun his tenure as a promoter as an understudy of his father, Herb, during the 1930s, he took over following the latter's death in 1942. Owen was a promoter of the Sam Muchnick type, unflinchingly fair to his talent and possessing a code of ethics rare in wrestling circles. The Pacific Northwest was capably run for decades without shady dealings, and Owen was greatly respected within the NWA, serving on the board of directors several times. His membership card in the Alliance was issued in 1951, making him one of the longest-reigning associates, and by the 1980s he was fast approaching his 50th anniversary in the business. His range of knowledge and experience made him a valuable cog in the national organization.

Wrestling at the Portland Sports Arena offered an addictive blend of athleticism and vibrant drama, and Owen never lacked top-named performers. Luther Lindsay, Stan Stasiak, Maurice "Mad Dog" Vachon, Moondog Mayne, and Dutch Savage were always reliable draws, and a young Roddy Piper was heavily influenced during his time in Portland. Loyal viewers of Owen's innovative television program on KPTV, featuring memorable commercials by sponsor Tom Peterson, saw the development of exciting angles and religiously packed the arena to see the culmination of intense feuds.[77] Regional champions and visits by the touring NWA world titleholders added box-office appeal, and crowds usually popped when a national attraction visited town. Altogether, with stable TV and a good crop of grapplers, Owen insulated himself from the pitfalls that had taken down San Francisco, Tulsa, and other original NWA territories.

Another Oregonian, Tex Hager, also held membership in the NWA during the 1950s, and booked a territory that included Idaho, Utah, and Washington. After he folded around 1959, his cities were divvied up by several enterprising promoters. The same went for Dave Reynolds, who controlled Salt Lake City and towns in both Wyoming and Colorado for a time. Outside of the stability Owen brought through his Portland booking office, most of these western states were loosely operated, and figured into the territories of various promoters through the years. Dean Silverstone's Superstar Championship Wrestling picked up a number of vacant towns, Seattle and Tacoma among them, in the late 1960s and ran as an independent outfit for about a decade. Many others cities were left without big-time wrestling. Travel was part of the problem, as good drawing towns were too far for wrestlers to make any money, and the weather conditions during winter months was brutal.

Salt Lake City was abandoned essentially because of its location. The closest major city regularly engaged in a prospering circuit was Denver, more than 500 miles away by car. Sporadically, indie promoters tried to make money in the region, such as when Eric the Great, Toma Red Cloud, Judy Grable, and Rod O'Neil appeared at the State Fairgrounds Coliseum in the summer of 1979.[78] But on the whole, Utah was mostly without wrestling until April 8, 1982, when the AWA, as part of its western expansion, claimed Salt Lake City. An enthusiastic crowd of 7,000 people turned out to see former Brigham Young University hero Ken Patera and many other TV stars, in what was the renaissance of pro grappling in the region. Sportswriter Lee Benson of the *Deseret News* remembered the old-time wrestling of the 1960s and, after seeing the AWA show, noted, "The years haven't changed the act."[79] And that was a major selling point for fans.

North of Portland, Vancouver, British Columbia, enjoyed more than a half century of remarkable wrestling history. Legends Frank Gotch, Stanislaus Zbyszko, Dan McLeod, and Ted Thye made appearances there, going back to the early 1900s, and the sport maintained a terrific popularity throughout the region. Cliff Parker, around the time of the NWA's formation, stabilized Vancouver as an affiliate, with booking ties to Don Owen in Portland and Stu Hart in Calgary. Interested in protecting the reputation of pro wrestling, Parker issued a challenge to the local populace in 1954, claiming that a wrestler could easily "demonstrate his favorite or any hold on the doubting fan" to prove the sport's legitimacy.[80] It isn't known how many people actually took him up on the offer, but Parker got his point across. He took Rod Fenton, recently an NWA member in Arizona, as a partner late in the 1950s and, in 1968, sold to Sandor Kovacs and Gene Kiniski. Kiniski, the NWA world champion from 1966 and 1969, was originally from Edmonton but made Vancouver his home, and he drew sizable audiences as the defending champ. His witty interviews, villainous tactics, and impressive wrestling abilities were on display against fan favorites and heels alike, and Kiniski never failed to deliver. Multiple-time world championship claimant Don Leo Jonathan was also a big star across British Columbia. The 6-foot-6, 300-pound behemoth won the local singles and tag team titles on numerous occasions. In 1977, Kovacs sold his shares in the territory to Al Tomko, who had previously promoted in Winnipeg as an affiliate for the AWA. Tomko implemented a different formula for his promotion, booking himself as the champion, and as a result, the once-thriving region began to suffer at the box office. Fans that knew the difference between the old style of grappling in Vancouver and Tomko's efforts were disappointed by the transformation and began to look elsewhere for their wrestling fix.

Many people gravitated toward Stu Hart's Stampede promotion, which, by 1983, was running shows in Vancouver at the PNE Agrodome. Hart was a legend in the business, first as a wrestler and then as the owner of the Foothills Athletic Club in Calgary, Alberta, beginning in 1952. The Calgary promotion was highly successful, and Hart was well respected as a trainer. The basement of his home, known as the "Dungeon," is where he taught his pupils the art of submission grappling, and his graduates were not only skilled performers, but capable shooters. Among his notable students were Fritz Von Erich, "Superstar" Billy Graham, and Wilbur Snyder. He also mentored his sons, and Bret, Bruce, Smith, Keith, and Owen Hart each followed Stu's career path into the squared circle. With a heavy influence of Hart family grappling talent, along with upstarts Davey Boy Smith, Bad News Allen, and Honky Tonk Wayne (Honky Tonk Man), wrestling under the Stampede banner flourished.

On the other side of Canada, in the Maritimes, another family ruled the roost. They were the Cormier brothers, better known by their wrestling names Rudy and Bobby Kay, Leo Burke, and the Beast. In 1969, Rudy established the Eastern Sports Association and the promotion International Wrestling. Al Zinck, his business partner, became the promoter of record, and the celebrated quartet of siblings maintained active careers. Burke was arguably the most popular, and he held the North American championship six times. He also was a strong regional challenger to world champions Terry Funk and Jack Brisco. International Wrestling closed up around 1979, and Emile Dupree's Atlantic Grand Prix Wrestling took over the territory. Burke was also a star for Dupree, capturing the local U.S. title three times. With programs at the Halifax Forum, the Jean-Louis Levesque Arena in Moncton, and Truro Stadium in central Nova Scotia, AGPW kept fans entertained in the Maritime territory in the early 1980s.

When considering the Canadian territories, one would be remiss not to place a rather large spotlight on Montreal and its tremendous wrestling history. The city, and its surrounding region in Quebec, was the proud home of pro grappling for generations, spawning legends Emile Maupas, Eugene Tremblay, Henri DeGlane, and Yvon Robert. Promoter Eddie Quinn was in charge of the region when the Montreal territory was officially recognized by the National Wrestling Alliance in 1949. Following Quinn's unceremonious exit from wrestling in 1963, Montreal was taken over by Johnny Rougeau and his International Wrestling Association.[81] During the early 1970s, the famous Vachon brothers, Maurice and Paul, opened Grand Prix Wrestling, offering a second brand for area fans.

Wrestling in Montreal was incredibly robust. The lineups included a young Andre the Giant, Killer Kowalski, Don Leo Jonathan, Edouard Carpentier, and, of course, the Vachons themselves. But by the late 1970s, both promotions closed, and pro wrestling in Montreal saw a gigantic turnaround in popularity. In 1980, though, Gino Brito, Frank Valois, and Andre the Giant formed Varoussac Promotions, launching their own incarnation of International Wrestling. And despite being an indie group, they featured a deep roster of talent. Andre's ties to the WWF allowed New York wrestlers to appear with regularity, and WWF champion Bob Backlund was among those to wrestle in Montreal. In 1982, Brito and his partners returned wrestling to the Montreal Forum, the city's top indoor venue, after several years' absence.[82] It was a major score for International Wrestling, and the promotion locked in a deal ensuring they would control the Forum exclusively going forward.

Another territory with a rich heritage was Puerto Rico, which was part of the Caribbean extension of Championship Wrestling from Florida for years. In 1973, Carlos Colon and Victor Jovica founded Capitol Sports Promotions and joined the NWA six years later. The promotion ran operations in San Juan, Bayamon, Caguas, Ponce, and many other towns and featured a host of internationally known stars. The regional North American championship was held by Bruno Sammartino, Gorilla Monsoon, Mr. Fuji, and Abdullah the Butcher, among others. Colon, an enormously popular performer, won it eight times. In July 1982, Abdullah claimed to be the heavyweight champion of the world but was quickly dethroned by Colon on July 24. With exciting athletes and rowdy brawls, Puerto Rico was the stage for intense grappling action, and local fans were hooked.

Lastly, nearly 6,000 miles away from San Juan, Hawaii developed under the leadership of Alex Karasick during the 1930s. Like Florida and Puerto Rico, Hawaii was a prime destination for wrestlers because of its beauty and weather. In addition, for wrestlers venturing overseas to Japan, Honolulu was the perfect midway spot to earn extra money. Karasick worked with partners in Japan, and those connections continued under his successors, Ed Francis and Lord James Blears (Mid-Pacific Promotions) beginning in 1961. Steve Rickard ultimately bought the promotion in 1979 and soon had a falling-out with well-known grappler Peter Maivia, who started up his own company, Polynesian Pro Wrestling. Rickard returned to New Zealand and Maivia built a highly profitable operation. On June 12, 1982, the 45-year-old Maivia passed away, and his wife, Lia, and booker Lars Anderson continued the promotion's success.

If you pull back even further and look at wrestling on a global scale, Japan, Mexico, the United Kingdom, Australia, South Africa, and many other countries featured some level of big-time professional wrestling. Organizations were well defined in those locations, offering their own heroes and popular feuds to excite and grow the fanbase. By the end of 1982, the belief that the sport was, indeed, in some kind of decline was hard to imagine. Well over a dozen booking offices in the U.S. were doing pretty good business, and although daring promoters were looking at expansion, the NWA continued to protect the integrity of the territories. But 1983 would see a change for pro wrestling, and there was nothing the NWA, with all of its finely crafted bylaws, could do to stop one enterprising promoter from taking on the world.

CHAPTER SIX

A NEW ERA IN PROFESSIONAL WRESTLING

The establishment of the American Wrestling Association in 1960 was a landmark moment in the history of pro wrestling. Verne Gagne, a grappler since 1949, was behind the bold move, one of only a handful of star-caliber performers with the clout, business sense, and political capital to successfully (and peacefully) branch off from the National Wrestling Alliance. An NCAA champion and Olympian, Gagne was a hot commodity in pro rings from day one, and he was a pawn in many promotional quarrels during the 1950s. After making his bones as a leading box-office attraction, he began to push back at the bully tactics of power-hungry promoters. Having served in the U.S. Marine Corps during World War II, Gagne was no pushover, mentally or physically. He liked the idea of being in charge, and the AWA gave him that freedom.

Beginning with a humble circuit in and around his home state of Minnesota, Gagne's AWA grew to include the Dakotas, Wisconsin, Nebraska, and sections of Illinois, Iowa, and Colorado. In late 1965, he teamed with Wilbur Snyder and Dick the Bruiser, two fellow wrestlers who had also launched an independent promotion in Indiana, and purchased the Chicago territory from Fred Kohler.[83] That investment gave both the AWA and Snyder and Bruiser's WWA (World Wrestling Association) a stranglehold on a top media market with the potential of millions in gate receipts over the long run. The move signified Gagne's willingness to increase his market share and put his organization on the national stage. He targeted Los Angeles in 1969, and although the scheme was well intentioned, it failed financially.[84]

In 1981, Gagne returned to California with an invasion of the Bay Area, and by the middle of 1982, he was firmly in the driver's seat with regular shows at San Francisco's Cow Palace. The AWA then annexed Salt Lake City and Las Vegas, completing its path from Minneapolis to the Pacific Coast. Gagne's crew was impressive, and live events featured world champion Nick Bockwinkel, Pat Patterson, Ray Stevens, Rick Martel, Andre the Giant, and the promotion's leading fan favorite, Hulk Hogan. Hogan was the public's choice to replace Bockwinkel as titleholder, and a title switch was seemingly just a matter of time. In April 1982, Hogan nearly won the belt in St. Paul, but AWA president Stanley Blackburn vetoed the decision, much to the chagrin of spectators. People remained hopeful, and in terms of riding Hogan's popularity, shifting the title to him appeared to be sound.

But Hogan wasn't a technically sound grappler in the vein of former AWA champions, and Gagne was hesitant. As a 10-time titleholder himself, Gagne brought credibility to the championship, similar to what Lou Thesz did for the NWA belt, and he didn't believe punch-and-kick brawlers like Hogan were genuine enough to represent his group. There was no question that Hogan was a much-improved grappler since his time in the WWF. He was the kind of guy whose sheer charisma in interviews and advertising could build a strong house, and his drawing power was nearly unrivaled anywhere in the business. His 1982 appearance in *Rocky III*, which grossed more than $122 million domestically, combined with his showings in Japan, made him an internationally recognizable name. Despite these immense positives, Gagne remained tentative.

A vigilant businessman, Gagne strengthened his political influence by purchasing stock in St. Louis and forging important relationships with promoters in Toronto, Houston, San Antonio, and Memphis. Further expansion wasn't out of the question either. In early 1983, much of Gagne's energy went into promoting Super Sunday, a massive program slated for the St. Paul Civic Center on April 24. He booked Hogan and Bockwinkel yet again, and the stage was set for the most-anticipated title bout in years. An estimated 20,000 fans packed the arena, with another 5,000 at a nearby venue watching on closed-circuit television. The total gate was an astronomical $300,000, the largest in AWA history, and the audience wanted nothing more than to see Hogan finally win the belt. They got what they wanted, at least momentarily. Hogan unleashed his famous legdrop on Bockwinkel and scored a three count as the crowd erupted into a cosmic explosion. The celebration was cut short, however, when it was announced that AWA president Stanley Blackburn was once again reversing the decision. Hogan was disqualified for tossing his opponent over the top rope, and Bockwinkel was still champion. To many observers, it was simply unbelievable that Gagne went back to the well and reused that particular finish in such an important bout. The reverse-decision disqualification was anything but satisfying to fans, and the atmosphere of jubilance immediately turned to anger. AWA loyalists were dismayed by the turn of events, but Super Sunday concluded on a high note when Gagne himself returned to the ring to partner with his old rival Mad Dog Vachon in a bout against rulebreakers Jerry Blackwell and Sheik Adnan Al-Kaissie. Needless to say, the good guys won.

Gagne wasn't always right, but he was resolute, and had decades of experience and accomplishments to support his way of thinking. For 20 years, he had pushed himself as a headliner, and fans responded to his routine style of working. But by the early 1980s, wrestling was changing at a rapid pace, and people weren't looking for authentic wrestlers. They wanted larger-than-life personalities, and Hogan represented that side of the pro wrestling spectrum. But the AWA was Gagne's ship to command, and the successes and failures were his to own.

The same went for Wilbur Snyder and Dick the Bruiser in their Indiana-based World Wrestling Association. Since 1964, the WWA had been a thriving regional promotion, with big outlets in Indianapolis and Chicago and extending into Ohio, Kentucky, and Michigan. Bruiser was the center attraction, and his wild style never ceased to entertain. He held the WWA world title 13 times during the course of his career.[85]

Other champions included Gene Kiniski, Blackjack Lanza, Baron von Raschke, Ernie Ladd, and King Kong (Bruiser) Brody. The best in the business toured through Indianapolis, and the territory thrived throughout the 1960s and '70s. In 1982, Snyder retired, but Bruiser continued on. His booking style was unchanged, and his own placement within the promotional structure remained the same. He was still on top, and the lack of strong, youthful newcomers narrowed the playing field, especially when compared to out-of-town promotions featured in WWA cities on cable. The WWA was losing momentum, and considering the amount of competition, it was a poor time to be facing a decline.

Ex-wrestler Angelo Poffo ran another independent promotion out of Lexington, Kentucky. His company, International Championship Wrestling, was considered to be much more of an "outlaw" group with few ties to other organizations. During the summer of 1979, he filed an antitrust suit against more than a half dozen established promoters claiming there was a wrestling monopoly.[86] In the meantime, he promoted upwards of 30 towns in Kentucky, many of them in rural communities, and also ran programs in surrounding states. His two top stars were his sons, Lanny Poffo and Randy Savage, and both had reigns with the ICW world heavyweight championship. Angelo, who set a consecutive sit-up record in 1945 (6,033) and held a claim to the U.S. title during the 1950s, was still getting in the ring himself, competing as the Masked Miser. He was determined to make ICW a success, but, like Dick the Bruiser in Indiana, he was in a practically unwinnable situation. There was cooperation between some non-NWA and NWA booking offices, and relations were pretty good between Alliance members and the AWA and WWA. Dick the Bruiser, notably, appeared regularly in St. Louis for Sam Muchnick. But when it came to pure "outlaw" organizations, there was little to no cooperation. Since 1948, NWA members had worked to protect each other from any rogue entity that could gain too much power and jeopardize the balance of professional wrestling. To date, the organization had been successful in minimizing exterior threats, but with the marketplace changing in a cable TV environment, paranoia amongst NWA affiliates was growing by leaps and bounds.

Georgia Championship Wrestling had promoters all over the map dealing with the consequences of *World Championship Wrestling* on WTBS. The Gordon Solie–hosted program was immensely popular, and the stars of Georgia were national wrestling celebrities. Reaching into Ohio, West Virginia, and Pennsylvania, it advertised its live shows as "A New Era in Professional Wrestling." Booker Ole Anderson was leading the charge, and he knew cable TV opened the door for a coast-to-coast promotion. Spurred on by high ratings and the fact that house show gates on the road were bettering those at home, Anderson was motivated to take a bigger step in expansion, and the Georgia circuit almost became of secondary importance.

Coincidentally, another Georgia-based outfit was looking to branch out, but this one had yet to stage a single show. The group was Global Wrestling, run by Ann Gunkel, and by early November 1982, she had pitched a new syndicated TV show to 14 different stations in the western United States. In fact, in a special memo to station managers, Gunkel claimed to "have the exclusive West Coast franchise from the National Wrestling Alliance to promote live wrestling cards in the states of Arizona, California, Hawaii, New Mexico, and Nevada."[87] *Global Wrestling* made its TV debut in Tucson in December 1982 and in Phoenix in January 1983, and later in New Mexico and California. The show went on the air in Florida as well, with Gordon Solie as announcer. Eddie Graham instituted a Global tag team title, and talks began about a special heavyweight title tournament. On February 4, 1983, Gunkel reached out to NWA secretary Jim Barnett and asked for all of world champion Ric Flair's available dates for 1983, 1984, and 1985.[88] Her idea was to use Flair on both Global TV and in live events. With respect, Barnett denied the request, stating that it was unfair to NWA members to book Flair so far in advance.[89] In a follow-up letter to Blair Television, the syndicator of *Global Wrestling*, NWA attorney Tench C. Coxe explained that Gunkel's outfit was not officially a member of the Alliance, dispelling the earlier claim.[90]

With enthusiasm waning, Graham dropped the Global experiment in May 1983, but Gunkel was not ready to throw in the towel. By that time,

GCW's Ole Anderson was taking a unique approach to his expansion plans. He arranged for his "A" squad, the wrestlers Georgia fans knew and loved, to tour nearly exclusively outside of the Peach State and return only for important Omni Coliseum shows and weekend WTBS TV tapings in Atlanta. But otherwise, Georgia would see an entirely new lineup of talent, headed by Bill Dundee and manager Jim Cornette and known as "Georgia Superstars." This outfit fulfilled dates on the normal circuit and were featured in a separately produced TV program from Chattanooga. Anderson, meanwhile, led Tommy Rich, Mr. Wrestling II, and the top stars of his group across Ohio, West Virginia, Pennsylvania, and then, surprisingly, to Texas.

Texas was new ground for GCW. Anderson worked a deal with Joe Blanchard of Southwest Championship Wrestling to share talent, and with Blanchard's USA Network coverage, the two had an incredible lock on cable TV. It should be noted that back in March 1983, Blanchard's son Tully had called Jim Barnett about NWA membership for Southwest Championship Wrestling. Barnett explained that a formal application had to be submitted six months prior to the annual convention, and since the 1983 meeting was to be held in August, Blanchard had to wait until the summer of 1984 for consideration.[91] That was approximately 17 months away. Southwest couldn't wait that long. The promotion was in a fight for its life, battling World Class in an all-out war for the territory. For Southwest to find an ally in GCW was interesting, as Anderson's group was an official member of the NWA. As far as most people knew, GCW president Jim Barnett was a high-powered officer in the Alliance, but Anderson wasn't on the same page as Barnett. There had been infighting between the two for years, and by this juncture in 1983, Barnett wasn't calling the shots, Anderson was. And Ole was apparently taking a renewed look at the wrestling scene, even calling into question his allegiance to the NWA. In July 1983, Dave Meltzer acknowledged the rumor that GCW had withdrawn from the Alliance in his *Wrestling Observer Newsletter* and noted that the *World Championship Wrestling* telecast failed to mention that Harley Race won the NWA belt in June.[92] It was strange, to say the least. There was another facet to the budding Anderson–Blanchard combine, and that was the fact that Ann Gunkel was also in on the deal.

Gunkel attended a Southwest Championship Wrestling TV taping in early July 1983.[93] She appeared on camera for an interview and promoted a combined Georgia–Southwest program under the Global banner in Albuquerque on July 6. Interestingly, though, a local advertisement in the *Albuquerque Journal* promoted "champion" Ric Flair, though Flair was in South Carolina fulfilling dates for Jim Crockett.[94] The hype was completely baseless and didn't reflect well on Global. In the main event, hero Tommy Rich battled his archnemesis, Buzz Sawyer, with Tully Blanchard, Ole Anderson, Larry Zbyszko, and Stan Hansen appearing on the undercard. Anderson and his Georgia workers appeared in several other western cities, and there were preliminary talks of touring Salt Lake City, Denver, and Southern California. The latter never happened.

Georgia's talent pool was experiencing high turnover in 1982 and '83, with some wrestlers leaving for Japan and others for neighboring territories. The loss of the Masked Superstar, Bruce Reed, and Paul Orndorff was significant, and Anderson's roster was considered too thin for a sustained national campaign. Neither Blanchard nor Gunkel were in any position to supplement the talent needed, and the entire proposition was doomed to fail. Anderson was in a precarious position and his promotion was losing much more than it was gaining by the endeavor. His home territory was weakened by the "Georgia Superstars" project, which area loyalists felt was a step down from the usual offering. Anderson was risking the alienation of his core audience in his attempt to reach new fans far outside the southeast.

On top of that, several important on-air angles were lambasted, particularly Killer Tim Brooks's victory over Orndorff for the National heavyweight title and his subsequent "sale" of the championship to Larry Zbyszko for $25,000. In the tag team division, Anderson was setting up a title run for Matt Borne and Arn Anderson, but Borne was arrested in Columbus, Ohio "on a fourth-degree felony charge," according to the Associated Press, forcing an immediate change in direction.[95] Ole Anderson brought in a pair of powerful weightlifters from the Midwest, dubbed them "the Road Warriors," and named Paul Ellering their manager. Hawk and Animal, as they were known, were physically intimidating in and out of the ring, and their charisma made up for their rawness. Anderson gave them the National tag team belts, claiming they'd won a tournament in Chicago, and the "Roadies" were soon to become the hottest tandem in pro wrestling. As for the Georgia–Southwest Global deal, it ended quietly.[96] Their expansion effort was over.

The WWF was faring a little better. The investment Vince McMahon Jr. made in southern California was paying off, and the territory was experiencing a revival. An estimated 3,000 people saw the promotion's regional debut in San Diego on March 5, 1983, and the Los Angeles Sports Arena improved upon that number by 1,000 the next day. Andre the Giant was undoubtedly the biggest sensation. He won battle royals and handicap matches on both cards, while WWF champion Bob Backlund went over Ray Stevens and Buddy Rose in separate affairs. Behind the scenes, McMahon relied on Arnold Skaaland, Pat Patterson, and Chief Jay Strongbow to organize and run events, and Mike LeBell assisted with publicity and booking prelim talent.

Attendance improved to 5,500 in Los Angeles on April 23, and superstars Jimmy Snuka and Mil Mascaras were highlight attractions. There was another big-time name on the bill, former three-time National champion Paul Orndorff. Known for his appearances on WTBS for GCW, Orndorff was a noteworthy addition to the WWF. But as it turned out, Orndorff wasn't kickstarting a big run for McMahon. He was filler and jobbed to a local guy, Billy Anderson, on the undercard. The next day in San Diego, he drew with Chief Jay Strongbow. These matches were highly forgettable, but for anyone paying attention, there was logic behind the way Orndorff was booked. Around this time, the talk of GCW invading Los Angeles was still prevalent. If GCW's former champ couldn't win over prelim workers on a WWF show, what did it say about Georgia's level of talent in comparison? Back in the kayfabe era, these details were critical to promoters.

McMahon didn't miss a chance to potentially devalue his rival, and the move was demonstrative of his hard-nosed approach to the business. Of all promoters, Ole Anderson had proven to be the biggest thorn in his side. First it was Ohio, then Pennsylvania, and now with pending operations in Baltimore and Los Angeles. And although the latter endeavor didn't bear out for Anderson, his efforts in the east continued undaunted by the growing power of the WWF. Anderson was also hard-nosed, and he was all too ready to fight fire with fire. During the summer of 1983, he booked a special preliminary match for Augusta, Georgia.[97] On one side it was Chief Joe Lightfoot, a well-known journeyman, and on the other a relative unknown with a surprising name: Vince McMann. It is not known if this was a comedic bout or if Lightfoot took on the symbolic duties of a GCW representative in pummeling "McMann" into submission. For those present with insider knowledge, it was probably entertaining either way.

The McMahon–Anderson rivalry wasn't the only one making news in 1983. In St. Louis, the philosophical differences between Larry Matysik and Bob Geigel fractured their working relationship, and Matysik went out on his own.[98] He incorporated Greater St. Louis Wrestling Enterprises, and reached out to fellow indie promoters for talent.[99] He found receptive allies in Joe Blanchard (SCW) and Angelo Poffo (ICW) and, without television, launched his promotion on June 18, 1983. He featured two claimants to the world title, ICW champion Randy Savage and SCW champion Adrian Adonis, and a solid lineup of wrestlers. King Kong (Bruiser) Brody was his top star, but the show failed to live up to expectations when Brody's opponent, Blackjack Mulligan, didn't appear. The wrestling war in St. Louis was already lopsided. That was because eight days earlier, a truly memorable program had been held at the Kiel Auditorium by Geigel's St. Louis Wrestling Club.

Geigel, the NWA president, in the interest of protecting his business, persuaded his colleagues to authorize a world heavyweight title switch for his June 10 show, the aforementioned Harley Race victory over Ric Flair. The changing hands of the NWA belt drew immense attention to his local brand, overshadowing Matysik's outlaw group, as he intended. He also pushed Race for a particular reason. Not only was he a trusted friend, but he was also tied with Lou Thesz with six reigns as NWA titleholder. (For Thesz, it was his combined National Wrestling Association and National Wrestling Alliance titles.) Thesz was connected to Matysik's group and appeared as a special referee on his June 18 show. To garner a little retribution against Thesz for this perceived lack of loyalty, Geigel gave Race his seventh reign, establishing a new record and making an important mark in history. Again, in the kayfabe era, people in the business took this stuff very seriously.

The St. Louis Wrestling Club had the political connections, the TV, and the finances to outgun Matysik from day one. The group's talent-sharing arrangement through the NWA was another pivotal advantage, and in advance of the June 10 program, Pat O'Connor told a reporter that they were booking "every magic name in wrestling."[100] The lineup included Andre the Giant, David Von Erich, Roddy Piper, Big John Studd, and Dick the Bruiser. Despite the odds, Matysik was determined to fight on. He landed a local television outlet and ran four shows at the Checkerdome that summer. His tireless efforts weren't lost on fans, and his ratings and attendance improved dramatically, while the opposite happened to his opponents. It was a unique reversal, and Matysik, with his stable of lesser-known workers, was making life hard for Geigel and his partners.

The strength of the NWA was being tested on all fronts. The cooperation of members, particularly when one affiliate was up against a non-Alliance opponent, was holding steady to a certain extent, but there was only so much talent to go around. Territories including Florida and Georgia experienced a shortage of good wrestlers, and neither was in any position to seriously assist a distant colleague. Geigel did receive outside support, but it wasn't powerful enough to give him a decisive victory. And if the NWA president was having trouble squashing an independent operator in one of his principal cities, what did it say about the overall health of the Alliance?

There was another problem too. On May 10, 1983, Frank Tunney, a principal NWA leader going back decades, suddenly passed away during a vacation to Hong Kong.[101] His importance to the Alliance couldn't be overstated, as he was not only a member of the board of directors and the second vice president, but an incredible mentor. When it came to making decisions about the future of the NWA, Tunney was never compelled by an insatiable need to make money or to gain status for himself. He generally cared about the organization and wanted his allies to achieve the same kind of success he had. Wrestling had always been good to him, and with Sam Muchnick retired, Tunney had embraced his role as the group's senior voice of reason.

But with Tunney gone, the NWA caucus in August 1983 was going to be anything but reasonable and rational. Tensions were high, and the overall composition of the organization was going to change by the end of the three-day session at the Dunes Hotel on the Las Vegas Strip. That was apparent on day one, August 21, during the initial meeting of the board of directors, when Jim Barnett resigned as the organization's secretary and treasurer, giving up one of the most powerful positions in pro wrestling.[102]

As the booker for the world heavyweight champion since 1975, he was the go-to man within the Alliance, and was considered to be the center of the NWA's political hierarchy. Barnett was involved in all high-level discussions and sent the champion through the various territories as evenly as he could to keep affiliates happy. He had been an official member since 1969, but his ties to the Alliance dated back to the early 1950s.

Barnett's move was prompted by at least two factors. His difficulties with Ole Anderson, a fellow Georgia Championship Wrestling shareholder, were a root cause for animosity, and whereas Barnett was vacating the board of directors at the 1983 convention, Anderson was joining it.[103] But Barnett had another reason to step down. He planned to link up with Vince McMahon Jr.'s Titan Sports in efforts to both stifle Anderson and expand the WWF. After all, McMahon was already at war with Anderson, and how better for Barnett to gain a little revenge than to help the WWF strengthen its national position? Barnett retained his stock in GCW and attended the remainder of the convention, but his plans to aid McMahon remained secret.

The board of directors meeting saw another resignation, this time by Mike LeBell.[104] Since going into business with McMahon Jr. in late 1982, LeBell's role in wrestling had significantly diminished. He was a figurehead in southern California, if anything, and his veteran standing was his only contribution to the Alliance. A third member of the board, Frank Tunney, had passed, and a fourth, Vince McMahon "Senior," was in a questionable spot because his son was actively battling another dues-paying NWA member. During the general meetings over the next two days, the outspoken Anderson didn't bite his tongue when it came to this topic and addressed McMahon's apparent conflict of interest between his devotion to the Alliance and the controversial maneuvering of his son. Members also discussed a number of other serious issues, including the drug problem within wrestling, the development of new talent, and doubling annual dues from $100 to $200.[105]

For the umpteenth convention in a row, the television situation was heavily debated, and, according to the meeting minutes, it was determined "that there was really no remedy available" to prevent "over-saturation of wrestling television programming." Surprisingly, Bob Geigel declared that there was "nothing wrong" with competition and reminded members that antitrust accusations could arise from the NWA uniting against any particular rival.[106] His comments were somewhat politically correct, and considering his rivalry in St. Louis, he knew better than anyone what the toll was in a heated war for territory. Perhaps a renewed concern about government oversight was the reason members weren't exhausting every possible avenue to put foes out of business. This, in itself, was evidence that the Alliance was weaker than it had been. But the fear of prosecution was definitely nothing to scoff at.

Geigel spoke about McMahon Jr.'s tactics without naming names, explaining that there was a fundamental problem with paying "unjustifiable sums" to television stations, arena managers, and to the wrestlers themselves to acquire a territorial advantage. He felt it was "unwise" and told members that history demonstrated "that such practices in a market [would] probably kill it."[107] On the whole, NWA affiliates were expecting 1984 to be a difficult year, but plans they believed would be helpful to their collective box office were already in motion. "Nature Boy" Ric Flair, the charismatic blond heel with a skilled ring presence, was being pushed back toward the championship, and Jim Crockett was laying out a brilliant script in the Mid-Atlantic region to make that happen.

The NWA completely overhauled its board of directors at that convention with only two of seven members returning. Anderson, Crockett, Mike Graham, Don Owen, and David Von Erich were the newcomers, and only Dory Funk Jr. and Victor Jovica remained. Of all the changes, McMahon's departure was the most intriguing. Many wondered what his role was in his son's plans, if they were indeed working side by side. Not everyone was aware that Titan Sports had purchased McMahon Sr.'s Capitol Wrestling Corporation and that by June 1983, McMahon Jr. owned the World Wrestling Federation outright.[108] McMahon Sr. was no longer in charge of a major promotion, and the only reasonable move left was to offer his resignation and head into semi-retirement.

On August 31, 1983, from his picturesque Fort Lauderdale home, McMahon Sr. did just that. He sent a letter to Geigel informing him of his immediate resignation, noting: "I wish continued success to you and my many friends in the Alliance."[109] No doubt he meant it. McMahon was that kind of man, thoughtful and considerate. His son was laying the groundwork for a remarkably risky plan, and McMahon Sr. was aware of his ideas. The grandiose scheme was well beyond anything he'd ever attempted during his decades in the business. His biggest maneuver had been getting into New York and acquiring booking rights at Madison Square Garden. In the 1950s, that was a huge accomplishment. But his son wanted a far bigger prize. And as a result, the wrestling industry was about to turn upside down.

CHAPTER SEVEN

"THEY SURE GOT RID OF ME"

The writing was on the wall. Vince McMahon Sr.'s decision to leave the National Wrestling Alliance was confirmation that his son was no longer abiding by any of the old handshake agreements. It appeared to be proof that Vincent Kennedy McMahon was going to ignore the existing structure of organized pro wrestling and test the perseverance of promoters all over the United States and Canada. Concerned territorial heads with longstanding ties to McMahon Sr. went to their phones and sought conciliation. They wanted promises from him that his son was not plotting takeover attempts of their regions. But what could the elder McMahon promise? He possessed no stock or membership in any organization and was privately battling cancer.

Already with notable feathers in his cap, McMahon Jr. and his new ally Jim Barnett were ready to push the envelope, and Ohio was the central battleground. The WWF had been working on a full invasion strategy for more than a year and acquired a local station, WAKR-23 out of Akron, with reach to Cleveland, on January 8, 1983.[110] The following month, McMahon's workers debuted at an Akron high school.[111] The promotion added regular shows in East Liverpool and Struthers, both near the Pennsylvania border. Eight months later, within a week of the NWA convention, the WWF renewed its Ohio expansion, and having Barnett around was a major benefit. On Saturday, August 27, 1983, the WWF debuted on WCPO-9 in Cincinnati, the same station Barnett had used back in the late 1950s and '60s. Barnett still had plenty of contacts in the area and, with a sellable product hyped by the fact that it was "from New York City," he bowled over station executives and secured TV time.

An established Georgia Championship Wrestling town, Cincinnati was quickly followed by an assault on Dayton, and Ole Anderson was in danger of losing two of his prime cities to the WWF. McMahon and Barnett shrewdly prompted the management at Dayton's WKEF-22 to cancel *World Championship Wrestling* on Saturday afternoons and replace it straightaway with the WWF's *Championship Wrestling*. A short time later, an official from the Hara Arena, the main wrestling venue in Dayton, informed GCW that the WWF had also signed an exclusive deal with the facility, thus leaving Anderson completely out in the cold.[112] On October 8 and 9, Andre the Giant led the charge into Cincinnati and Dayton, and his gigantic footprint captured the imagination of local fans. As for Barnett, his value was apparent to the WWF, and he made a public appearance at a TV taping in Allentown as a demonstration of his new loyalty.[113]

McMahon had another ace up his sleeve. On the morning of Sunday, August 28, 1983, a new WWF offering replaced Joe Blanchard's Southwest Championship Wrestling telecast on the USA Cable Network. *All-American Wrestling* made its debut with McMahon himself serving as the host. The patriotic-themed program was a stunner to fans expecting grappling from San Antonio, but Blanchard could no longer afford the costly payments to the network, and McMahon swooped in. The first hour of the telecast introduced viewers to the WWF champion Bob Backlund, including snippets of his bouts against "Superstar" Billy Graham, Ken Patera, Jesse Ventura, and Adrian Adonis. McMahon put over Backlund's achievements, his work ethic, and his popularity. By showing his victories over Adonis and Ventura, well known in SCW and AWA territories respectively, he bolstered his credibility in non-WWF regions.

Notably, though, the WWF wasn't a stranger to the USA Network. It had been broadcasting taped WWF footage from Madison Square Garden on Monday nights for some time, and the Sunday presentation gave them complete coverage. Adding in the reach of WOR, McMahon held a dominating share of the cable market with GCW's program on WTBS being the only real national competitor. *All-American Wrestling* would ultimately become a compilation program with footage from the Garden, the regular Pennsylvania tapings, and, surprisingly, matches from outside WWF territories. Notwithstanding his dispute with NWA member Ole Anderson, McMahon featured bouts from Florida, World Class, and the Mid-Atlantic territories (all Alliance affiliates), plus matches from the AWA and Mid-South regions. McMahon talked up the wrestlers — Ric Flair, the Von Erichs, and Hulk Hogan among them — giving other promoters' stars national exposure on his outlet.

The sharing of precious national TV time with fellow promoters was a gentlemanly maneuver for McMahon, and he certainly didn't appear to be the impulsive threat people were making him out to be. That left two questions — did the McMahons only leave the NWA because of the WWF's ongoing feud with GCW, and did they still plan to cooperate with Alliance members to ensure mutual prosperity? At the time, the answer to both questions seemed to be "yes," and a high level of cooperation remained in place. Nevertheless, GCW wasn't going to sit idly by. Ole Anderson poured his stars into Ohio cities and strengthened his talent-sharing relationship with Jim Crockett. But fans were going to choose which promotion to support in places like Cincinnati and Dayton, and with good competition, the wrestling public was undoubtedly the winner.

In a December 1983 article, sportswriter Michael Paolercio of the *Cincinnati Enquirer* didn't offer an opinion regarding the wrestling war after witnessing a WWF show at the Cincinnati Gardens.[114] He did, however, take a nonserious approach to the "pseudo mayhem," and noted the passion of enthusiasts in the crowd. The madcap characters of the WWF inspired reaction; whether it was the simple awesomeness of Andre the Giant, the high-flying of Jimmy "Superfly" Snuka, or the aggressive behavior of Sgt. Slaughter, fans were usually fully connected to the action in the ring. Slaughter, who had made his return to the WWF earlier in the year after a lengthy absence, was one of the promotion's top heels, and fans loved to shout "Gomer" in his direction. Other newcomers to the organization in August–September 1983 included the Masked Superstar, Tony Atlas, and the Iron Sheik, three former stars for GCW.

Again, there was no coincidence about these signings. McMahon wanted to use Anderson's former wrestlers against him in Ohio, and this tactic would become a staple in the WWF arsenal. In terms of McMahon acquiring more territory, Detroit was high on the list, and its geographic location made it a central priority. Barnett's history in the Motor City helped, and in the closing weeks and months of 1983, the WWF contacted George Cannon, the 51-year-old proprietor of the Superstars of Wrestling promotion to discuss a possible deal. Cannon, a former wrestler and manager, known for his Crybaby gimmick and his 300-plus-pound frame, was receptive to McMahon's initial inquiry. His SOW promotion had seen the same decline that the Sheik had faced in Detroit, and despite great determination, he was unable to recapture its former glory.[115] An amiable guy with far-reaching contacts in the business, Cannon had solid TV and arena contracts, but getting steady talent was a problem. He'd worked with groups from Montreal, Indianapolis, and elsewhere to attract a better turnout, without luck. He'd heard the rumors of GCW's planned invasion of Detroit, so striking a deal with McMahon made even more sense to him. McMahon sold Cannon on a three-way deal, with one-third going to Titan Sports, one-third to Cannon, and the remaining third to the Olympia Stadium Corporation, the administrator of Detroit's two main venues, Cobo Hall and the Joe Louis Arena.[116] For an annual take of upwards of $60,000, Cannon would remain involved in promotions, handling the local operations on behalf of the WWF. But there was another aspect to the agreement, one with far greater ramifications.

For years, Cannon ran a popular TV show entitled *Superstars of Wrestling* across Canada and parts of the U.S. He was still generating original content in 1983, and McMahon not only wanted to assume production rights to the local presentation on channel 9 (CBET) out of Windsor, but hoped to utilize the new program — also called *Superstars of Wrestling* — in other cities as well. Particularly, the show would be used as the WWF's main telecast in newly signed markets. With remarkable production values, much more sophisticated than the grainy efforts of Cannon and other promotions, *Superstars of Wrestling* was going to make a powerful first impression on fans all over North America. Cannon agreed to the stipulations of the deal and primed Detroit for the WWF's debut on December 30, 1983. On that evening, just over 2,000 people saw Andre the Giant, Jimmy Snuka, and Rocky Johnson win a three-fall victory over the Wild Samoans and Samula. On the undercard were two of Cannon's stars, the Great Wojo and Chris Carter.

McMahon also added northern California to his circuit by achieving TV on channel 36 (KICU), serving the San Francisco Bay Area, and he ran a live event in San Jose on September 30, 1983. Inclement weather may have stifled the attendance, but 2,000 were on hand to see Andre the Giant topple Big John Studd and Jimmy Snuka beat Don Muraco by count-out. Regional favorite Pat Patterson was also on the card, winning over Alexis Smirnoff. Smirnoff, incidentally, participated in one of the WWF's most memorable promotional efforts for San Jose, occurring during an appearance on channel 36's *Prize Movie* TV show. Interviewed by host Steve Dini, Smirnoff became a bit rambunctious, and the two men launched into an unscripted and impromptu wrestling match on set. The chaotic scene was great publicity for the WWF, and nobody was hurt in the melee. Dini later said Smirnoff couldn't have been nicer off-camera.[117]

Not every expansion idea McMahon had worked out. He was said to have approached NWA member Don Owen of Portland with a buyout proposal sometime in late 1983, but Owen turned him down.[118] If he'd attained the Pacific Northwest, he would've controlled the entire coast. Around November 1983, he reportedly offered NWA world heavyweight champion Harley Race $250,000 to abandon the Alliance and join the WWF.[119] The money was alluring, but Race refused to turn his back on the NWA and remained loyal. His defection would have been crippling to the Alliance and given McMahon extraordinary momentum in his expansion endeavors. Although the offer was made in secret, those in the know had proof that McMahon Jr. wasn't exactly cooperating with the NWA to ensure mutual success. His aggressive actions were one-sided and, in effect, a de facto state of war existed between the WWF and the NWA. It just wasn't yet public knowledge.

In fact, NWA-affiliated wrestlers continued to appear on the WWF's *All-American Wrestling* program going into 1984. But McMahon was thinking far outside the box, and the motivated staff of Titan Sports was working to make his vision a reality. Thirty-three-year-old Howard Finkel was the company's very first employee, and his face and voice were well known to fans.[120] From Newark, New Jersey, Finkel worked as a ring announcer for McMahon Sr. before being hired by Titan in 1981.[121] In addition to lending his familiar voice to various events, he narrated TV voice-over promos, helped with talent, and added his creative input wherever it was needed. Finkel was joined by Ed Cohen, who was six years younger and Titan's second official employee.[122] A 1978 business graduate of Roger Williams University in Rhode Island, Cohen shared McMahon's ideals when it came to brand development. He saw the potential for growth and approached wrestling from a fresh, outsider perspective.

Altogether, McMahon and his team implemented a new business model for professional wrestling, and in doing so, strived to replace nearly all the industry's old philosophies with new ideas and formulas. Even the lexicon had to change — beginning with the word "wrestling" itself. Over time, their business became "sports entertainment." His wrestlers were not athletes, but either "sports entertainers" or simply "talent," and fans were "consumers." It was the job of Titan Sports to market its product to the masses, and it was going to use every creative way known to mankind to generate sales.

The repackaging of wrestling was an essential element of Titan's uphill climb. Since the popular qualities of the sport were already well known to the public, there were two segments of people: those who loved wrestling and those who hated it. There was a unique middle ground for casual fans, but McMahon wanted to widen the WWF's audience by completely reformulating wrestling's image. He wanted families, not cigar-smoking, beer-guzzling roughnecks, and he was willing to sanitize his promotion even at the risk of losing longtime supporters. To old-school promoters and fans, that was a huge step in the wrong direction. McMahon didn't see it that way and planned to force wrestling's evolution by redefining how the sport was marketed, presented, and perceived.

At its core, the WWF was already far more colorful than rival promotions, and McMahon's talent roster was formulaic. He had his popular babyfaces, a group of clean-cut wrestlers who smiled and shook hands with fans. Then there were the rulebreakers, a group of snarling heels constantly gaining heat for their brutal actions. Categorizing the wrestlers even further, McMahon had wrestlers pigeon holed by their cultural heritage — Native Americans (Chief Jay and Jules Strongbow), Asians (Mr. Fuji, Tiger Chung Lee), Samoans (Afa and Sika), and Puerto Ricans (Pedro Morales) — or by a performance specialty — masked wrestlers (Masked Superstar, Invaders), high flyers (Jimmy Snuka), and muscular performers (Ivan Putski, Tony Atlas, Don Muraco). Each wrestler fulfilled a specific need in the WWF's machinery. And if a wrestler left the organization for one reason or another, McMahon simply filled the gap with someone else. McMahon liked to capitalize on current events, and with Russia and Iran always in the news in the 1980s, he promoted heels Ivan Koloff and the Iron Sheik. Interview segments were peppered with pop culture references to make the WWF appear trendy. TV squash matches were purposely short to provide the audience with instant gratification. The star grappler of the bout would dominate the offense and crush his opponent with a noteworthy finishing move, which the commentators incessantly talked up. They would hype his ongoing feud or his climb up the WWF ladder, giving the impression that he was a wrestler to watch in the future. The balance between the action in the ring and the crafty salesmanship of the commentators was one of the WWF's strengths, and McMahon himself was a master in the way he advertised his wrestlers. Managers Fred Blassie and Captain Lou Albano were also exemplary in that regard.

Titan Sports also experienced a physical overhaul in the latter stages of 1983, when the company uprooted from South Yarmouth, Massachusetts, and moved to Greenwich, Connecticut.[123] The building was 35 miles from New York City, less than an hour's drive, and gave them good access to JFK, LaGuardia, and Newark airports. The proximity to New York made the sales pitch that Titan was based in the Big Apple almost true. New York had always represented wrestling's biggest money territory and carried a lot of weight in the industry. The new headquarters went hand in hand with Titan's new national goals.

Part of his consolidation included a handful of new organization-wide policies. For one, he placed a ringside ban on all non-Titan photographers, a move that dramatically affected the way the media covered the promotion.[124] McMahon's reason was simple: he wanted to create his own WWF periodical, and on July 5, 1983, Titan Sports Publications Inc. was incorporated in Massachusetts.[125] The WWF had long enjoyed a partnership with Norman H. Kietzer of Minnesota, the publisher of the widely popular *Wrestling News* magazine. As part of that collaboration, Kietzer was responsible for two WWF souvenir arena programs, *WWF Championship Wrestling* and *Major League Wrestling*. In 1983, Mike LeBell's longtime assistant, Jeff Walton, joined Kietzer as an editor and was a big help in coordinating WWF material for the various publications. Following the ban on photographers, there was speculation that Kietzer was going to publish a WWF-only magazine since he already had the mechanisms in place. But legend has it that McMahon wanted him to cancel his agreements with other promotions to do so. Kietzer was the central hub for high-quality programs and worked with the AWA, Mid-South, and the NWA, and he wasn't interested in working only with the WWF.[126] As a result, McMahon abruptly severed his ties with the Minnesota outfit and launched *Victory Magazine*, published out of Greenwich, with Edward D. Helinski and Jeff Walton as editors. This project would ultimately evolve into *WWF Magazine* in 1984. The in-house publication was a great tool to put over talent, featured photographs of all the popular stars, and advertised merchandise, a revenue stream increasingly valuable to Titan.

Surprisingly, McMahon authorized his magazine editors to feature a limited amount of content about other territories, including an article entitled, "The Von Erichs: A Dominant Family of Wrestling" in the inaugural issue of *WWF Magazine* during the spring of 1984. Like the footage of outside territories on *All-American Wrestling*, the articles seemed to compound the confusion about the WWF's relationship with other promotions. On one hand, Titan seemed to be heading toward an isolationist policy at odds with other territories, and on the other, McMahon propped up the stars of World Class or Florida on TV and in print, sharing his national exposure with NWA members Jack Adkisson and Eddie Graham. Perhaps these gestures by McMahon Jr. were the last vestiges of his father's friendship with these longtime associates. But promoting non-WWF superstars was another way to garner interest in new territories. For instance, having an article on the popular Von Erichs was a surefire way to increase magazine sales in the Dallas market, and help familiarize those fans with the WWF roster. The Von Erichs were also on TV in many WWF cities through syndication, and McMahon might have been looking for crossover viewers.

On the booking side of things, McMahon Jr. wanted to strengthen his creative team by hiring a first-class matchmaker. There were a number of options, but McMahon Sr. had a man in mind and, as a favor to his son, reached out to George Scott.[127] Scott, at 54 years old, had more than three decades of experience in the business, both on the mat and behind the scenes. He was long known as one-half of the Scott brothers tag team, along with his real-life sibling, Sandy, and prior to plying his trade in the Mid-Atlantic region, he had honed his craft as a booker alongside Stu Hart in Calgary. Back in 1973, Scott had taken the reins of Jim Crockett Promotions and transformed it from a middle-of-the-pack organization into arguably the hottest, most-talked-about territory in the country. His task wasn't easy. He actually rewired the promotion from the ground up and slowly altered Crockett's antiquated booking philosophies into a cool and stylish new system. He pushed young guys like Ric Flair, Jimmy Snuka, Ricky Steamboat, and Roddy Piper, while relying heavily on veterans like Johnny Valentine and Wahoo McDaniel. The mixture of talent offered intriguing feuds, and Scott was careful to protect his wrestlers with sensible scenarios that consistently piqued the interest of fans over a period of years. Even with some redundancy of matchups, his creative methodology kept Crockett thriving into the early 1980s, and his influence remained after his 1981 departure. Scott spent time in Georgia and Oklahoma before receiving the call from McMahon Sr., and he happily accepted a job on the WWF's payroll.

Ticket sales for WWF shows fluctuated throughout 1983, but it didn't take long for the core audience to warm up to a hot angle. The reemergence of heel Sgt. Slaughter made a big impact on the organization, and his Marine Corps drill instructor gimmick drew immense heat. He chased Bob Backlund's WWF title for some time but never scored a three count to win the belt. Jimmy Snuka was involved in a chase of his own, and his ongoing feud with Intercontinental champion Don Muraco grabbed headlines throughout the year. The two wrestled all over the territory with many finishes ending in count-out or disqualification, before culminating in a series of cage matches. Another attention-grabber in the WWF arsenal was Andre the Giant battling the 6-foot-10, 350-plus-pound Big John Studd. Though these matches consisted mostly of punches and kicks, the two mountainous men colliding created a good visual for spectators.

It is important to note that George Scott had a good working history with most of the WWF locker room. Slaughter, Snuka, Studd, Tony Atlas, Masked Superstar, and the Iron Sheik had each spent time in the Mid-Atlantic territory and witnessed Scott's magic firsthand. Scott went in knowing the strengths and limitations of his wrestlers, and for a booker, that was invaluable information to have, making his transition all the easier. At the forefront of the roster was Bob Backlund, well into his fifth year as champion. Like the heavyweight titleholders for the NWA and AWA, Backlund was the face of the WWF, and his sincere, role-model persona had made him a box-office superstar. But to some fans, his clean-cut traits were wearing thin, and they wanted a stronger personality at the top.

Backlund, since defeating "Superstar" Billy Graham in 1978, had been a credible champion on the mat, respectful of the fans, and utterly humble. The WWF's rotating heel challengers worked as effectively for him as they had for Bruno Sammartino, and Backlund lived up to all of Vince McMahon Sr.'s expectations. McMahon Sr. had always been an enthusiastic supporter of the Minnesota grappler, and Backlund had great respect for the man who'd given him the belt. During an interview in 1985, Backlund told a reporter, "I owe [McMahon Sr.], second to my father, more than anyone in my life."[128] His 2015 autobiography was also dedicated to McMahon.[129] McMahon Jr. had been on board with Backlund as well and spent the entire first episode of *All-American Wrestling* in August 1983 touting him as the best in the world.

But by December, McMahon Jr. was ready to make a dramatic decision. Backlund, he concluded, was a great champion, but to successfully market the WWF to a larger part of North America, a change was in order. The promotion needed a more charismatic star, and McMahon had someone in mind. He first had to get the belt off Backlund to a transitory titleholder, and he quickly scripted a TV angle between Backlund and the Iron Sheik, setting up a match at Madison Square Garden the day after Christmas. Backlund, ever the professional, helped lay out the finish for the important bout, which would see him caught in the Sheik's powerful camel clutch.[130] With little hope of escaping, his manager Arnold Skaaland would throw in the towel to signify his defeat. That's exactly how it played out. Backlund was dethroned before a shocked crowd of 24,500 people at the Garden.

The following day McMahon made another historic move when the World Wrestling Federation invaded St. Louis, the heart of the National Wrestling Alliance, and planted its flag. On December 27, McMahon led his company into the famed Khorassan Room at the Chase-Park Plaza Hotel, the site of Sam Muchnick's long-running *Wrestling at the Chase* television program, and staged a WWF TV taping. The arrival of the WWF on sacred NWA ground was disconcerting to Alliance officials, and Bob Geigel, the local NWA representative, was in for the fight of his life. His promotion had barely outlasted the competition of Larry Matysik, who ran opposition through the end of October before closing up. Matysik, interestingly, was initially in on the WWF's St. Louis deal as a partner, but McMahon chose to go it alone and locked in deals with KPLR-TV (channel 11) and the ballroom at the Chase Hotel.[131]

Kevin Horrigan reported on the WWF's arrival in the *St. Louis Post-Dispatch* on December 30, 1983, and called McMahon's promotion "The Beast of the East." He mentioned the extraordinary history of wrestling in St. Louis and acknowledged that McMahon wanted to "recapture" the stylishness and popularity the sport lost when Muchnick retired. "St. Louis isn't that much different from other major markets," McMahon was quoted as saying. "We can bring in new talent, more sophisticated marketing techniques and a new approach. The consumer isn't going to suffer. The consumer is going to be the winner."[132] However, some people would've argued that St. Louis was greatly dissimilar to other wrestling cities. It was an entity all its own, and the hardcore local audience was definitely against outlandish gimmicks, too much in-ring drama, and anything that insulted their intelligence. They were the people who supported credible champions like Jack Brisco, Pat O'Connor, and Lou Thesz. Although Bob Backlund and the Iron Sheik had legitimate backgrounds, the WWF was the polar opposite of Muchnick's promotion in just about every way. Fans who grew up watching the NWA now had a contrasting alternative, and whether they'd be swayed by McMahon's cartoonish roster remained to be seen.

McMahon's move into St. Louis had an even greater significance, which resonated deeply in the wrestling world. His effort was a full-scale declaration of war against the NWA and the territorial system, and no one could dispute that he was expanding nationally. And McMahon's

December 27 taping in St. Louis managed to declare war on Verne Gagne's American Wrestling Association at the same time. He did it by signing Gagne's most captivating box-office superstar, Hulk Hogan, a man who'd been waiting in the wings for a run at the AWA world championship for months. Hogan was jumping to greener pastures in the WWF, and McMahon was riding a huge wave of momentum.

Larry Matysik, in Kevin Horrigan's article in the *St. Louis Post-Dispatch*, noted, "The talk in the business is that [McMahon is] trying to take over everything. The question is, can one outfit take over an operation that's been run by dozens of independents? I don't know, but they sure got rid of me."[133] The last part of his comments was unsettling to a certain degree, but as facts would have it, before it was all said and done, scores of others would say the same thing.

CHAPTER EIGHT

THE GREAT TV EXPANSION OF 1984

The landscape of professional wrestling changed in 1983. Whether the modifications were good for business as a whole remained open to debate, and the answer you received really depended on who you asked. The World Wrestling Federation logo was shining bright in St. Louis and Detroit, two old-time NWA strongholds, and Vince McMahon Jr. was organizing a series of maneuvers that would stun critics and enthusiasts alike. Just before the year ended, McMahon made an appearance on the WWF's "Victory Corner," a brief TV interview segment used to promote the organization's periodical, *Victory Magazine*.[134] After acknowledging the massive changes that had already taken place, McMahon made a stunning prediction to host Robert DeBord: "I see 1984 as being perhaps the most turbulent year in professional wrestling." He added that there might be a "virtual flood of wrestling talent into the World Wrestling Federation the likes of which we've never seen before."

Any type of mass migration of top talent to the WWF was going to create turbulence of the highest order, as Hulk Hogan's jump from the AWA did. Hogan was Verne Gagne's cash cow, and a man he took great credit for building up. "Hogan I created and molded," Gagne told *Minneapolis CityBusiness* in 1986. "He's a guitar player. You know what his athletic background is? Little League."[135] No one could dispute that Gagne had given Hogan room to mature as a grappler and fan favorite. During Hogan's first run in the WWF, he showed glimpses of greatness but was limited as a heel before closing out his tenure unceremoniously in April 1981. He joined the AWA several months later and saw his career take off in feuds with world champion Nick Bockwinkel, Jesse Ventura, and Jerry "Crusher" Blackwell. In addition, he enhanced his abilities and confidence with a string of tours for New Japan Pro Wrestling.

Hogan became one of Japan's top *gaijin* (foreign) performers, and he worked high-profile matches with Bob Backlund, Andre the Giant, Dusty Rhodes, and New Japan founder Antonio Inoki. In June 1983, he defeated Inoki by knockout to win the first ever IWGP championship, and five months later, he teamed with Inoki to triumph in the annual MSG Tag League tournament.[136] Reportedly, it was around this same time in Japan that Hogan was approached by Vince McMahon Sr. about defecting to the WWF. Hogan was dismayed by his recent problems with Gagne, specifically over money relating to his New Japan deal and regarding the sale of merchandise.[137] Gagne's failure to push him over the top to the world title was another slight. The WWF offer came at the right time. His commitment to the AWA ended in mid-November 1983, and he was free to accept McMahon's proposal to return.

On December 27, 1983, before a sold-out audience at the Chase Park Hotel in St. Louis, the Incredible Hulk Hogan emerged from the dressing room in his trademark yellow outfit to Survivor's "Eye of the Tiger," the theme of *Rocky III*. As the crowd cheered, he stepped through the ropes and locked up with prelim wrestler Bill Dixon. The match lasted only three minutes and two seconds, but Hogan displayed his strength and charisma, and briefly flashed a working knowledge of ring science. Put over by the commentators and adored by the audience, Hogan was right in his groove, landing his legdrop and scoring a pin in quick time. After the bout, Hogan spoke with "Mean" Gene Okerlund, who had also defected to the WWF from the AWA, and hyped up a future live event in St. Louis. Before the interview was over, though, Hogan said he wanted a future shot at the world champion, who by that point was the Iron Sheik.

Hogan was ushered into a prominent role on WWF TV in January 1984. He teamed with Bob Backlund to defeat Tiger Chung Lee and Mr. Fuji on an episode of *Championship Wrestling*, and it was clear he was as over in McMahon's promotion as he had been in the AWA. Backlund was in line for a rematch with the Sheik at Madison Square Garden on January 23 but was forced to pull out because of "injury." Hogan was given the match in his place, and after five minutes and 40 seconds of grappling, the Hulkster pinned his foe and captured the WWF belt for the first time. The throng of 22,000 fans at the Garden went nuts, and it really felt like it was the dawn of a new era.

Gagne missed the boat. Hurt by Hogan's defection, he called the Iron Sheik, whom he'd helped train back in the early 1970s, and asked him to "punish" Hogan in their Garden bout as a measure of revenge, according to Hogan's 2009 autobiography.[138] But the Sheik passed on the idea. The loss of Okerlund was painful to Gagne as well. He had been the voice of the AWA's *All-Star Wrestling* program and interviewed stars prior to big shows. Gagne later told a reporter that he had offered to match Okerlund's WWF salary to keep him in the AWA, and the latter agreed. "The next day, he was announcing for the WWF," Gagne added. "He's an ass."[139]

Okerlund, like Hogan, had seen the writing on the wall. The WWF, he believed, was the better opportunity. "The local [AWA] show here on Channel 9," Okerlund explained to a Minneapolis reporter in 1984, "has left-handed matches in a garage in front of 85 people." In contrast, Titan was "a first-class operation . . . Everything's totally professional. It's network-quality programming. [We have] 12 or 15,000 people for the shows that we air on television."[140] Mean Gene couldn't have been more right; the WWF's TV production was light-years ahead of the AWA's. Gagne had been running TV tapings for years from the KMSP studios, and his program was arguably one of the most technologically challenged and uninspired wrestling shows of the time. Vince McMahon Jr. took great pride in his TV superiority and worked overtime to expand the distribution of his product. As it broke down, his plan essentially encompassed four tiers of broadcasting: network TV, syndicated TV, basic cable, and pay cable. But going into 1984, his focus was on the expansion onto stations in non-WWF territories, in another bold move against established rival promoters.

"My major step was television on a local basis," McMahon told *Sports Illustrated* in 1991. "We already had our network in the Northeast and we started selling these shows to stations in other fiefdoms. In Chicago, in Los Angeles, the WWF brand of wrestling was something new. We had better athletes, more upscale and more charisma."[141] While cable programs reached a great number of people across state lines, the local broadcasts honed in on a specific market and could be utilized to promote live events. And with Okerlund on board, he became the primary interviewer to advertise these shows, speaking with wrestlers and managers and customizing the content for each market. It was a critical job, and Okerlund often did several hundred interviews a week.

"The ability to tie things on TV in with local shows and somehow make the wrestlers seem a part of the community is a key," Dave Meltzer of the *Wrestling Observer Newsletter* explained in 1990.[142] That was the principal function of Okerlund and localized programming. They wanted to connect to and draw in regional fans. Basil DeVito Jr., the vice president of marketing for Titan Sports, told a reporter in 1991 that the WWF was a hybrid organization, "national in scope, but local in impact." He explained: "The same TV stars you see on the tube come right to your hometown. Vanna White doesn't come to Peoria. The NFL doesn't come to Peoria. But Hulk Hogan comes to Peoria, in person. And unlike big league stars, WWF wrestlers are never in an off-season. Those guys are performing 350 nights a year."[143]

The great TV expansion of 1984 began on January 14, when the WWF's newest program, *Superstars of Wrestling*, made its debut in Chicago (a longtime AWA–WWA city) on WFLD-32 on Saturday mornings at 8:30. Over the next two months, the WWF secured television spots for *Superstars* in Louisville (WDRB), Nashville (WCAY), Little Rock (KLRT), and New Orleans (WNOL) as McMahon's sales team reached out to many upstart independent stations. They were warmly received by the TVX Broadcast Group, an eastern North Carolina outfit, and expanded onto a number of their stations, including Norfolk (WTVZ), Richmond (WRLH), and Memphis (WMKW). On April 7, 1984, McMahon gained ground in another big market, Dallas, and *Superstars* began broadcasting on Saturday mornings at 9:00 on channel 21, KTXA. In the span of four months, the WWF encroached on the territories of Verne Gagne, Jerry Jarrett, Bill Watts, Jim Crockett, and Jack Adkisson, among the most powerful promoters in the world.

In looking for support in these towns, the WWF imperiled the stability of the local promoters. McMahon was now in a fight for talent, ratings, and, most importantly, the interest of fans. It was just a matter of time before he added these cities to his national circuit and challenged his rivals head to head. Jim Crockett, whose Mid-Atlantic territory was just down the coast from McMahon's northeastern lair, was well within striking distance. Crockett dealt with the threat of outside competition by proactively strengthening his promotion. In July 1983, he did away with canned studio TV tapings and moved his made-for-television matches into arenas, improving his company's image. The effort was costly, upwards of a million dollars for a new TV truck, but it was a necessary investment.

After Crockett's top star Ric Flair lost the NWA title to Harley Race during the summer of 1983, a perfectly executed booking plan played out over a series of months building up to Crockett's biggest show ever, Starrcade, on November 24 (Thanksgiving night) in Greensboro, North Carolina. People wanted to see the 34-year-old Nature Boy regain the championship, and his popularity throughout the region soared. He feuded with Race, Bob Orton Jr., and Dick Slater, and called upon Roddy Piper and Wahoo McDaniel to help even things up. By Thanksgiving, fans were eager to see their hero achieve retribution on Race in the confines of a steel cage.

Starrcade '83 lived up to the hype, both in the ring and at the box office.[144] The Greensboro Coliseum was packed to the rafters (15,447) and tens of thousands — estimated between 30,000 and 80,000 — watched the show on closed-circuit television. The event was wrestling's first million-dollar gate and a huge boost to Crockett and the anti-WWF movement. In the ring, Flair emerged victorious, as anticipated, winning the NWA belt in a bloody bout. Roddy Piper beat his longtime foe, Greg Valentine, in another violent epic, this one under dog-collar chain rules.

The popular Ricky Steamboat and Jay Youngblood also triumphed, winning the world tag championship for the fifth time with a technical win over the Brisco Brothers. While there was room for trivial complaints, Crockett's great storytelling made history, and Starrcade would become an annual event, continuing for the next 17 straight years.

But a month later, on December 25, 1983, Steamboat, one of Crockett's top fan favorites, retired from wrestling and vacated his claim to the world tag title. Piper, another hero in the Mid-Atlantic region, was scooped up by Vince McMahon Jr. in what would be the latter's second major talent raid. Crockett spent time turning Valentine babyface to make up for the losses, and then McMahon grabbed him too. With Flair on the National Wrestling Alliance circuit defending the world title, and criticism that much of the upper roster of JCP was too old, Crockett needed to bring in talent. Promoters in Georgia, Mid-South, and San Antonio helped him out with the deficiencies, and the Road Warriors, Junkyard Dog, Stan Hansen, and Tully Blanchard made their local debuts.

The Georgia territory struggled in 1983, as the company's focus was on western expansion. But booker Ole Anderson had returned to the basics and put all his energy into his core cities, while still not giving up on progress in Ohio. Unafraid to make a move against McMahon, Anderson sought to advance into Washington, D.C., and Baltimore in addition to Pennsylvania. On his TV programming, he featured brief clips of current WWF wrestlers from old Georgia footage, showing the grapplers being pummeled by prelim-level opponents. Though the full match had always ended with the bigger name winning, Anderson would cut the finish and tell the viewing audience that the preliminary wrestler had won. Smart wrestling fans were not amused by the crude promotional tactic.

Nor were they pleased with the promotion's show at the Omni Coliseum in Atlanta on November 6, 1983.[145] Then NWA world champion Harley Race was slated to appear and defend his crown against Tommy Rich. An estimated 4,000 people turned out, only to be told Race was a no-show and Ted DiBiase was appearing instead. No refunds were offered. Some questioned whether Race had been booked for Atlanta at all. The champ was coming off a tour of Japan and was likely getting some much-needed R&R. Georgia officials could have managed the entire affair differently, but didn't, and the last minute switcheroo was a big disappointment. Further no-shows in Ohio, including a situation in Columbus where Abdullah the Butcher *and* Mr. Wrestling II didn't appear, were also harmful to the promotion's credibility.

Two weeks before Race's nonappearance, Anderson had scored a huge hit with "The Last Battle of Atlanta," the end to the long-running feud between Tommy Rich and Buzz Sawyer. More than 10,000 fans turned out for that event. On Thanksgiving, for the sixth annual holiday tag team tournament, another 12,000 enthusiasts were on hand. But on December 4, Omni crowds dipped to under 2,000, and they were not much better on Christmas (2,500). The overexposure of Rich, plus the high-positioned roles of Ronnie Garvin and Killer Brooks were unpopular, and even Anderson was getting too much air time. The promotion needed new talent and storylines, and Anderson responded. He pushed Ted DiBiase to the National title and Jake Roberts to the TV championship, and he saw gold in the Road Warriors. Both Roberts and the Warriors had been part of Paul Ellering's Legion of Doom stable, and on camera, they were a major thorn in Anderson's side.

The massive 6-foot-4, 350-pound King Kong Bundy along with Stan Hansen and Brad Armstrong were top fan favorites, in addition to Tommy Rich. Rich had lost a loser-leaves-town bout to DiBiase on Christmas, but he was still active in the territory under a mask, appearing as Mr. R. The real identity of the shrouded hero wasn't much of a secret. On February 18, 1984, the hooded grappler received a shot at DiBiase's National belt, but during the fracas, much to the shock of the titleholder, Rich made an appearance outside the ring. His opponent was really Brad Armstrong, and as the champion reeled from astonishment, he suffered a pinfall and lost the title. Notably, two days before this match, Anderson had run his first show in Baltimore at the Civic Center with a solid lineup. Larry Zbyszko was booked against his mentor's son, Bruno Sammartino Jr., in an effort to draw WWF fans. But gaining superiority in Baltimore, which had been part of McMahon's circuit for two decades, was a huge challenge.

To make a point in response, McMahon scheduled nearly every big gun talent he had for Baltimore's Civic Center on March 3, 1984, and drew a complete sellout. Aside from Andre the Giant, Jimmy Snuka, Don Muraco, and Roddy Piper, his world champion (Hulk Hogan), Intercontinental titleholder (Tito Santana), and world tag champs (Tony Atlas and Rocky

Johnson) were all on the bill. It was an extraordinary display of firepower. Anderson refused to give in, and on April 7, he returned to the city with NWA champ Ric Flair defending against former kingpin Jack Brisco. Whereas Baltimore was a battleground city with the box-office advantage going to McMahon, the reverse occurred in Altoona, Pennsylvania. There, GCW made a deal with disgruntled former WWF affiliate promoter Gene Dargan and quickly won over the hearts of local fans.[146]

In the interest of keeping things fresh, Anderson routinely shared wrestlers with the Mid-South office run by the polarizing Bill Watts. Headquartered in suburban Tulsa, Watts operated in five southern states: Oklahoma, Louisiana, Mississippi, Arkansas, and part of Texas. His promotion drew consistently well in New Orleans and Houston, and although not a member of the National Wrestling Alliance, Mid-South was considered a friendly peer of the NWA. Watts didn't need membership in a national organization to be successful, having proven to be one of the brightest minds in the industry. He churned out arguably the best wrestling TV show found anywhere on a weekly basis. It was a no-frills production, sans pointless interview segments and wasted time. The show was built around steady action, and Watts, known for his commanding personality, micromanaged the telecast to ensure everything ran according to his vision.

And the result was unanimous. Viewers in New Orleans delivered better than a 40 share in TV ratings, and *Mid-South Wrestling* was respected by the wrestling-smart community and average fans alike, an often difficult balance to strike. Watts was a traditionalist, and he preached to his locker room the importance of credibility in wrestling. His roster had to strictly adhere to kayfabe protection, and anything that diminished the integrity of his promotion was dealt with through fines and dismissals. For instance, warnings went out that fan favorites could never be seen in public with villains — not in bars, restaurants, or in the same rental car. A lot of wrestlers were friends behind the scenes, but Watts forbade any public interaction to maintain the illusion of the in-ring feuds.

Watts was an intelligent promoter and knew his audience. He teased their emotions with creative storylines and mixed wrestling fundamentals with wild brawling. Like the WWF's formulaic methodology when it came to talent, Watts had a blueprint all his own. He filled his cards with edgy heels, personable babyfaces, and general tough guys. The wrestlers he pushed earned his respect and trust, but at the same time, he was keenly aware of the marketing potential of key performers. Junkyard Dog, an African-American grappler with off-the-charts charisma, was singled out because of his immense potential and began his star-making climb in 1979.[147] Junkyard Dog became an unparalleled hero throughout the South, and his supporters were as diehard as they came. Watts played his cards right, avoiding overexposure, and JYD was still going strong in 1983–84.

But even his superstar status couldn't bump attendance for a show at the Superdome in New Orleans on November 19, 1983, and only 8,000 people turned out, the smallest-ever wrestling crowd for that venue. Dusty Rhodes, David and Kerry Von Erich, and Mr. Wrestling II were also on the card, in addition up-and-comers the Road Warriors and Magnum T.A. Mr. Wrestling II and Magnum T.A. were involved in one of early 1984's hottest feuds, and the slowly developing angle was an example of the consideration Watts put into his booking strategy. The two wrestlers were leading fan favorites in Mid-South, and the veteran masked grappler had taken his 24-year-old partner under his wing. On December 25, 1983, the pair toppled Butch Reed and Jim Neidhart for the regional tag team championship.

In the weeks that followed, Mr. Wrestling II became jealous of his protégé, especially after Magnum was named the number-one contender to the North American title held by the Junkyard Dog. Magnum gave his mentor his title shot, but Mr. Wrestling II cheated his way to a victory, cementing his heel turn. Ultimately, Magnum ended up battling and defeating the man he'd admired for so long in an emotional battle on May 12, 1984. The angle played out in gripping fashion and captured the attention of fans throughout the region.

Watts was fully aware of Vince McMahon Jr.'s manipulations and, in early 1984, the WWF achieved local TV deals in two of his top towns, New Orleans and Little Rock.[148] But as far as Louisiana was concerned, Watts was politically protected and unworried about any future invasions. That was because the Louisiana Athletic Commission only issued a single wrestling booking license for the entire state, and Watts had it. Mid-South was the only game in town for live events within Louisiana. In Tulsa and Oklahoma City, Watts continued his business dealings with Dallas promoter Jack Adkisson and booked the Von Erich boys whenever he got the chance. David, Kevin, and Kerry Von Erich were enormously popular and almost guaranteed sellouts. But Watts knew there was a dark side to the Von Erichs, and in June 1983, the public became aware of it too.[149] On June 25, Kerry Von Erich returned to Dallas from his honeymoon in Mexico and was found to be carrying more than 300 pills and 10 grams of marijuana.[150] He was locked up and charged, and details of his incarceration were revealed by the Dallas media. Kerry's arrest was representative of a wider drug abuse problem by the Von Erich brothers, and insiders who'd been around the trio knew it to be true. The crippling effects of substance abuse had the brothers headed down a gloomy path.

But in terms of the success of World Class Wrestling, their problems couldn't have come at a worse time. The promotion was in the midst of a financial boom unlike anything it had experienced before, and the Von Erichs were ring royalty. Their faces were plastered on the covers of national wrestling magazines, and the syndicated Dallas TV program increased their fame in cities far from Texas. Adkisson had struck gold with the protracted Von Erich–Freebirds war, and David, Kevin, and Kerry battled Michael Hayes, Terry Gordy, and Buddy Roberts across the territory with exceptional returns.

Three major "Star Wars" shows were staged at the Reunion Arena in downtown Dallas in 1983, and each drew more than 19,000 spectators. On June 17, 21,000 paid $300,000 at the gate to see Kevin Von Erich challenge the NWA world heavyweight champion Harley Race in a highly charged bout. The match ended when David Von Erich entered the ring to stop Race's onslaught on his brother, who had suffered an arm injury, and established David as the next logical contender to the NWA belt. Both David and Kerry became champions before leaving the building that night in Dallas, David going over Jimmy Garvin for the Texas title and Kerry winning the American tag straps from Hayes and Gordy with Bruiser Brody as his partner. On November 24, World Class returned to the Reunion Arena, and this time Kerry beat Hayes in a loser-leaves-town match before 19,000 fans. Garvin was also involved in a hot feud with English wrestling sensation Chris Adams, and the two traded the American heavyweight championship several times.

There was another big happening that night. Nineteen-year-old Mike Von Erich, the fourth son of Jack Adkisson, made his wrestling debut and defeated Skandor Akbar. Tall and skinny, Mike was immediately embraced by the home crowd, and he worked through his greenness to display vast potential. The following month, on Christmas night, World Class staged its final Reunion Arena program of the year, with 19,675 people eager to see David Von Erich dethrone Ric Flair for the NWA belt. The audience didn't get the finish they wanted, but David did end up with a DQ victory, solidifying his place as a top world title challenger. As in Mid-South, sportsmanship and credibility were principal elements of the Dallas promotion. Adkisson was extremely protective of wrestling's insider secrets and went out of his way to shield his sons from anything that would cast a negative shadow on their careers or his business, including allegations of drug abuse.

Rumors circulated that Adkisson was working behind the scenes to influence the NWA hierarchy to give David a run with the world title. As mentioned earlier, David was actually a member of the NWA board of directors, and he was in maybe the most unique position of any active professional wrestler for that reason. For Adkisson, getting one of his sons the championship was a primary goal, and there was speculation that David was going to beat Harley Race for the championship sometime before the end of 1983. However, those plans changed when Flair regained the NWA belt at Starrcade in November. If David was getting the championship — and it was still a big if — the title change was probably going to occur sometime in early 1984.

Part of Adkisson's close network of allies was the head of All Japan Pro Wrestling, Shohei "Giant" Baba, a three-time NWA world champion himself. Baba and two of his protégés, Jumbo Tsuruta and Genichiro Tenryu, had captured the attention of Dallas fans during the June 17, 1983, Reunion Arena show. As part of the talent exchange between the promotions, wrestlers also went to the Far East. On February 10, 1984, David Von Erich arrived in Tokyo to begin a three-week tour for Baba. But before the first show took place, he was found dead in his hotel room. The 25-year-old's death stunned the international wrestling community. It was determined that Von Erich had suffered from acute enteritis (inflamed intestine), which may have triggered a heart attack. There was gossip that his death was caused by substance abuse, and Kevin didn't waste any time telling a reporter that his brother was "in no way, shape, or form involved in drugs."[151] Von Erich's tragic death reverberated to all corners of the wrestling world, and fans in Dallas took it especially hard. More than 3,000 people attended his funeral, and Ric Flair, Dory and Terry Funk, and Verne Gagne were among those on hand to pay their respects.

The wrestling business lost another influential figure during the first half of 1984. Vincent James McMahon, the founder of the World Wide Wrestling Federation, and the man who had unified the northeastern territory into one thriving operation, passed away on May 27, 1984. At 69 years old, McMahon Sr. succumbed to cancer after a long fight and was laid to rest at Our Lady Queen of Heaven Cemetery in North Lauderdale, Florida. Across the wrestling landscape, admiration for McMahon poured in from his peers, pundits, and the public alike, and his accomplishments spoke for themselves.[152] No other promoter in history had ruled the metropolises of the Northeast single-handedly like he had, and when his son purchased the WWF in 1982, he acquired wrestling's greatest enterprise.

Over his last year, it is believed that McMahon Sr. fielded many calls from contemporaries who wanted to know what his son was up to. Individuals like Verne Gagne, a longtime associate with a track record of good business dealings with the elder McMahon, paid a heavy price in McMahon Jr.'s late 1983 talent raid.[153] Bob Geigel was hammered in St. Louis when the WWF arrived, and McMahon Jr. not only seized a prime TV spot, but resumed wrestling at the Chase Hotel. And throughout the early part of 1984, as the WWF targeted local TV acquisitions, a new group of promoters were coping with the harsh new realities. Although McMahon Sr. had remained an advisor to his son, his days calling the shots were over. He'd earned universal respect over the course of his lengthy, hall of fame career, and now with his death, it was up to his son to sink or swim in the new wrestling environment he was creating. Either McMahon Jr. would reshape the industry, or he was going to fail miserably, and the business was going to snap back to its original configuration without much fallout. The latter was unlikely, but the jury was still out.

CHAPTER NINE

AN INDUSTRY
AT WAR

The wrestling industry was facing a level of competition unlike anything before, and promoters were scrambling to ensure their businesses didn't descend into chaos. The competition wasn't only from Vince McMahon Jr., but from each other as well. Although promotional unions such as the National Wrestling Alliance maintained the peace amongst affiliated members, there was still enough anxiety to keep everyone on their toes. The threat of a deep pocketed rival with national aspirations was hard to comprehend, and there was no established precedent in terms of a proper defense. Many years earlier, the NWA had been powerful enough to curtail oppositional groups, and often simply intimidated foes by its size and strength. The Alliance flaunted its authority at times, and with exhaustive political ties, vast cash resources, and a steady leader like Sam Muchnick, the organization stopped many adversaries in their tracks. By

1984, though, the NWA was lacking nearly all of those attributes and was susceptible to any number of problems, including internal dissension.

Promoters were coping with an increased number of challenges during an extraordinary period in history. First and foremost, they absolutely had to keep their top talent happy. With the open option to migrate to a non-NWA promoter, for better pay and national publicity, wrestlers were viewing the road to the WWF a little differently than they had in years past. The NWA could no longer threaten a grappler with blacklisting, as they'd done in the 1950s.[154] The loss of a headline wrestler like Hulk Hogan on basically no notice was crippling. Verne Gagne, who had his star booked weeks in advance with good presales, crushed fans expecting to see Hogan live. Gagne didn't help matters by not quickly changing local advertisements when he knew Hogan was going to be a no-show.

With good reason, people were less prone to support a promotion that pulled the bait-and-switch routine. In early 1984, Jim Crockett lost Roddy Piper and Greg Valentine to the WWF, and it was no secret that McMahon was actively hunting for more big names to add to his roster. When wrestlers did jump to the WWF, organizations had to replace their losses. Up and down the lines, the talent ranks tightened. Gagne called on a semi-retired friend, 57-year-old the Crusher, to help fill the void left by Hogan, but in most situations, promoters pulled in workers from other groups. It was an accordion effect — one promotion after another was hurt by the talent grab, leaving vacancies all over the place.

Smaller independents, such as International Championship Wrestling out of Lexington, Kentucky, were the last rung on the talent ladder. Serving parts of Kentucky, Tennessee, Indiana, and Illinois, ICW had been a direct opponent of NWA and AWA-affiliated promoter Jerry Jarrett since 1978. There was legitimate hostility between the two operations, and the rivalry between ICW's Randy "Macho Man" Savage and Jerry "The King" Lawler was a feud just waiting to be exploited. In late 1983, facing heavy financial hardship, ICW owner Angelo Poffo made a deal with Jarrett, and Savage debuted on Memphis TV in early December. Of course, Savage wanted a piece of Lawler, and the invasion angle was a huge hit with fans. An explosive, brash persona, Savage was taking a big step toward greater fame and, over the following months, he feuded with Lawler, captured the Mid-America and International titles, and garnered mainstream attention.

As for Lawler, by early 1984, he was in the midst of his 36th reign as Southern champion, and his lengthy feud with Jimmy Hart's First Family dominated Memphis headlines. He battled the likes of Lord Humongous, Sabu the Wildman, and future superstar Rick Rude. In one particularly memorable storyline, Lawler was prompted to team with heel Jos LeDuc, who was also managed by Hart, and on March 12, 1984, they beat J.J. Dillon's Zambuie Express for the AWA Southern tag team belts. On the whole, Jarrett's Memphis promotion was never dull, with spirited gimmicks (Man Mountain Link, Harley Davidson, and the Executioner, for example), hot matches, and solid talent. Jarrett also featured King Kong Bundy, Dutch Mantell, Austin Idol, and the Rock and Roll Express. The Fabulous Ones were popular as well, but they were on the way out, and they ventured to the AWA during the latter part of March.

Memphis and the AWA had maintained a good partnership for nearly six years, and Lawler was a principal challenger to AWA world champion Nick Bockwinkel. The arrivals of the Fabulous Ones, Larry Zbyszko, and several others were part of Verne Gagne's effort to reignite his territory following a disastrous period of uncertainty. Since late 1983, with the exit of Hulk Hogan and Gene Okerlund, fans had let AWA officials know just how unhappy they were. Attendance dipped in most cities on the circuit, and on January 15, 1984, the audience in the AWA's homebase of St. Paul booed fan favorites unmercifully.[155] Jesse Ventura, a strongman heel with a gift for gab, was roundly cheered, and Gagne reportedly asked Ventura to turn hero in the wake of Hogan's departure. Ventura rejected the idea.

Looking to strengthen the promotion's alliances and bring in new faces, Gagne reached out to an old friend, Eddie Einhorn, a minority owner and president of the Chicago White Sox. Back in the 1970s, Einhorn headed an independent promotion known as the International Wrestling Association and ran opposition to the major organizations. His ideas were fundamentally strong, but he faced too many hurdles in bucking the establishment, and the IWA folded. Einhorn had been a TV executive prior to joining the Sox in 1981, and he and Gagne discussed the possibility of creating a nationally syndicated wrestling show. Their talks were at the preliminary level, but it was an exciting avenue that both men wanted to further pursue.

Out in San Francisco, the AWA was losing ground and took a big loss on January 31, 1984, when only 1,000 people attended a show at the Cow Palace. The WWF didn't seem to be doing much better. Vince McMahon lost his local TV on San Jose's channel 36, but refused to give up. In late February or early March 1984, he traveled to San Francisco and met with James Gabbert, owner of channel 20 (KTZO), the station that broadcast Gagne's weekly program, *All-Star Wrestling*. McMahon offered to pay Gabbert $2,000 a week to feature WWF content in place of the AWA.[156] In contrast, Gagne was providing his show for free, and though Gabbert had been cleaning up in commercial time, the WWF was proposing the weekly fee (inflated to as much as $5,000 in some reports) *plus* all advertisement revenue. Gabbert agreed to the proposition, and since Gagne didn't have a contract, the WWF immediately took over the timeslot on Saturday mornings, leaving the AWA high and dry.

As if losing Hogan and Okerlund weren't bad enough, having his San Francisco television outlet ripped out from underneath him was a personal affront to Gagne. And since the AWA was already committed to a Cow Palace show on March 24, 1984, and now had no TV to promote the event, the program was a predestined box-office bomb. Gagne did manage to obtain a new station (channel 26) about a week prior to the card, but the March 24 effort drew only 900 people. The WWF added a second TV outlet in northern California, signing on with a Sacramento station, and entered that city for a live event on March 9. On April 30, 1984, McMahon debuted in Oakland, and the WWF drew an impressive 10,200 spectators. Andre the Giant won an 18-man battle royal, which also included Hogan, Jimmy Snuka, and Pat Patterson. Hogan was victorious as well, winning his singles bout against Tiger Chung Lee.

The AWA survived the turbulence. Nick Bockwinkel stepped off the throne after a loss to Jumbo Tsuruta in Tokyo on February 23, 1984, and for a variety of reasons, gates began to rebound in March. Chicago fans responded to the reunion of the Crusher and Dick the Bruiser tag team, and on March 4, more than 18,000 people packed the Rosemont Horizon. The Freebirds, Stan Hansen, Jerry Lawler, and Montreal stars Dino Bravo and Rick Martel were part of the supporting cast. Amazingly, an even larger crowd was on hand in St. Paul on March 25 to see Crusher and Greg Gagne best Jerry Blackwell and Sheik Adnan El Kaissey. There is little doubt, however, that Verne Gagne was jolted by a tidbit of news in the *Minneapolis Tribune* on April 15, 1984. The blurb stated that a new program entitled *Superstars of Wrestling* was going to appear on channel 11 on Saturday evenings.[157] With *Superstars* now on the TV lineup, it could only mean one thing: The WWF was on its way to the Twin Cities.

From an outsider's point of view, McMahon's hostile actions toward the AWA appeared to be nothing short of a vendetta. But according to Gene Okerlund, who spoke with a Minneapolis reporter in May, such a claim was far from the truth. "Vince McMahon Jr. . . . doesn't want to drive [the AWA] out of business," he explained. "Verne Gagne and Wally Karbo are still going to be able to exist."[158] Needless to say, Gagne wasn't going to express any kind of gratitude for that statement. A world-class athlete in his younger days, he was no stranger to legitimate competition, and was fully prepared to defend the Twin Cities and the rest of his territory from WWF aggression. He didn't need anyone reaffirming the future of his company, and later told *Minneapolis CityBusiness*, "We were here before the WWF and we'll be here long after they are gone."[159]

McMahon's Minnesota incursion could've been much worse for Gagne. Apparently, when the WWF boss first got to the Twin Cities, he visited the office of Stu Swartz, general manager of KMSP (channel 9), the home station for the AWA. Once there, he offered a six-figure, upfront cash payment to replace the AWA with WWF programming. A deal of that magnitude would've made anyone stop in their tracks, but Swartz ultimately declined the offer. Undisturbed, the ever-motivated McMahon took his business over to WTCN (channel 11), which had been the flagship station for the AWA between the 1950s and '70s, and an agreement was made. *Superstars of Wrestling* debuted on April 21, 1984 at 6:00 p.m.

With so many former AWA stars on the WWF payroll, everyone knew a Twin Cities invasion was inevitable. Besides Hogan and Okerlund, McMahon had Sgt. Slaughter, the Iron Sheik, Don Muraco, and Andre the Giant, all AWA vets, plus recent signees Adrian Adonis, Dick Murdoch, and David Schultz. Featuring local wrestling veterans on WWF TV and at live events was part of McMahon's wider strategy going into new territories. To connect to fans who didn't necessarily know the WWF product, he wanted to highlight familiar faces, wrestlers who'd worked that region prior for regional promoters. These recognizable grapplers would help induce people to watch McMahon's production and serve as somewhat of a bridge between the wrestling they were used to seeing and the new WWF style. For many purists of the AWA and NWA, the WWF was quite dissimilar in terms of presentation, booking, and genuine action. To garner the attention of AWA and NWA loyalists, McMahon packed his cards with high-quality attractions and placed an emphasis on name value over in-ring skill.

The WWF wasn't Gagne's only concern. Unfavorable publicity surrounded an unscheduled brawl involving two of his stars, Ken Patera and Mr. Saito.[160] Instead of a headline match at a local arena, their bout occurred at a Holiday Inn, and their opponents were 15 Waukesha, Wisconsin, police officers. The April 6, 1984, incident saw both grapplers arrested after a lengthy battle. At least four officers were hospitalized, and one was forced to retire because of her injuries. Charged with multiple counts of battery, Patera and Saito were sentenced to two-year prison terms in 1985.[161] Gagne dealt with the challenges as they appeared and kept the AWA chugging along. On May 13, 1984, the day after the WWF debuted on WTCN, the world heavyweight championship changed hands at a show in St. Paul. Quebecer Rick Martel, a strong and athletic wrestling prodigy whom Gagne had taken under his wing, beat Jumbo Tsuruta to capture the belt — a decision by Gagne that attempted to dispel the conjecture that the AWA was nothing but an old man's promotion.

McMahon's aggressive actions continued to motivate rivals. Jim Crockett was in the best position to counter the push of the WWF by advancing into McMahon's northeastern stronghold from his Mid-Atlantic location. It also helped that Crockett's TV already reached the New York City area by way of WXTV (channel 41), a Spanish-language station. Viewers responded to the immense talent in Crockett's territory, and the show grew a large following. Crockett solidified his partnership with Ole Anderson and, in early May 1984, an ambitious 17-city national tour was announced on Anderson's WTBS cable broadcast.[162] Promoter Gary Juster appeared on camera in the segment, and was acknowledged as the NWA's representative in Baltimore and at the Meadowlands in New Jersey.

While that idea was in the works, few people knew that McMahon had already set the wheels in motion to secretly purchase Georgia Championship Wrestling out from under Anderson.[163] With help from Jim Barnett, a minority owner of the company, and the Brisco brothers,

McMahon obtained 51 percent stock and controlling interest in what was, in essence, the Georgia territory. Anderson temporarily blocked the purchase by obtaining a restraining order, and pending court action was the only thing holding McMahon back from officially taking charge and replacing *World Championship Wrestling* with WWF programming on WTBS. In no way did Anderson want to sell, especially to McMahon, but because of the structure of the company's articles of incorporation, he was in an extremely vulnerable spot. By May 1984, news of McMahon's actions broke nationally, and Anderson remained hopeful that a Georgia court would side with him and declare the sale unlawful.

Invading the Meadowlands was a big deal for the National Wrestling Alliance, which hadn't had much traction in that part of the country since "Nature Boy" Buddy Rogers ruled the roost in the early 1960s. Even then, the NWA name didn't hold much weight. But times had changed, and with WXTV and WTBS promoting their cause, Crockett and Anderson wanted to make the most of their opportunity. The proposed 17-city tour was scaled back to concentrate on an East Coast run from the Meadowlands beginning on May 29, 1984, and going through June 9 in Baltimore. The circuit included Roanoke, Atlanta, Raleigh, Norfolk, Richmond, and Greensboro, and saw the two promoters pool their resources at a crucial time to offset McMahon's first offensive in the Mid-Atlantic region. On May 31, the WWF was going to debut in Richmond, followed by shows in Winston-Salem, Norfolk, and Hampton.

Tensions were high. The talent grabs by McMahon hurt Crockett where it mattered most, and only worsened when Bob Orton Jr. left in March. A lot was riding on the NWA's Meadowlands show, and the spectacular was dubbed "A Night of Champions." Headlined by world champion Ric Flair defending against Ricky Steamboat (who had returned to the ring in March after being offered a $10,000 check by Crockett), the program featured the Road Warriors, Stan Hansen, Dusty Rhodes, and Wahoo McDaniel. As anticipated, Flair and Steamboat put on a wrestling clinic, one of their absolute best, and the undercard thoroughly entertained the 12,000 in attendance. Among the other competitors was Carlos Colon, a Puerto Rican superstar and holder of the World Wrestling Council Universal championship. Colon was a fantastic lure for Spanish viewers of WXTV, and he successfully defended his belt against Tully Blanchard.

Two nights later, the WWF stormed into the Richmond Arena and featured four former Mid-Atlantic stars: Greg Valentine, Sgt. Slaughter, Jimmy Snuka, and the Iron Sheik. (Andre the Giant, who usually spearheaded the WWF forays into new territories, was in Japan at the time.) Prior to McMahon's invasion, sportswriter Jerry Lindquist noted in the *Richmond Times Dispatch* that there used to be an "unwritten law" in pro wrestling when it came to promoters and the various territories: "You don't encroach on mine and I won't encroach on yours."[164] That law was broken by both the NWA and WWF. But the WWF didn't see the results they wanted in Richmond. The WWF drew a gate of only $6,000 on May 31, and a journalist called the effort "ill-advised." In contrast, Crockett, the reporter claimed, had recently drawn an $82,000 gate at the Coliseum.[165] With more recognizable performers, Crockett and Anderson held the advantage in the Mid-Atlantic States, but the turf war was just beginning.

Combining talent to outgun outsiders was an old promotional tactic, one that the NWA had used throughout history. By conjoining their rosters, promoters were giving fans a never-ending string of dream shows, and that was the upshot of heavy competition. Of all the battleground regions, there was no territory receiving a better blend of top wrestling talent on a monthly basis than St. Louis. Always known for its impressive lineups, St. Louis took on an even greater sense of importance after the WWF debut in December 1983, and in the fight for fan support, both McMahon and the NWA's Bob Geigel were pulling out all the stops. On paper, Geigel's appeared to be the stronger of the two operations. In early 1984, he was receiving the cream of the crop from at least five territories, in addition to the AWA, to help pad his programs. His coalition of stars included Flair, Harley Race, Dick the Bruiser, Dory Funk Jr., and AWA world tag team champions Crusher Blackwell and Ken Patera. King Kong (Bruiser) Brody was a significant attraction for Geigel's outfit since he'd previously worked for Larry Matysik's outlaw group, and his placement against NWA workers was notable for St. Louis fans. On January 6, 1984, Flair and Brody at the top of the bill drew a sold-out crowd to the Kiel Auditorium, Geigel's first in many months. The WWF was putting up a good showing as well with two TV tapings at the Chase Park Hotel and a local arena debut at the Kiel on February 10. Geigel tried to siphon off attendance by advertising his next big Kiel event, still a week away, on the same day as the WWF's show.[166] But attendance was respectable for both promotions, and neither was anywhere near ready to fold up shop.

The Von Erich Brothers were longtime favorites in St. Louis and important allies for Geigel. Kevin, Kerry, and David each had runs with the Missouri State championship, and were popular box office attractions. In addition, Jack Adkisson sent Chris Adams and Jimmy Garvin to St. Louis in 1984, with their respective valets, Sunshine and Precious. The quartet was engaged in one of wrestling's most talked about feuds, and gates were up all over Texas and Oklahoma because of the heat brewing between them.[167] The relationship between Adkisson and Geigel, as firm as it might have seemed, was being impacted by the influence of Vince McMahon. The latter made no attempt to hide the fact that he wanted to do business with the Von Erichs, and the possibility of working together seemed very real.[168]

Between April 22 and April 27, 1984, McMahon's top star, Andre the Giant, made three appearances for Adkisson in one of his final tours for a non-WWF affiliate. Adkisson also withheld his sons from the St. Louis wrestling war from January 7 through the end of May, as it would've shown preference for one promotion over the other. But with the WWF gaining TV in Dallas, and talk of a future invasion, Adkisson shut down any speculation and remained loyal to the NWA. Kerry Von Erich appeared for Geigel on June 1 and drew with Ric Flair. Notably, Kerry and Flair had been part of an even bigger match on a much bigger stage just a few weeks before. On May 6, Adkisson held a special memorial event for his late son, David, at Texas Stadium. The Parade of Champions show drew more than 32,000 spectators and Kerry went over Flair in the main event to capture the NWA world heavyweight crown. It was a touching moment, mixed with emotion and excitement, and finally a Von Erich was world titleholder.

Kerry's reign lasted 18 days. He lost a rematch to Flair in Japan on May 24. The title switch ensured Flair would be back in the U.S., wearing the belt, for the important Night of Champions program at the Meadowlands on May 29.

McMahon had another big surprise for the wrestling world. On the same night as the NWA's Meadowlands debut, he presented the first episode of his new weekly series, *Tuesday Night Titans*, on the USA Network. "Wrestling TNT" was the first of its kind, an entertainment-driven primetime interview and clip show featuring sit-down discussions with various stars, comedic segments, and lots of improvisation. McMahon hosted the program alongside former wrestler Lord Alfred Hayes. The debut episode included a visit with "Dr. D" David Schultz at home with his family, a cooking segment with the Wild Samoans, and a lengthy appearance by "Captain" Lou Albano. By the end of the two-hour program, it was clear that McMahon had created something both noteworthy and cringe-worthy.

The invasions continued, and the WWF targeted Jerry Jarrett's territory next. On June 24, 1984, McMahon held a loaded show in Memphis, showcasing the world, I-C, and tag champs, along with Andre the Giant, Big John Studd, Jimmy Snuka, and Mil Mascaras. Hulk Hogan's opponent in the main event was Moondog Rex, half of the Moondogs tag team, which had formerly held belts for Jarrett's promotion. Of all the regions McMahon had invaded, Memphis required a unique approach, and packing his cards with "New York" stars didn't win over patrons. Memphis fans responded to emotionally charged feuds, built with a steady hand, and acted out with precision. So the random booking of Hogan and Moondog Rex without any backstory or psychological investment was of no interest to fans. As a result, the WWF's draw in the Memphis area was remarkably unimpressive. Nevertheless, Jarrett was ready to combat the WWF in Memphis. He went all-out to prove his local supremacy, booking a special extravaganza billed as Star Wars '84 for the next evening at the Mid-South Coliseum. The venue was sold out, with 11,000 fans dwarfing the WWF's attendance of 1,200 at the Convention Center. Jarrett gave the fans nine big matches, among which were Lawler and Austin Idol against the Road Warriors, and the Fabulous Ones against the Pretty Young Things. The event was Jarrett's biggest to date, and the following month, Star Wars programs were staged in Nashville and Louisville as well, within days of the WWF's second local card. The Louisville show, on July 22, had eight matches, with Lawler teaming with pro footballer Ron Mikolajczyk against Rick Rude and Jim Neidhart in the headline bout.[169]

Florida was another unique territory with its own traditions. Promoter Eddie Graham was as old school as they came, and though wrestling fans loved his creative management style, the territory struggled in 1983, suffering from a lack of strong attractions. At one point, Dave Meltzer of the *Wrestling Observer Newsletter* described the territory as "crumbling," saying its rebound depended on a talent upgrade.[170] Things did pick up before the end of the year, and by early 1984, Graham was once again reaping hefty box-office rewards. Youngsters Barry Windham, Mike Rotunda, and Billy Jack Haynes were fast becoming his bread and butter, and Dusty Rhodes continued to carry the territory as the top fan favorite. On the heel side, Kevin Sullivan was doing a masterful job portraying a madman, supported by the likes of Jim Duggan, One Man Gang, and "Cowboy" Ron Bass. Ric Flair also made a number of impactful appearances.

In April 1984, Graham received Andre the Giant on loan from Titan Sports for a week's worth of appearances. Like Andre's visit to Jack Adkisson in Texas, this seemed like a gesture of goodwill to ensure the WWF and Florida remained on good terms. But, literally, the day before Andre began his tour, the WWF's *Superstars of Wrestling* show debuted in south Florida on WCIX (channel 6). This move could've been interpreted one of two ways. One, it was an added outlet in a cooperative enterprise benefiting both Graham and Vince McMahon, or two, it was really step one in the WWF's expansion into the territory. Two months later, on June 16, 1984, that question was answered when Hulk Hogan and his compatriots marched into the Hollywood Sportatorium in the suburbs of Fort Lauderdale. Possibly due to the respect McMahon, and his father before him, had for Graham, the WWF stayed away from the territory's primary city, Tampa, and instead focused on the southern part of the state. But Florida was now a battleground state.

The McMahons also had a long association with Don Owen of Portland. That didn't stop the WWF from placing *Superstars of Wrestling* on Portland's KPTV (channel 12) on April 27, 1984. But their good relations might have slowed any attempt by the WWF to operate in Oregon, for a little while at least. As far as Washington State was concerned, Owen's deep political connections did the rest of the work. Similar to the situation in Louisiana, Washington officials issued only a single license to promote wrestling, and Owen was locked in. Interestingly, Roddy Piper, who had made his bones working for Owen years earlier, didn't want to work shows in opposition to his former boss in the Pacific Northwest, though Owen reportedly gave Piper his blessing to do so.

McMahon invaded Minneapolis on June 17, 1984, with Hogan, Paul Orndorff, Tito Santana, David Schultz, and the tag team champions,

Adrian Adonis and Dick Murdoch, at the Met Center before an estimated 11,000 people. Also part of the show were Maurice "Mad Dog" Vachon and Jesse Ventura, recent signees from the AWA. In July, McMahon added two other AWA cities to his circuit after placing *Superstars of Wrestling* in Salt Lake City (KSTU-20) and Phoenix (KNXV-15). The WWF followed up with shows in Salt Lake and Phoenix on July 28 and July 29, 1984, and did fairly well in their debut presentations. The defections of Vachon, Ventura, and TV producer Al DeRusha, who joined the production team for *Tuesday Night Titans*, had drawn more blood from Verne Gagne. The war was costing him manpower and money and was highly personal.

In his 20 years promoting in the Twin Cities, Gagne had dealt with competitors before, but the WWF was a different kind of animal. It had the finances, the connections, and the talent — including many former AWA stars — to succeed. But a big question lingered in the minds of many anti-WWF promoters: was McMahon breaking federal antitrust law by taking over talent, venues, and TV stations from rival organizations? In the opinion of some, the WWF was fast becoming a monopoly. If McMahon was able to achieve half of what he was trying to accomplish, he would establish a wrestling syndicate that even the NWA in its heyday would have been proud to call its own.

CHAPTER TEN

ROCK 'N' WRESTLING

For any wrestling promoter not affiliated with the World Wrestling Federation, one word was of central importance by mid-1984, and that was "cooperation." A fusion of the most experienced minds in the business, fully united and motivated, seemed to be the best way to halt the WWF's advancement. To a degree, teamwork was already paying off in certain parts of the country. Jim Crockett and Ole Anderson had done well at the Meadowlands and were fortified up and down the East Coast. Jerry Jarrett and Bill Watts had coordinated their efforts and traded talent to nice benefits. Several promoters were sending talent to St. Louis to help Bob Geigel and his partners, keeping the NWA alive in a competitive head-to-head fight. But as the wrestling war intensified, and more territories were drawn into fracas, these businessmen realized it was time to take their cooperation to another level. Their future depended on it.

Earlier in the year, Verne Gagne and Eddie Einhorn discussed the implementation of a new nationally syndicated program to challenge McMahon in each of the major markets. With good placement on prime TV stations and a slickly produced show, they could potentially stop his momentum, regain their old stars, and even gain ground in the Northeast. The leaders of the NWA–AWA faction debated these strategies at a special meeting in Chicago in June 1984.[171] Gagne was joined by a handful of his longtime allies, including Crockett, Jarrett, Watts, and Einhorn, and by the end of the conference, everyone was seemingly on the same page. This union formed what would become Pro Wrestling USA, a syndicated television program and joint promotion. The best of their rosters would travel to a centralized location for a combined TV taping and then to supershows all over the country. As a result of the controversial Georgia Championship Wrestling deal, the NWA was on the cusp of losing WTBS, and needed to secure a national platform more than ever. Einhorn would act as the middleman between the promoters and Syndicast Services Inc., a New York–based syndication outfit. They still needed to locate a venue for the first TV taping, arrange talent, and book the matches, but with handshake agreements in place, the foundation for Pro Wrestling USA was set in stone.

A number of territorial stars were rumored to be on their way to "New York," among them Magnum T.A., Butch Reed, Jimmy Valiant, and Mike Rotunda. Bruiser Brody's name was also mentioned for a big feud against Hulk Hogan. From the WWF's point of view, a guy like Brody was a potential game-changer, and his jump to McMahon would've had ramifications from St. Louis to Japan. The WWF was getting a lot of mileage out of recent signees, specifically Paul Orndorff (who joined the WWF full-time in November 1983), Greg Valentine, Dave Schultz, and Bob Orton Jr. But none of the recent additions compared to the impact "Rowdy" Roddy Piper was having on the organization, and his character was developing into one of the most colorful in the industry.

Billed as the "Rowdy Scot" from Glasgow, Scotland, Piper was really born in Saskatoon, Saskatchewan, and was 29 when he joined the WWF in early January 1984. Coming off a run as a fan favorite in the Mid-Atlantic region, Piper became a fast-talking heel. His wit and bravado gave the WWF an immense personality, and he was a natural manager.

He seconded Orndorff and Schultz to the ring and soon became the host of his own TV interview segment, "Piper's Pit." He was aggressive, willing to fight at the drop of a hat, and usually made a mockery of his guests. In June 1984, footage of him blasting Jimmy Snuka over the head with a coconut was featured on TV, and was a perfect display of his ruthlessness. People loved his antics, and Piper was instrumental in helping the WWF turn a corner as it adopted a national touring circuit.

Far and away, though, Hulk Hogan was the most important figure in the organization. Hulkamania had gripped the imagination of fans, both the young and old, and his free-flowing charisma made him a natural attraction. Wearing bright yellow garb and flexing 24-inch "pythons," Hogan connected to audiences like few people in wrestling history and was incredibly marketable. In the ring, Hogan couldn't be compared to Ric Flair or other technically savvy grapplers. His style was that of a brawler, and supporters of the NWA and AWA criticized his lack of depth. But his fans didn't care. They weren't interested in seeing Hogan arm drag his opponent. They wanted to see him pummel the crooked foes, deliver a big boot, and land a legdrop for a pinfall. Then they wanted to see him cup his hand to his ear as the crowd celebrated around him.

During the first half of 1984, he feuded with Orndorff, Schultz, the Masked Superstar, and Big John Studd, and his matches were usually in the five-to-six-minute range. On May 21, 1984, Hogan and Schultz topped a show at Madison Square Garden before more than 24,000 people, and at the end of June, he sold out the Olympic Auditorium in Los Angeles, going over Orndorff in the main event. Hogan was billed as a native son of the Los Angeles area, hailing from Venice Beach, despite originally being from Florida. Venice Beach (home of the famous Muscle Beach) played better for his gimmick as a muscular, tanned superstar, and Hogan never missed a beat. On July 15, 1984, Hogan teamed with Andre the Giant to beat Studd, Adrian Adonis, and Dick Murdoch at the Meadowlands before nearly 19,000 fans, outdrawing the previous NWA effort by about 7,000. Sgt. Slaughter was another major fan favorite, having turned from the dark side to battle the Iron Sheik in a feud that stirred up plenty of patriotism. His popular drill sergeant persona would later become immortalized as a *G.I. Joe* character, in the TV cartoon and as an action figure. Slaughter and Sheik faced off many times in 1984, and their bouts were filled with passion, in the ring and from the audience. Bloodshed was a common sight in their hardcore cage and boot-camp matches. Former collegiate football star Tito Santana, a protégé of Hiro Matsuda, captured the WWF Intercontinental championship from Don Muraco on February 11, 1984, at the Boston Garden. Adored by fans, Santana reigned the entire summer, turning back an array of quality challengers. He was ultimately beaten for the belt by Greg Valentine on September 24 in London, Ontario. Valentine's manager, Captain Lou Albano, was as cunning as ever, and 1984 was a remarkable year in his hall of fame career.

Things began to take off when Albano was cast as pop sensation Cyndi Lauper's father in the music video for "Girls Just Want to Have Fun," a big hit on MTV beginning in December 1983. According to the *Los Angeles Times*, he was Lauper's "guru," and the singer herself admitted to being influenced by his words of wisdom.[172] With the video in heavy rotation, Albano reached a new realm of celebrity, and Lauper went on to win Best Female Video at the 1984 Video Music Awards. Lauper's manager David Wolff, a longtime grappling enthusiast, came up with a plan to drum up even more attention. His angle was scripted to do three things: generate interest, garner heat for Albano, and maximize sales for both Lauper and the box office.

Between May and July 1984, Albano began to take more and more credit for Lauper's success, claiming to be her manager and insisting the reason she was a superstar was all his doing. Then with unabashed misogyny he took it a step further by stating that women belonged in the kitchen. Lauper wasn't going to let that slide. She appeared on Piper's Pit and gave it right back to Albano, first verbally and then physically.[173] After things calmed down, Lauper issued a challenge. She said that she was going to find a woman wrestler to battle, and beat, anyone Albano wanted. She subsequently chose Wendi Richter, a spirited young grappler from Dallas, Texas. In opposition, Albano picked the Fabulous Moolah, the women's world champion, purportedly, since 1956. It was true Moolah was still claiming a belt she'd first won 28 years earlier, but her reign wasn't uninterrupted. She lost and regained the title several times.[174]

The stage was set, the lines in the sand were drawn, and the era of the Rock 'n' Wrestling Connection was officially launched. On July 23, 1984, MTV featured live satellite coverage of the Moolah–Richter bout from

Madison Square Garden in New York and drew the largest ratings, to date, in network history. Richter, accompanied by Lauper, was victorious in the match and won the WWF women's championship. "When Wendi won," Wolff later told a reporter, "the cheers were as loud or louder than any I've ever heard at a rock concert."[175]

Vince McMahon couldn't have been disappointed by the results of the Rock 'n' Wrestling experiment, and it meant tremendous publicity for the WWF. In terms of placing his company on a platform above his competitors, McMahon was getting it done by taking chances. No other promoters were even close, and honestly, many of the old-school territorial bosses likely would have scoffed at an angle involving a pop star because of how it went against the grain of traditional pro wrestling. But McMahon had no such qualms. This outside-the-box thinking gave the WWF an edge in the all-important 18- to 34-year-old demographic, as well as with teenagers. The WWF was entering a more robust consciousness, not only for madcap in-ring mayhem, but for entertaining angles involving celebrities. The July 1984 spectacle, the Brawl to Settle It All, was only the beginning of the wrestling and rock partnership.[176]

Throughout this entire period, in addition to his television responsibilities and regular management operations, Vince McMahon found plenty of time to further his expansion. Toronto, a major stop on the National Wrestling Alliance circuit dating back to 1949, was profoundly weakened by the death of Frank Tunney in 1983 and faced a steep decline in attendance. As it was, top-tier grapplers used to flock to Toronto to enjoy Tunney's world-renowned professionalism and fair payoffs. Following his death, the promotion was taken over by his son Eddie and nephew Jack, and continued to draw in workers from Jim Crockett and eastern Canada, but the pool of wrestling talent was stretched thin in 1984 and Toronto suffered, like many other cities. With things coming to a head financially, the Tunneys had to make a decision, and perhaps their choice was easy. The WWF had been on TV in the Toronto area since 1982, broadcasting from a Buffalo station, and was a known commodity to local fans. It also featured many former Toronto stars, guys like Roddy Piper, Greg Valentine, Sgt. Slaughter, and Jimmy Snuka who had appeared at Maple Leaf Gardens when the promotion was riding high. These were the individuals people wanted to see live, and the Tunneys realized an agreement with the WWF was their best option. On June 27, 1984, at a special press conference, the new WWF–Toronto pact was announced to the public. Toronto was a major acquisition for McMahon. In most other cases, his expansion included battleground cities with heavy competition. Toronto differed because, as in the previous deals in Los Angeles and Detroit, he gained a certain level of exclusivity. By working with the Tunneys, McMahon took over grappling at Maple Leaf Gardens and the popular *Maple Leaf Wrestling* television program on CHCH-11 out of Hamilton. Jack Tunney became chief of the WWF's Canadian operations and took an on-camera figurehead role as president of the entire promotion. He was an enthusiastic member of the organization, and talked up Hulk Hogan to a reporter for the *Financial Post*, saying, "Gorgeous George, Yukon Eric, Whipper Watson. They were big stars, but nothing like Hogan. He's big in every corner of the world."[177]

Maple Leaf Wrestling, as produced by the WWF, debuted within days of the agreement with the Tunneys, and the first live show at the Gardens on July 22, 1984, drew 10,000 people. Programs were staged every two weeks, and McMahon hired Billy Red Lyons, a popular ex-wrestler from Ontario, as a commentator and interviewer to give the WWF that local familiar face he wanted in new territories. Altogether, the WWF had sufficient manpower well known to area enthusiasts and expected big returns at the box office. McMahon had additional plans for Ontario and the rest of Canada. Beginning on July 10, he began holding TV tapings north of the border, the first in Brantford, Ontario, and then also in London and Hamilton.

The customary television tapings held in Hamburg and Allentown, Pennsylvania, were discontinued in May and June, respectively, ending a long-running tradition. New footage for *All-Star Wrestling* and *Maple Leaf Wrestling* originated from Ontario tapings, while *Championship Wrestling* was filmed in Poughkeepsie, New York. The *Superstars of Wrestling* program was predominantly recorded from the Kiel Auditorium in St. Louis with interviews and promos spliced into each episode. *Tuesday Night Titans*, with its formulaic interview setup, was taped in Baltimore before relocating to Connecticut, and for the wrestlers, producers, and hosts of the various programs, there was a great deal of traveling required. In fact, the weekly live event schedule had more than doubled, and Ed Cohen, the WWF's director of promotions, was responsible for booking the various arenas all over the country. "When I first came aboard, we were doing five events a week," Cohen told the *Greenwich News* in 1984. "Now we have 14 a week."[178]

As the WWF roster continued to grow, there were rumors that McMahon envisioned four different live shows every single day, an incredible proposition. The increased traveling, even with 14 programs a week, split with half the wrestlers on an "A" circuit and the others on a "B" circuit, was undoubtedly going to tax everyone in the locker room. There was some question of whether the overloaded schedule, and the wear and tear on the wrestlers themselves, impacted the quality of matches in the ring. "Physically, you find the body can take a lot more than people expect," Don Muraco told an Associated Press reporter in 1985. "The body is capable of enduring that kind of punishment and fatigue. The grind comes when you're trying to coordinate that with your home life."[179] He was often on the road eight days straight before returning home to his family. For one stretch of seven months, announcer Gene Okerlund said he traveled 160,000 miles.[180]

Special publicity events were also part of the lives of WWF employees. In May 1984, McMahon, Lou Albano, Roddy Piper, Sgt. Slaughter, and Freddie Blassie appeared on a regional talk show in Pennsylvania, *It's Your Turn Lehigh Valley*. The program, which originated on PBS station WLVT-39 and was shown in Philadelphia, featured a live studio audience and gave all five individuals a platform to work their gimmicks. Slaughter was adored by the crowd, Albano and Blassie drew boos, and Piper made a lot of the people laugh, especially when it came to questions about his kilt. Each individual on the panel remained in character, but they had a good time with the crowd, and probably endeared themselves a little more to fans by the end of the program.

Despite his personable efforts in the media, McMahon was highly unpopular with smart wrestling fans in non-WWF areas. In the Correspondents' Corner of the popular "dirt sheet" *Wrestling Observer Newsletter*, people sounded off about his maneuvering, voicing their concerns and complaints. Longtime enthusiasts, loyal to their home territories, were upset about the WWF's growing influence, hated the promotion's style of wrestling, and, as one correspondent noted, saw it as a "real threat to the stability" of the entire industry.[181] These fans hoped the

NWA and AWA would rise up and quell its march. "Cowboy" Bill Watts, head of the Mid-South promotion, turned correspondent for an early 1985 edition of the *Observer*, and surprisingly wanted to thank McMahon. He felt the business had grown stagnant and believed McMahon was forcing promoters to step up their game for a complete and total rejuvenation.[182]

On the other hand, some promoters continued to be wooed by McMahon's big cash offerings. As part of the WWF's Canadian expansion, McMahon reportedly offered Stu Hart $1 million for the Calgary territory (Stampede), including several wrestlers, TV timeslots, and arena rights.[183] Hart, who had bought his promotion in the early 1950s for $50,000, consented to the deal and held his final live Calgary event on September 14, 1984, at the Victoria Pavilion.[184] In the main event, his son Bret teamed with Dynamite Kid to beat Bad News Allen and Ron Starr in a cage match. The WWF picked up Bret Hart and Dynamite Kid in the Stampede purchase, along with Davey Boy Smith. *Maple Leaf Wrestling* soon replaced the local TV show, and in November, McMahon sent his troupe across western Canada, stopping in Calgary, Winnipeg, Regina, and Vancouver.

Montreal was another crucial Canadian city but was going to be a much harder acquisition. Already heavily fortified, the International Wrestling promotion run by Gino Brito and Dino Bravo (Andre the Giant had sold out early in 1984) was scoring sizeable houses throughout 1984. Featuring the Rougeaus, Abdullah the Butcher, Brito, Bravo, and stars from the AWA, IW was by far the hottest wrestling company in Quebec. The WWF, however, already had TV time in Montreal, stemming from the late 1983 deal with George Cannon, and fans watched McMahon's *Superstars of Wrestling* on CFCF-12. In late May 1984, with coordination efforts by Montreal native Pat Patterson, the WWF presented a live show at the Verdun Auditorium just south of Montreal, but the event was a financial bomb. McMahon tried a second time in June, but again, the WWF failed to show competitive strength against International Wrestling.

Meanwhile, back in Atlanta, McMahon received positive news about his "forced buyout" of Ole Anderson and the Georgia promotion. On July 11, 1984, the contracts were finalized and Titan Sports obtained Georgia Championship Wrestling and its immensely valuable timeslots on Superstation WTBS. Three days later, at 6:05 p.m., Freddie Miller, the longtime co-host of *World Championship Wrestling*, officially welcomed the WWF to the station.[185] Bewildered regular viewers of weekend matches on WTBS expected to see famed announcer Gordon Solie at the top of the show, but instead watched Miller introduce McMahon, who promised to bring "the greatest in professional wrestling entertainment." Over the next hour, WWF tag champions Adrian Adonis and Dick Murdoch, the Iron Sheik, Jesse Ventura, and Big John Studd made appearances in previously recorded bouts. Studd's opponent was the legendary Bobo Brazil, a former WWWF U.S. champion back in the 1960s, but the latter was pinned after just six minutes of action.

McMahon had succeeded in capturing a major prize in the world of pro wrestling and was now in charge of two influential cable outlets. As for Anderson and the NWA as a whole, they were pushed off the national stage with the scales of power tipping in the WWF's favor. But the initial reaction to what was later designated "Black Saturday" was not exactly positive. According to some reports, "thousands" of people phoned WTBS to gripe about the changeover from the NWA to the WWF. Alan Patureau of the *Atlanta Constitution*, in an article the following Tuesday, explained that "at least 83 viewers" had called to protest. McMahon had a response for the vocal grievances: "We'll show those complainers the difference between a major league and a minor league production, given time."[186]

Part of McMahon's agreement with WTBS included the stipulation that he'd present live studio wrestling taped in Atlanta, as Anderson had done in years past. Instead, he used the WTBS show, still named *World Championship Wrestling*, to feature pre-taped, out-of-town footage from various house shows and TV tapings. WWF officials believed the background crowds and noise from places like New York City, Philadelphia, and Minneapolis were important to illustrate that their promotion was indeed "big time." The arena settings made a greater impression on spectators in contrast to the studio efforts of southern promoters. Gordon Solie disagreed. "Technically, studio matches are far superior entertainment because they are designed for the viewer at home as opposed to the spectators in an auditorium," he told a reporter for the *Palm Beach Post*. "There really is no comparison."[187] To ingratiate itself with fans of GCW, the WWF made offers to the talent of the Georgia promotion, and snagged a handful of key names. The Spoiler, Les Thornton, Mr. Wrestling II, and the Brisco Brothers made appearances on the WWF's

World Championship Wrestling in the following months, as did a number of other Georgia alumni.

Also, continuing with the Rock 'n' Wrestling theme, David Wolff signed a managerial contract with the Fabulous Freebirds. The idea was to push Michael Hayes, a Freebird teammate of Terry Gordy and Buddy Roberts, as a musician and ultimately release an album through CBS Associated Labels. "Michael Hayes is a heavy metal rock 'n' roller, a very energetic performer," Wolff told the *Philadelphia Daily News*, "and the Freebirds are a wrestling equivalent — heavy brawlers. I think that wrestling and rock have a great untapped crossover market, and that a Michael Hayes can really bridge the gap."[188] The Freebirds, unlike during their time in Texas as adversaries of the Von Erichs, were fan favorites in the WWF, and both Wolff and Cyndi Lauper made appearances with the trio in August 1984. Anyone who knew the background of the Freebirds understood their incredible value, but a lengthy run in the WWF was not to be. For reasons likely spurred by creative differences, Hayes, Gordy, and Roberts left the promotion in September 1984 after a dozen or so tag matches.

Another newcomer, the 6-foot-7, 350-plus-pound Kamala, was brought in as a protégé of Fred Blassie and literally squashed enhancement talent with his massive splash finisher. He went on to feud with Andre the Giant. On July 31, 1984, both Brutus Beefcake and Ken Patera turned up in the WWF as heels at a Poughkeepsie TV taping. Patera was still facing court action based on the out-of-the-ring incident in Wisconsin while in the AWA, but his arrival was noteworthy nonetheless. Beefcake was a solid performer, and good things were in store for him headed into 1985.

And the WWF didn't stop there. On August 10, 1984, one of the most popular attractions in the territorial system, the Junkyard Dog, made his debut for McMahon in St. Louis. He was a huge acquisition and potentially crippling to the Mid-South promotion. JYD was beloved on a Hulk Hogan level in the South. His WWF entrance as a fan favorite balanced out a heel-heavy roster, and over subsequent months, he went to the mat against Paul Orndorff, Roddy Piper, Greg Valentine, and other top rule-breakers. David Sammartino, the bulky 24-year-old son of the "Living Legend" Bruno Sammartino, was also new to the WWF. He made his first in-ring appearance at a Poughkeepsie taping on September 11, 1984, the same night his father returned to the WWF as a commentator. Bruno

Sammartino had been embroiled in a real feud with McMahon for several years, involving legal action, but the two sides had reached an amicable resolution. Some believed that Bruno was brought back to bolster support in the New York area against Pro Wrestling USA.

Nine days before the WWF debut in Toronto, on July 13, 1984, McMahon entered Chicago for his first live event at the Pavilion on the campus of the University of Illinois. Chicago was considered firm AWA territory, and saw many wrestlers from Indianapolis as part of the WWA–AWA relationship. With local TV in place on WFLD since January, the WWF had made some inroads in the Windy City, but the promotion was hurt by two things. First, the WFLD telecast was on Saturday mornings at 8:30, which was far from an optimal timeslot. Second, the growth of cable television was developing slower in Chicago than in most major cities, and the wrestling populace there wasn't seriously influenced by McMahon's offerings on USA Network. The AWA was way out in front, drawing sizable crowds at the Rosemont Horizon, and a lot needed to happen for the roles to reverse.

On the other side of the wrestling universe, Ole Anderson didn't take his ouster from the Georgia promotion lying down. He immediately started a new company (Championship Wrestling from Georgia), gained local TV on WGNX-46, and, with help from Ann Gunkel, obtained an early Saturday morning timeslot on WTBS beginning in early August 1984.[189] The following month, he began taping from the WTBS studios in Atlanta, filling the void left when McMahon decided to use out-of-town footage. The reacquisition of a cable TV slot was enormous for the NWA, and Jim Crockett joined several other members in support of Anderson.

But with the WWF putting a toehold on wrestling in Canada, adding Atlanta and Chicago to its overall war efforts, and profiting from connections to cable stations WTBS, MTV, and USA, the battle for wrestling superiority was as hot as ever.

CHAPTER ELEVEN

COOPERATION AND CRISIS

Two weeks after the WWF made its Florida debut at the Hollywood Sportatorium, Championship Wrestling from Florida responded with an all-star event at the Orange Bowl in Miami, about 25 miles away. The show was called "Lord of the Ring" for its headline bout between NWA world champion Ric Flair and Dusty Rhodes, and the two faced off for a prize ring and $100,000. CWF owner Eddie Graham received help from several fellow promoters and imported Wahoo McDaniel, Dick Slater, and the Road Warriors for the June 30, 1984, happening. An estimated 10,000 people were on hand as Rhodes scored the popular victory, winning the final fall by disqualification and capturing the title of Lord of the Ring.

When Vince McMahon's army returned to the Sportatorium on July 21, the NWA held a show of its own a little ways north at the Sunrise Musical Theater. Drawing a near sellout, the NWA program was unfortunately marred by gunfire during a tag bout between Rhodes and One Man Gang against Ron Bass and "Superstar" Billy Graham.[190] One man was shot, and fans rushed from the venue fearing for their lives. Across the county in Hollywood, Hulk Hogan went over Big John Studd, and Paul Orndorff, Tito Santana, Bob Backlund, and Mil Mascaras were a part of the under-card. In September, the conflict shifted to Miami with both promotions staging cards there on September 22. The NWA featured Flair and Rhodes again at the Miami Beach Convention Center, while Andre the Giant wrestled Roddy Piper in the main event at the Knight Center. The NWA won the attendance battle 8,000 to 2,000.

McMahon's war against Championship Wrestling from Florida was waged on several different fronts. On the television side of things, he suc-ceeded in replacing the decade-long run of CWF's *Lucha Libre* program on WNJU (channel 47) in New York City with *Superstars of Wrestling*. While it didn't affect Eddie Graham's efforts down south, it undoubtedly resonated with the Florida boss nonetheless. As far as talent went, Buzz Sawyer and Billy Jack jumped from Florida to the WWF, but both enjoyed extremely short tours. Billy Jack received heavy promotion on WWF tele-casts but only made a couple live appearances before leaving for personal reasons. Sawyer was expected to help the promotion in Georgia and Ohio, and even had Captain Lou Albano as his manager, but his employment for McMahon was brief.

Another major blow to Florida occurred when Dusty Rhodes bowed out of the territory for the Mid-Atlantic region, ending his long tenure as the top box-office draw and hero. Some months later, the WWF gained the upper hand on the CWF in West Palm Beach when officials at Graham's main venue (WPB Auditorium) decided not to renew its lease with the CWF in favor of McMahon. The facility, under the NWA banner, had seen attendance drop from 4,000 to less than 1,500 per show, and general man-ager Randy Carillo told the *Palm Beach Post*, "We're going from a mom and pop store to a national organization."[191] WWF officials liked the sound of that. But for anyone affiliated with the NWA, it was harsh commentary, demonstrating the growing perception that the WWF was big league.

In the northwest part of the Sunshine State and extending into Alabama, the Gulf Coast promotion maintained its territorial strength under the lead-ership of Ron Fuller. Filming TV matches from WTVY Studios (channel

4) in Dothan, Southeastern Wrestling offered a good roster of young talent and older stars. NWA king Ric Flair regularly appeared on the local television program and set up arena main events. The patriarch of the famed Armstrong clan, Bob Armstrong, made a miraculous return to the ring after sustaining severe facial injuries in a weight-lifting accident. He went on to beat Fuller for the Continental championship.[192] Future Hall of Famer Arn Anderson was gaining a lot of experience in the region and held the Southeastern tag team title three times with Jerry Stubbs in 1984. Their principal rivals were the R.A.T. Patrol, made up of fan favorites Johnny Rich, Scott Armstrong, and Tonga Kid. In addition, Austin Idol, an ever-colorful performer, won the Southeastern heavyweight belt from Vic Rain in July 1984 and held off the challenges of Rip Rogers and Boris Zurkov.

The Southeastern territory was not immune to the WWF's expansion. *Superstars of Wrestling* aired in Birmingham on Sunday evenings at 7:00 on WTTO (channel 21), and Vince McMahon's first live show in the city was on August 30, 1984. The card was topped by Andre the Giant going over Big John Studd and also highlighted the Junkyard Dog, the Spoiler, and WWF tag champions Adrian Adonis and Dick Murdoch. But Fuller was an old-school battler and held his own Birmingham event that same night. His program saw Idol win a cage match over Rogers, and Ted DiBiase, who was said to be the culprit behind Bob Armstrong's injury (turning the real-world accident into an on-camera angle), beat Bob's son Brad. Notably, in early October, the Tonga Kid jumped to the WWF to feud with Roddy Piper in defense of his injured "cousin" Jimmy Snuka.

Over in Dallas, the territory was hurt by the loss of the Fabulous Freebirds to the WWF. Jack Adkisson was already dealing with lower than expected box-office returns following the reign of Kerry Von Erich as the NWA world champion, and losing his top heels added to his problems. The emergence of Gino Hernandez, a 26-year-old wrestling ace, mitigated a bit of the sting. Hernandez was a tough rulebreaker, and within two months of his arrival, he was pushed to both the American and Texas heavyweight championships. His win of the Texas belt came as a result of a San Antonio tournament on June 23, 1984, and he pinned NWA titleholder Ric Flair in the finals. Jake Roberts joined Hernandez as a primary adversary for the Von Erich brothers, but the turn of Chris Adams in September drew the real headlines. Adams, coming off his lengthy feud with Jimmy Garvin, was the perfect opponent for Kerry, Kevin, and Mike Von Erich in singles and tag team bouts.

Terry Gordy and Buddy Roberts, two-thirds of the Freebirds, returned to Dallas after their short-lived stint in the WWF and resumed their war with the Von Erichs. The various combinations of these stars built up box-office sales at the Cotton Bowl and Reunion Arena for Adkisson between October and December 1984. Much was being made about the WWF's syndication efforts, but Adkisson was growing an equally impressive national network. By the fall of 1984, he had four dozen affiliates, including stations in Boston, St. Louis, Atlanta, Chicago, and Minneapolis. The arrival of an outside TV show, specifically one as good as *World Class*, unnerved promoters fearing invasion. Verne Gagne of the AWA, already being pushed to his limits by the WWF, was panicky about Dallas TV in two of his main cities. Adkisson could use local television as a springboard right into the Twin Cities for live shows, as the WWF had.

But Adkisson was not really in the best position to expand outside of Texas, lacking the finances and the depth of talent. His wrestlers were engaged on the circuit around Dallas and still going into San Antonio in the war against Joe Blanchard's Southwest promotion. There were other factors at play, fueling the wheels of paranoia and speculation. Adkisson was surprised to find that several of his fellow NWA associates supported Blanchard, a nonmember, by sending him wrestlers to use against World Class in San Antonio. That move heightened Adkisson's need for support, and although he was working with Bill Watts, he was reportedly again considering a partnership with the WWF. From Gagne's point of view, if Adkisson joined up with McMahon, the World Class TV show in Minneapolis and Chicago would become a huge promotional tool for combined Dallas–WWF live events. Needless to say, Gagne was preparing for all contingencies and acted with a measure of aggression. He got his *All-Star Wrestling* telecast a weekend slot on KRLD-33 in Dallas, opening up the opportunity for future AWA shows there. If Adkisson made a move in his territory, he'd respond in kind.

Meanwhile, Joe Blanchard was getting just enough help to survive. At one point, his San Antonio company seemed to be on its last legs against the superior Dallas outfit, but Blanchard not only pulled through it, he was starting to gain small victories. But, altogether, few active wrestling bosses suffered as much as Blanchard did in 1983–84, starting with the loss of his national cable outlet on USA and his failed effort with GCW. But that wasn't all. San Antonio tried to go into Dallas in 1983, but one show drew less than 50 people. The much-hyped world championship Blanchard had created with help from Lou Thesz was abandoned, and he started to lose ground at home as Adkisson entered San Antonio with his cast of popular stars. The Southwest promotion was hemorrhaging money and only sustained itself by crafting hot feuds that kept the attention of loyalists. 1984 was more successful, however, and even though Blanchard's son Tully was earning a reputation in the NWA, Southwest was improving its core circuit. During the feud with World Class, Blanchard's promotion imported Tommy Rich, the Road Warriors, Carlos Colon, Kevin Sullivan, Bruiser Brody, and the Rock and Roll Express. Heading into 1985, there was no end to the war in Texas, but Blanchard was in a much better position to protect San Antonio.

In the Midwest, Dick the Bruiser and his World Wrestling Association were in an incredibly vulnerable spot.[193] Bruiser, at age 55, was considered to be over the hill, but he continued to main event in WWA cities in Indiana. A few embarrassing incidents in late 1983 and into '84 damaged his promotion, one being the appearance of his world heavyweight champion Bobby Colt on the undercard of a WWF show in Dayton, Ohio. Colt was pinned by journeyman S.D. Jones, and the credibility of the WWA title was clearly diminished. Colt dropped the belt to Spike Huber on January 7, 1984, and Huber, who was Bruiser's son-in-law, spent a little time in the WWF as well, between March and June 1984. Huber was actually propped up as a young up-and-comer by McMahon himself during an episode of *All American Wrestling* on May 20, 1984.

The WWA remained a favorite for regional fans, but its roster was practically devoid of nationally recognizable stars, and any chance of it competing beyond its limited Midwestern base was out of the question. So when the WWF started looking to expand into Indianapolis, Bruiser had little recourse. That's when Verne Gagne entered the picture. He locked up Indy's big venue, the Market Square Arena, and moved into Indianapolis early in June 1984. The AWA ran monthly into October, but fans were unimpressed even with an uptick of talent, and the draw hovered between 550 and 1,000 people. Bruiser's WWA still outdrew the outsiders.

But on November 17, 1984, Vince McMahon snatched Gagne's TV time on WTTV-4 on Saturday mornings at 10:00, and the WWF debuted live two months later on January 19, 1985.

Hurt by constant no-shows and a flat TV show, Gagne was at a great disadvantage. Yet despite the overt negatives, the AWA was still powerful, shown by its ability to obtain big-named free agents, including Bruiser Brody and the Road Warriors. The Warriors, by this juncture, were the hottest tag team in North America, maybe the world, and boosted the box office wherever they went. Strongman Tony Atlas left the WWF and became one of the first major name grapplers to jump away from McMahon during his expansion. Atlas joined the AWA, hoping to find better opportunities, but returned to the WWF before the end of the year. The AWA was embroiled in a difficult defense of two western locales: Salt Lake City, which the WWF invaded in July, and the Bay Area in northern California. Attendance in Salt Lake started slow for McMahon, but he was drawing just under 7,000 by November. The AWA was only slightly more popular, luring 9,200 for a show in October 1984.

Out on the West Coast, McMahon was dominating his competition. Of the six shows held in Oakland between April and November 1984, four of them had crowds better than 10,000. Gagne, in contrast, was flailing in San Francisco at the Cow Palace. His attendance was less than 1,000 at times, but for a special tag team battle royal on November 11, 1984, rose to 6,800. But after six no-shows, the AWA fell back down to 1,200 in December. Fans weren't putting up with unreliable talent and inconsistent booking, and the AWA needed to make a number of philosophical changes to regain the trust of area spectators. Gagne continued his efforts to make the AWA competitive elsewhere, attaining a timeslot on the newly instituted The Sports Network (TSN) cable channel in Canada and hinting at a northeastern invasion, targeting McMahon unilaterally.

Going it alone was contrary to the Pro Wrestling USA idea promoters had established in Chicago months earlier. That initiative essentially was meant to create a coalition for syndicated TV and live events in opposition to the WWF. But cracks in the relationship between Gagne and Jim Crockett were apparent during the summer of 1984, and Crockett was forced to cancel his second Meadowlands show planned for August 21. Crockett and Gagne came together in Las Vegas that same month for the NWA's annual convention at the Dunes Hotel. They were joined by NWA president Bob Geigel, Don Owen, Ron Fuller, Mike Graham (representing his father, Eddie), Shohei "Giant" Baba of All Japan, Lia Maivia of Honolulu, Steve Rickard of New Zealand, and Larry O'Dea of Australia, plus Ric Flair, Dusty Rhodes, Dory Funk Jr., and Harley Race. Meshing their ideas, hashing out grievances, and reaffirming their support for each other, the members in attendance once again charted a strategy to combat McMahon.

"Competition is good," Georgia promoter Fred Ward explained to *Wrestling's Main Event* magazine. "But if the WWF thinks it can come into the cities that we've had for so long and be successful they will be in for an awful surprise. The people throughout the world know that the NWA stands for excellence in wrestling. We will stick together for the survival of our support. In fact, starting next month we will get even bigger than ever before. We've got quite a surprise in store that will benefit all the fans throughout the world. We plan on having even bigger and better matches throughout the rest of 1984 and for many, many years to come."[194] Organizers set a September 18 date for the initial taping of *Pro Wrestling USA*. Jerry Jarrett hosted the important event at the Mid-South Coliseum in Memphis, and 25 matches were arranged for future broadcast.[195]

The talent on the card was stunning. Former NWA world champions Harley Race and Dory Funk Jr., ex–AWA world titleholder Nick Bockwinkel, and current AWA champ Rick Martel wrestled on the show. "Superstar" Billy Graham, a former WWWF kingpin, grappled in two squash bouts, and former NWA and WWF titleholders Terry Funk and Bob Backlund, respectively, made appearances. The Road Warriors, Jerry Lawler, Butch Reed, Tommy Rich, Mr. Saito, Tony Atlas, and Eddie Gilbert were also part of the TV taping, representing the AWA, Memphis, and Mid-South. Announcer Jack Reynolds mentioned Backlund's championship past during an interview segment, and it was obvious they were trying to reestablish his credibility in the Northeast, where he'd once ruled. The first episode of *Pro Wrestling USA* debuted on the high-profile New York City outlet WPIX-11 on September 29.[196] The anti-WWF group was on its way.

The new promotion was covered in *USA Today*, and the wrestling war was front and center. Gagne, the executive producer for the syndicated show, affirmed that there was "room for both" his group and the WWF in the marketplace. Though known for his old-school methods, Gagne told the reporter there would be fresh concepts on the telecast, such as video packages and profiles. "We're keeping up with the times," he admitted.[197] For Gagne, the Pro Wrestling USA experiment was going to be instrumental for his AWA as well, and he soon replaced his small-scale studio offerings for his syndicated *All Star Wrestling* show with arena matches from the PWUSA tapings.[198]

Jim Crockett staged the second *Pro Wrestling USA* taping in Spartanburg, South Carolina, on October 23, 1984, and the ever-popular Ricky Steamboat made his first showing for the group. Former WWWF champion Ivan Koloff made an appearance and teamed with his "nephew" Nikita, a 25-year-old strongman from Minneapolis and a real bright spot in the Mid-Atlantic region. In his own promotion, Crockett was rebuilding in 1984, and the arrival of Koloff, Tully Blanchard, and Dusty Rhodes rejuvenated his booking scheme. In August, Barry Windham, the talented son of Blackjack Mulligan, jumped from Florida, and Crockett had big hopes for the youngster. It was believed he was on a path to win the U.S. title, but instead, Windham left the territory on little-to-no notice and joined the WWF. Mike Rotundo, Windham's tag partner in Florida, followed suit.

The turnover in manpower, plus the loss of Toronto to the WWF, was painstaking, but Crockett was resilient. He still had one of the best rosters in the business, headed by NWA world champion Ric Flair, Ricky Steamboat, and Wahoo McDaniel, who had been renewed by a heel run. On Thanksgiving night, November 22, 1984, the second annual Starrcade event was held at the Greensboro Coliseum. In the main event, Flair was matched against Rhodes in a bout for a million-dollar purse with former boxing champion "Smokin'" Joe Frazier as special referee. While Flair–Rhodes wasn't on par technically with Flair–Harley Race from a year earlier, it still drummed up plenty of excitement, and the prize money only added to the anticipation of fans. Nearly 16,000 people attended the spectacular, with thousands more watching via closed-circuit television. After a good battle, Frazier stopped the match because of a cut near Rhodes's eye, and Flair was given the victory.

Crockett remained motivated to fight the WWF in the Northeast. Twice in June 1984, he held small-town shows in New Jersey. His plans to return to the Meadowlands fell through, and his scheduled dates in the Bronx, Queens, and Long Island were canceled under questionable circumstances in late November. In any case, his Spanish-language TV show in New York wasn't helping Crockett much, and he needed the Pro Wrestling USA connection on WPIX to shore up future business. Crockett then made a three-way pact with Ole Anderson and Jerry Jarrett in October 1984 to share talent and equally benefit from Anderson's Saturday morning telecast on WTBS.[199] He also wanted to secure a timeslot on TSN in Canada and was willing to pay for a timeslot, but the network went in another direction and, as noted, added the AWA to its weekly schedule.[200]

In Kansas City, NWA president Bob Geigel knew a WWF invasion was imminent and was doing everything possible to maintain his local control. Throughout 1984, to strengthen a roster that paled in comparison to outside territories, he imported recognizable stars for shows at the Memorial Auditorium, Memorial Hall, and Kemper Arena, and he had his ups and downs. One show in March logged a $100,000 gate, but his regular Thursday night shows at the Memorial Hall — part of Kansas City wrestling tradition going back decades — saw a steep decline in attendance, and he scaled back to once or twice a month. As expected, McMahon obtained TV in Kansas City, on KEKR-62, and arranged for a show in July 1984. But dismal advance sales forced a cancelation, and again in August. McMahon finally got the right kind of momentum going and pushed into Kansas City on September 29 with 5,500 people on hand to see Andre the Giant, Roddy Piper, Junkyard Dog, and the Brisco Brothers.

The pressure on Geigel to successfully repel the New York impresario was immense, and it got the point that he was seriously considering walking away. According to an article in the *Kansas City Times* in December 1984, he actually accepted terms to sell the KC office outright to McMahon, but the deal was never finalized. Instead, the hostilities intensified. On November 29, the two sides went head to head but ended in a stalemate, with the WWF drawing 820 fans and Geigel 970. "This [war] has cost us a lot of money," Geigel explained. "I've gone out of my way not to knock the guy (McMahon) in public, although he's on a dead-end street, or at least I hope he is. I have instructed my people not to say a thing bad about any of them." A public relations official for Titan Sports issued a statement, declaring that the WWF was more akin to the "major leagues" than to the regional operation, but Geigel didn't let that comment slide. "At first, they thought [the WWF wrestlers] were big time, from Madison Square Garden, and we were run of the mill," Geigel said. "Now they've seen the 'big time' and seen that the 'big time' isn't really the big time."[201]

One of Geigel's important Pacific allies, Lia Maivia of Honolulu, along with her booker Lars Anderson, had attended the annual NWA convention in Las Vegas. Maivia's Polynesian Championship Wrestling was a shining example of how cooperation benefited a promotion. In 1984, with help from outside territories, her company saw average attendance at the Blaisdell Arena jump threefold, and crowds popped for supershows at the NBC Arena during Maivia's Summer Series '84 campaign.[202] The Von Erichs were big favorites, particularly because the World Class syndicated show had been on in Honolulu for months, and people couldn't wait to see them in person. Chris Adams, Jimmy Garvin, and Michael Hayes flew in from Dallas, and Seiji Sakaguchi and Tatsumi Fujinami came from Japan. Other participants included Bad News Allen, Matt Borne, Masked Superstar, and Mark Lewin.

On December 19, 1984, Jimmy Snuka and Andre the Giant, two WWF workers, wrestled for Maivia, and Andre won a 20-man battle royal. Maivia's son-in-law, Rocky Johnson, was active on the WWF circuit for most of 1984 and was a longtime mainstay in the promotion. At least for the time being, Hawaii was not in McMahon's expansion plans, a fact that was probably more attributable to its distance from the U.S. mainland than anything else. Generally speaking, it was difficult to find many territories not being directly impacted by the WWF one way or another. The promotion's TV reach was on an unheard-of level in professional wrestling history. In addition to national outlets on WTBS and USA, a local WWF show was on air in nearly 100 markets by the end of 1984.

TV overexposure was a worry not only for the WWF, but for pro wrestling as a whole. Twelve years before, in 1972, a promoter warned of its effects, explaining, "Too much television almost killed us off 20 years ago, but we won't make that mistake again. We use television now, but we limit the exposure to give fans just a taste so they'll come out for the live matches."[203] That promoter was none other than Vince McMahon Sr., who'd been through the turbulent 1950s, when TV sent wrestling into the stratosphere of success and then caused its downfall. People became bored by the wrestlers, the matches, and the same old script. Was McMahon Jr. setting himself up for the same kind of fall? Verne Gagne believed so. "I see history repeating itself," he told a reporter for *Minneapolis CityBusiness*. "There's no new talent, you've seen them all before. And fans get a little confused, it's so diluted."[204]

Veteran Baton Rouge promoter Jimmy Kilshaw, an associate of Bill Watts's Mid-South promotion, told a local journalist in 1985 that oversaturation was already hurting their operations, with attendance down an average of 500 people: "If [the overexposure] keeps up, it'll burn the population out on wrestling. It's making big bucks now, but [McMahon] will cut his own throat."[205] In the past there had been a saturation point for pro grappling, but McMahon didn't seem to care. At any rate, that was the impression. But McMahon was more cunning than people realized. While he did offer full matches on his various telecasts, he usually withheld superstar bouts and his top-running feuds. Hulk Hogan, Andre the Giant, and other upper-echelon talent made TV appearances but only to whet the appetite of eager fans. Thus, if they wanted to see more of their favorite performers, people would have to buy tickets.

Of course, traditionalists didn't like it. They hammered the WWF for its general practices and unconventional theatrics. But the WWF had no interest in straight-laced wrestling content. McMahon and his cohorts were offering "sports entertainment," a blend of in-ring action with memorable characters and storylines. He was appealing to a new audience, building up the interest of casual fans, and introducing his style of wrestling to young people.

McMahon had massively increased the public's awareness of his company's brand, and WWF was fast becoming the most recognized wrestling organization in North America. By the end of 1984, wrestling was a hip enterprise headed for its most lucrative financial year to date. McMahon undoubtedly had his opponents, but even his rivals had to acknowledge the immense interest he was bringing to the sport. To remain competitive, they needed to take a few pages from the WWF's playbook and capitalize on the opportunities being afforded. The game was changing, and McMahon was far out in the lead.

CHAPTER TWELVE

WRESTLEMANIA

Longtime Houston promoter Paul Boesch was first lured into the business as a grappler in 1932 by Jack Pfefer, a man who knew talent when he saw it. In the years that followed, he toured North America, facing the best in the business, and became a fine journeyman. After serving distinctly during World War II, Boesch resumed his career, only to suffer serious injuries in a car accident in 1947 near San Antonio.[206] Boesch gave up his active wrestling career to focus on announcing, refereeing, and booking matches in Texas. By that juncture, the native New Yorker now had the Lonestar State in his blood, and Boesch made Houston his permanent home. In the 1960s, Boesch assumed control of the Houston office and had good relations with NWA and AWA officials. He broke off his longstanding trade agreement with Jack Adkisson in 1981, cutting off appearances by the Von Erichs, but Boesch didn't miss a beat. Despite not having a booking office of his own, he remained an influential player because of his partnership with Bill Watts and the Mid-South group. Boesch focused on giving Houston fans a professional operation, and the strength of Watts's roster kept enthusiasts happy. Cards featured Magnum T.A., Butch Reed, the Midnight Express, the Rock and Roll Express, Jim Duggan, and Steve Williams, among others, and Houston never seemed to be at a loss for great matches. But as 1984 passed, Boesch and Watts had to deal with the WWF, as *Superstars of Wrestling* debuted in several of Watts's key cities.

Breaking ground in Texas, Titan Sports secured TV outlets on two independent stations owned by Grant Broadcasting, channel 20 (KTXH) in Houston and channel 21 (KTXA) in Dallas–Fort Worth. The WWF made its first live appearance in Houston on December 27, 1984, with a Dallas program scheduled for the next evening. In preparation for the WWF's arrival, Boesch and Adkisson put their past grievances aside and, along with Watts, arranged a defense. They planned to directly compete against McMahon in both Houston and Dallas and booked several recent castoffs from the WWF: Billy Jack, Kamala, Terry Gordy, and Buddy Roberts. In Houston, Butch Reed won a massive two-ring battle royal and Kerry Von Erich beat Gino Hernandez, while Hernandez went over Kevin Von Erich in Dallas. As for the WWF, they offered their "B" lineup with Andre the Giant, Greg Valentine, Tito Santana, and Big John Studd, drawing under 3,000 people in each city.[207]

The WWF's "A" players, including Hulk Hogan, Roddy Piper, Junkyard Dog, and Jimmy Snuka, were in St. Louis on December 27 before returning to New York for a huge spectacular the next night. The show sold out Madison Square Garden and the adjoining Felt Forum, and Hogan pinned the former WWF champ the Iron Sheik in the main event. JYD, Barry Windham, Mike Rotundo, and Antonio Inoki won singles matches, and a tag bout between Piper and Bob Orton Jr. against Snuka and the Tonga Kid ended in a double disqualification. There were two other happenings of note, and the first was clearly scripted. Cyndi Lauper returned to the WWF and buried the hatchet with Captain Lou Albano, giving him a gold record for helping raise money for charity. Piper wasn't caught up in the sentimentality of the moment and ended up breaking the record over Albano's head. He also hurled Lauper to the ground and slammed her manager, David Wolff.

The other occurrence at the Garden took place backstage, out of the view of the crowd, and to this day, there is still conjecture about whether it was all spontaneous or preplanned. Reporter John Stossel was at the event doing a story on pro wrestling for ABC's newsmagazine *20/20*. He went in for an interview with reputed heel "Dr. D" David Schultz, who was in no mood for games. Stossel asked about the veracity of wrestling, and the 6-foot-4 grappler proceeded to slap him twice in the head.[208] From Stossel's point of view, it was a genuine attack, but there was question whether Schultz's actions were part of a purposeful attempt to garner media attention. If you believed that any publicity was good publicity, then this idea was a winner. But looking at the ramifications of the incident for Schultz, Stossel, and the wider reputation of pro wrestling, the entire episode was a major catastrophe.

For his actions, Schultz was suspended by the New York State Athletic Commission, fined $3,000, and, less than two months later, was let go by the WWF.[209] Stossel suffered hearing damage in both ears and received a six-figure settlement from the WWF. Wrestling was hammered by the national media, with pundits wondering if it was "too violent." Disgruntled ex-wrestlers, such as Eddy Mansfield, joined in the condemnation, discussing how matches were predetermined and the practice of blading.[210] The Schultz–Stossel incident wasn't the only costly out-of-the-ring miscue to hit Titan Sports in early 1985. Hulk Hogan appeared on the cable talk show *Hot Properties* and demonstrated a front chinlock on host Richard Belzer. The maneuver caused Belzer to lose consciousness, and his body fell headfirst onto the studio floor, causing a head injury. This situation also triggered a lawsuit, with a financial settlement favorable to the victim. It was negative press all the way, and everyone wanted to forget these incidents ever happened.

In December 1984, the WWF was active in 15 previously off-limits territories, and was currently battling opposition in 11 of them, demonstrating the turbulence of the times. One thing was becoming apparent for the WWF, though, and that was that big-name talent alone wasn't going to sustain the box office in newly forged regions. Booking patterns left a lot to be desired, as the undercards of arena shows often appeared to have been arranged in slipshod fashion. "Good guys" were pitted against "bad guys" with no further rhyme or reason. And to make things worse, it was typically one "name" wrestler paired with a preliminary-level worker, only diminishing the importance even more. The finishes were painfully predictable.

With all the superstars on the roster, enthusiasts expected better in-ring action, and in a lot of cases, they just weren't getting it. So after the initial excitement wore off, and Hogan and the other leading stars made their initial impression, there wasn't much left to speak about. In the battleground cities, a disappointed wrestling fan could cross town the next time and watch the competition instead. For the WWF to keep them coming back, it had to improve its TV-to-arena booking, and ensure there was not only basis for the matches at the top of the card, but up and down the bill as well. Matchmaker George Scott took on a larger role in 1984 to improve on these deficiencies, and he undoubtedly had the talent to work with. There were huge personalities with incredible charisma, high-fliers and skilled scientific grapplers — he just had to get the pieces into the correct positions and establish a sound game plan for a few months at a time.

Generally, the WWF was doing many things right, and the organization operated with heightened professionalism. At the arena, there was the odd no-show, but nothing like the problems Verne Gagne had in the AWA. "If a fan comes to see Hulk Hogan and he isn't on the card, we give him his money back," explained Ed Cohen, a Titan Sports official, in late 1984. "We make sure nobody goes home feeling cheated."[211] Even if a fan favorite lost in the main event, they were usually put back over with a little post-match revenge or time to pose in the ring, practices that continue to this day after live shows go off the air.

Back in the Northeast, McMahon's home territory, the WWF had long maintained a sense of community, particularly in smaller towns. The WWF worked hand in hand with local groups and was generous in donating funds from special events to charity. In this transitional era, it was extraordinary to hear Howard Finkel's voiceover promotion of WWF stars at a high school gym on WOR-TV, but that was the nature of the business. As the years passed, Vince McMahon put an end to the school-gym era. As for WOR-TV, it was reported that McMahon was paying the station as much as $5,000 a week for television time in 1984, up from $1,750 a few years before.

Compensating stations was a commonplace practice for Titan Sports, and it was costing the company a fortune. If you take just three stations from the vast WWF TV empire, WOR, KHJ in Los Angeles, and KSTU in Salt Lake City, the combined payment schedule for a year amounted to $494,000. The WWF had somewhere between 90 and 100 stations, and though they weren't paying every one of them, it was still a huge amount to invest across North America. But the local promotion was translating into serious earnings in many markets. To use the example of Los Angeles, if the WWF made a minimum net profit of $40,000 at the gate for 10 shows a year, it would earn $400,000. The annual cost of TV on KHJ was $130,000. Of course, there was tremendous overhead, but a strong box office could pay sizable dividends.

In some cases, Titan Sports offered their program to a station free of cost, and gave the operator seven of the 12 minutes set aside for commercial spots. The station would then sell that time to local businesses to make a good profit without spending a dime. Titan kept the remaining commercial time for their national advertisers. It was a mutually beneficial arrangement, and TV station sales departments easily sold advertising during WWF broadcasts thanks to the important demographic it reached. The major deals Titan made with national advertisers brought in a lot of income for the company and easily offset the original production costs for its television operations. Finally, the extended promos individualized for each market drew fans to the arenas where Titan Sports made its real money.

On the cable TV side of things, the WWF's relationship with WTBS out of Atlanta remained contentious through the end of 1984 and into '85. The problems began when Vince McMahon decided to use out-of-town footage for his two weekend telecasts instead of holding full tapings at the WTBS studios like his predecessor. McMahon spliced in interview footage from WTBS, but it just wasn't up to par in the eyes of station owner Ted Turner, who wanted the same commitment Georgia Championship Wrestling had given him since the 1970s. But McMahon was intent on doing things his way, and there the issues began. Over time, two other problems arose. First, Turner believed the ratings for *World Championship Wrestling* and *The Best of World Championship Wrestling* should have been higher, though both shows were in the top five highest-rated shows on cable. Additionally, Turner and other station officials didn't like that McMahon worked so closely with one of its main rivals, the USA

Network. Needless to say, USA was equally peeved about the WWF being on WTBS and MTV.

The difficulties between the WWF and WTBS didn't stop there. Apparently, Titan wanted to run commercial advertisements that it had obtained independently during the broadcasts, but WTBS blocked them from doing so. The station was paying the promotion a production fee and was not interested in sharing commercial time. They compromised by offering the WWF commercial time at a reduced rate, which could be resold to advertisers. McMahon agreed and the matter was seemingly settled. But in early 1985, WTBS officials insisted the WWF become exclusive and drop affiliation with the USA Network.[212] McMahon declined. In response, station officials eliminated the discounted commercial time and began charging the full rate.

Under the circumstances, the long-term connections between the two entities appeared to be in doubt. In contrast, USA Network officials, aside from the WTBS issue, had always been happy with the WWF. McMahon's promotion was featured three nights a week, encompassing four and a half hours of content, and was the highest-rated program on the network. "The last six months have been incredible," said Mark Braff, director of communications for the USA Network, in early 1985. "It wasn't that long ago that people would watch [wrestling] on television and not talk about it the next day at work. Now if you don't watch it and can't talk about it the next day, you're not chic. It has actually become mainstream."[213]

McMahon's multifaceted expansion campaign was working. He was increasing physical ground in terms of his wrestling circuit, boosting his television reach through basic cable and syndicated TV, enlarging his talent roster, and strengthening the international awareness of the WWF as an entertainment company. "Vince is just doing what everyone else wanted to do," explained Red Bastien, a West Coast agent for the WWF. "It's like lots of other things. One time there used to be a lot of small farms, with 20 acres, 40 acres. Then the co-ops came in and bought them up. Look at the oil companies and the food stores. They buy up the little ones. Wrestling isn't any different from those. And wrestling is big time again. It's reached a new height because of Vince's marketing genius. Vince says he doesn't have enemies; they do."[214]

"They're mad at me because now they have to work for a living," McMahon told *Sports Illustrated* in 1985.[215] In an interview with the Associated Press, he explained, "You've always had that territoriality. There is some carryover from that old era into what we're doing now. We've encountered some difficulty in some markets."[216] Attendance was lower than anticipated in a few areas, causing McMahon to reanalyze his approach. But, on the whole, he was seeing great success. "It's just become a real phenomenon," said Larry Robinson, the box-office manager at the Anaheim Convention Center. "TV's what's making it. The TV people have figured out what the American people are watching and they're causing it to happen. We had 8,900 seats for wrestling in February [1985]. And we filled them."[217]

"Demographics," McMahon told the *Los Angeles Times*, "they're simply incredible, although ours are beyond what an MTV might be. Ours are about 18 to 40, and 40 percent of that is women. I've always maintained that our demographics are broad-based Americana. Really what we're trying to do is put pro wrestling in the proper vehicles so that professional people will feel it's all right to [enjoy]. I don't think it's a question of America suddenly awakening to a new phenomenon. They're awakening to a new level of it."[218] In Los Angeles, the WWF's 10 hours of television every weekend was certainly helping its cause. As amazing as that was, McMahon still wasn't done trying to enhance his TV operations, specifically looking at a possible network deal as well as advancing into pay-per-view. By early 1985, these two goals were much more than a distant thought; they were really close to becoming a reality.

On the commercial broadcasting end of things, the WWF was attracting substantial attention, the most since the late 1940s, when televised pro wrestling first captured the public's imagination. On March 17, 1985, *Sports World* did a feature episode on grappling. That same month, Vince McMahon had a high-profile interview on *Late Night with David Letterman* (March 28, 1985) and Hulk Hogan and Mr. T, co-star of the *A-Team*, hosted *Saturday Night Live* (March 30, 1985). All four programs were on NBC, and it was apparent there was a budding relationship between the network and the WWF. Officials soon began preliminary talks for a joint venture, and the return of pro wrestling to network TV appeared to be just around the corner. Meanwhile, the WWF's media blitz in February and March 1985 was building toward the organization's biggest program to date, WrestleMania, scheduled for March 31, 1985, at Madison Square Garden in New York.

Like Jim Crockett's Starrcade or Jack Adkisson's Star Wars, WrestleMania was billed as a one-of-a-kind spectacle highlighting the very best of the organization. That was absolutely true, but McMahon was ready to take the concept of a supershow to an entirely new plateau. He lined up celebrities like Muhammad Ali, Billy Martin, and Liberace, played up the Rock 'n' Wrestling angle again with Cyndi Lauper, and launched a massive media campaign to hype WrestleMania everywhere. McMahon and his staff arranged an extensive array of closed-circuit television venues across the country and also stepped into the realm of pay-per-view for the first time. Pay-per-view, which gave fans the ability to watch live events from the comfort of their own homes, was in its infancy, and only a few cable outlets were offering the service.[219] But "PPV" was definitely the wave of the future, and McMahon was on the ground floor.

In the main event of WrestleMania, Hogan and Mr. T beat Roddy Piper and Paul Orndorff, thrilling the 19,121 fans in attendance. Andre the Giant won over Big John Studd in a special bodyslam bout for a $15,000 prize. (Studd was managed by Bobby Heenan, a recent major signee from the AWA.) Junkyard Dog won by count-out over Intercontinental champion Greg Valentine, and fan favorites Barry Windham and Mike Rotundo dropped their tag team belts to Nikolai Volkoff and the Iron Sheik. In addition, the show featured a handful of newcomers, King Kong Bundy and manager Jimmy Hart among them. But the real surprise was Ricky Steamboat, a longtime employee of Jim Crockett, who'd debuted for McMahon earlier in March. Steamboat was a major addition to the promotion and a blow to the NWA at the same time. WrestleMania established a new benchmark for a pro wrestling extravaganza, and the bar was raised in each subsequent year.

In the weeks leading up to the first WrestleMania, a lot of uncertainty surrounded the event, with questions of whether it would achieve the kind of success needed for Titan Sports to meet its heavy financial obligations. In fact, McMahon was gambling with the future of his company by putting all of his eggs into one basket, and if the venture failed, Titan was likely facing bankruptcy. The public was unaware of the financial realities, but insiders had been wondering about the WWF's ability to maintain its enormous operating costs for a while. It was rumored that Titan took a heavy financial loss in 1984 as its spending far exceeded its income.[220]

McMahon's financial resources had been a mystery to pundits and his opposition since the wrestling war began. Wrestling insiders were amazed by the depth of his pockets as he acquired new TV outlets and talent, and his WrestleMania investment only added to the whispers. The northeastern wrestling circuit was known as the biggest moneymaker of all territories, and Vince McMahon Sr. had been considered one of the richest promoters in the business. There was speculation that McMahon Sr. had bequeathed his son millions of dollars, and it was that fortune McMahon Jr. was using to expand the WWF. But the truth was he was doing it all on his own without a grand inheritance, and by WrestleMania, he was deeply in debt. Titan Sports, however, wasn't destined for failure, and McMahon's shrewd maneuvering saved his company from financial insolvency.

A timely payment from Antonio Inoki's New Japan Pro Wrestling, as compensation for WWF stars appearing for the latter's promotion in Asia, was of considerable help.[221] In recent months, things in that part of the world had become quite sticky when Hisashi Shinma, a matchmaker for Inoki, broke off and formed his own company, the UWF. Shinma had been acknowledged as the figurehead president of the WWF prior to Jack Tunney, and after breaking off relations with Inoki, he wanted to take his WWF ties with him. Inoki didn't want to relinquish his lengthy association with McMahon and, ultimately, a new six-figure deal was signed that maintained the status quo.

McMahon worked out another deal involving his WTBS contract, adding to the economic lifeblood of his company at a crucial time. With Jim Barnett as a mediator, he agreed to sell his WTBS timeslots (and production contracts) to Jim Crockett Promotions for $1 million. Said to have made $500,000 on the transaction, McMahon didn't walk away from Atlanta completely.[222] He secured placement for the WWF on WAGA-TV and held local shows at the Omni Coliseum through July. Although the money garnered from New Japan and JCP was significant, McMahon wasn't on the losing side of WrestleMania. The event grossed in the neighborhood of $4 to 6 million, though the total was inflated to $12 million in media reports.[223]

For McMahon, the good news kept pouring in. NBC came to terms for a pilot episode of *Saturday Night's Main Event*, replacing *Saturday Night Live* on May 11, 1985, and if successful, additional programs were possible later in the year. The pre- and post-show coverage for WrestleMania, combined with news that wrestling was returning to network TV, gave the WWF incredible national publicity. Arena managers, television executives, insiders, and even the wrestlers themselves were taking notice of the unparalleled heights McMahon had reached.

But not everyone was thrilled. Veteran sportswriter Bob Broeg called WrestleMania the "worst thing to hit wrestling since Gorgeous George" in the *St. Louis Post Dispatch*. He believed that Lou Thesz, at 68 years old, "probably could beat the show-business bums of the day," and stated, "Maybe if Sam [Muchnick] had stayed on the job, Vince McMahon's boy wouldn't have muscled in from Broadway."[224] Many wondered how Muchnick, who left the business in 1982, would've dealt with McMahon's rise if he had still been at the helm of the NWA. Having turned 79 in August 1984, Muchnick remained interested in the sport and watched the closed-circuit feed of WrestleMania at the Kiel Auditorium. Later, he admitted that he'd received "overtures from various circles to return" to his old job. "I don't like the style in the ring these days," he explained, "such as the knocking down of referees and fights breaking out outside the ring."[225] Both elements were commonplace in the WWF.

Nick Roberts, who promoted in West Texas for years, maintained that "Texas-style pro wrestling" was "more serious and sportsmanlike" than what McMahon had to offer. "To me, what he's doing is a bizarre kind of thing," Roberts said. "It's like he's making [wrestling] a burlesque nationally. But then he plays to huge metropolitan areas. The tempo of living and way of life is completely different."[226] George Cannon, a WWF-affiliate promoter in Detroit, praised McMahon as a businessman but wasn't blown away by the sensationalism and gimmicks. "Personally, I don't like it," he explained, "but I understand their reasoning."[227] Former multiple-time world champion Killer Kowalski said it best in a 1985 article in the *Burlington Free Press*: "The bottom line is money, and if something works and will make money, I say do it. I give all the credit to Vince for the surge [of the WWF]. He's done it himself."[228] But like many of his colleagues, Kowalski preferred the old style. "I think the people want to see wrestling," he said. "They want to see holds, moves, and punches. Action is what they're looking for. I can remember wrestling Bruno Sammartino for an hour once. I had a 90-minute match with Lou Thesz in Houston. I was exhausted after that. It just kept going and going and going. Now, the matches last two, three, four minutes. Sometimes they have a long match and it goes eight minutes. What the hell is that? There's nothing involved there. There's no wrestling going on, and that's what the people are paying to see."[229] *Washington Times* journalist Dan Cox wrote, "The WWF is beginning to look more and more like a circus and less and less like a wrestling organization. It's a shame the Three Stooges aren't alive today, they would fit in perfect in the WWF."[230] The editor for *Inside Wrestling*, Max Rottersman, told a reporter in 1985, "In the long run, I think the WWF is going to fall flat on its face. They do the oddest things — with one hand they're doing a lot for themselves, but with the other hand they're taking it away."[231]

Alliance promoters wanted to reassure fans that "real" pro wrestling was still alive and well. "Mr. T and rock singer Cyndi Lauper were used by the WWF [to] get them national attention," Henry Robinson, an NWA affiliate promoter, told the *Cleveland Plain Dealer*. "They also used Muhammad Ali and Liberace at WrestleMania with the idea that they'd draw more people. What they've done is wrong. You won't catch the NWA using singers and actors to get attention. Fans come to pro wrestling matches to see wrestling, and using an actor like Mr. T in a wrestling match isn't fair to wrestling fans. You know, most of the WWF wrestlers, Hulk Hogan and Rowdy Roddy Piper included, were once with the NWA. Hogan is very muscular, but our NWA champion, Ric Flair, doesn't have to flex his muscles and pose in the ring. He wrestles."[232] And for many people, that was the most important difference of all.

CHAPTER THIRTEEN

THE ONLY GAME IN TOWN

Heading into 1985, the territorial system was at its weakest point in decades, and only a handful of promoters were maintaining a level of competitiveness with McMahon. Elsewhere, it was just a matter of survival. The Florida territory had seen its share of turmoil, but was one of the strongest affiliates of the NWA, and remained a viable force under the leadership of Eddie Graham. Like many other old-time promoters, Graham hated how the business was changing and was defending two of his cities (Miami and Jacksonville) from WWF aggression. But a number of his stars had left for more profitable opportunities, Dusty Rhodes among them, and a combination of factors, some personal and some business, left Graham deeply depressed. Six days after his 55th birthday, on January 21, 1985, Graham died from self-inflicted wounds. The news couldn't have been sadder to the wrestling community and the scores of people he'd either influenced or helped through his extensive philanthropy. "There's never been a man better known or better liked in this industry, worldwide," Jack Adkisson told a reporter for the *Orlando Sentinel*.[233] Mike Graham did his utmost to follow in his father's footsteps. "I loved my dad and he was my best friend until the day he died," Mike said in a 2004 article. "Everyone in the industry respected my father."[234] With Graham's death, Championship Wrestling from Florida passed into the hands of trusted veterans Hiro Matsuda and Duke Keomuka, and the region maintained its fundamental strengths.

The Freebirds reunited in Florida in January 1985 as fan favorites but turned heel two months later to feud with Mike Graham, Bugsy McGraw, and Brian Blair. Blair, a native of Tampa and a protégé of Graham and Matsuda, had spent nine months in the WWF the year before but never got above the undercard. He captured both the Florida and Southern heavyweight championships during the first half of 1985. Another home-grown talent, Hercules Hernandez, a powerlifter with immense might, also won both of Florida's main singles belts, going over Blair in May and Hector Guerrero in June. Hernandez's time in the Florida promotion was cut short after a backstage fight with booker Wahoo McDaniel in July, and he was dismissed.

McDaniel's jump to Florida came after a lengthy tour of the Mid-Atlantic region for the Crockett Family. In June 1984, he turned heel and, on October 7, won his fifth and last United States heavyweight championship. He reigned until March 23, 1985, when he lost the strap to up-and-comer Magnum T.A. in Charlotte. McDaniel and Ricky Steamboat were big losses for Crockett, but JCP was being revitalized by the work of Magnum T.A., Tully Blanchard, and Nikita Koloff. Arn Anderson arrived from the Southeast territory and formed a successful tag team with his "relative" Ole Anderson, and with Dusty Rhodes and Ric Flair added to the bill, Crockett was flying high once again. Ole Anderson's full-time position in the company was interesting, coming as a result of Crockett buying Ole's Championship Wrestling from Georgia upstart group. Thus, JCP inherited control of the National heavyweight, tag team, and TV titles.

At the same time, Crockett assumed the rights to Anderson's TV outlets and venues in Georgia (including Atlanta), Ohio, Pennsylvania, and Maryland. The expansion was important, and Crockett knew the growth of his syndication network to would help balance out his heavy cable

TV presence on WTBS. He landed stations in Philadelphia (WPHL-17) and Los Angeles (KDOC-56), opening up the door for targeted promotions and live events. JCP debuted in Philadelphia on February 5, 1985, with former WWF champion Bob Backlund in the main event as a tag partner for Rhodes against Ron Bass and Black Bart. JCP also went into Anderson's old haunts of Pittsburgh, Altoona, and Baltimore for the first time. Crowds were anywhere from 500 to nearly 6,000, a little better in Baltimore, and Crockett Promotions sold out the CYO Center in Trenton, New Jersey, with more than 1,700 fans on February 14.

Elliot Murnick, one of Crockett's key associate promoters, explained to a local Trenton reporter the difference between their promotion and the WWF: "We try to give the fans what the marquee says — wrestling. We work on the premise that these people are our loyal viewers, and we want to give them the chance to see the best. This is our way of saying thanks. We're not in competition with the WWF, although they probably feel we are. We want to give the fans an alternative." Local promoter John Milligan was delighted by the ticket sales, and George O'Gorman, of the *Trentonian* newspaper, deemed the show "impressive."[235] Press coverage was quite the opposite in Pittsburgh. On May 28, 1985, Gerry Dulac ripped NWA wrestling in the *Pittsburgh Press*, the day after a Crockett program at Three Rivers Stadium. The headline attraction was Ric Flair defending his world title against Magnum T.A., and the Nature Boy retained by disqualification in 56 minutes of action. In another bout, Tully Blanchard and Dusty Rhodes battled to a double count-out. Dulac wrote, "This was the NWA, the rival organization that takes fading stars . . . from the World Wrestling Federation and attempts to turn them into drawing cards." He noted that Hulk Hogan was the real world champion and asked, "When was the last time someone saw Ric Flair on stage at the Grammy Awards?" He added, "In essence, the NWA is doing nothing more than hoping the popularity of the WWF will eventually spill over into its ranks, waiting for the day its wrestlers can make videos with [Cyndi] Lauper."[236]

In response, incensed fans wrote letters to the editor, and two were published in the June 2 edition of the paper. "Since when has appearing at the Grammys been a necessary facet to become a fine wrestler?" one asked. "The NWA appeals to the diehard wrestling fan, who just enjoys watching a good match of mayhem and chaos," wrote another. "The WWF, on the other hand, appeals to both the diehard fan and those who like to be involved with the 'in' thing. Wrestling, as promoted by the WWF, is definitely 'in,' but this audience consists of those who know nothing of the sport. Dulac is obviously from that audience."[237] With attendance of 2,500, JCP's stadium effort in Pittsburgh proved to be a financial failure. Such an endeavor made much more sense in Charlotte, and on July 6, 1985, JCP drew 27,000 fans to Memorial Stadium for the Great American Bash. Ric Flair went over Nikita Koloff and Dusty Rhodes topped Tully Blanchard in a cage, winning the NWA world TV title in the process. The Road Warriors, the reigning AWA world tag champs, wrestled their NWA counterparts, Ivan Koloff and Krusher Khruschev, to a double-disqualification. The appearance of Hawk and Animal illustrated that the on-again, off-again relationship between Crockett and Verne Gagne was on. In fact, the AWA and JCP were working together in the Northeast, pairing talent to boost the box office. One of their biggest assets was Sgt. Slaughter, who abruptly left the WWF in December 1984 in the wake of various differences, including his percentage of merchandising for his character.

Slaughter was hugely popular — big business for the WWF — and his jump to the AWA was remarkable during a time of war. It only made sense for the AWA to use Slaughter as their top attraction going into northeastern cities, not only for solo shows, but for Pro Wrestling USA programs as well. On February 24, 1985, he single-handedly won a tag team battle royal at the Meadowlands in New Jersey, and four months later, Slaughter captured the Americas championship, a patriotic honor created with him in mind from Larry Zbyszko.[238] The AWA booked a weeklong tour of New Jersey and New York in March 1985, and Pro Wrestling USA ran the Meadowlands five more times that year. But even shows featuring Slaughter, the NWA and AWA world champions, the Road Warriors, the Koloffs, Jerry Lawler, and other superstars didn't guarantee sellouts.

Mid-South's Bill Watts agreed in principle with the union behind Pro Wrestling USA, but it was an unruly mess behind the scenes, and he kept his distance.[239] He was doing pretty well for himself as it was, and his promotion enjoyed a brief two-month run on WTBS between March and May 1985, achieving the highest ratings for any wrestling show on the station. Watts also discussed a partnership with Ted Turner, to take over the WWF's timeslots and create an even larger national footprint.

However, Vince McMahon's deal with JCP negated that plan. Watts held no ill will, though, and touted NWA wrestling during his last episode on May 26. From April to November, Watts worked with the NWA and AWA, bringing world champion Ric Flair to his territory a dozen times, in addition to Sgt. Slaughter and Road Warriors.

Mid-South still had a competitive lineup. Ted DiBiase, Jim Duggan, and Jake Roberts were at the top of their game, and Watts produced many hot angles for his two syndicated programs, *Mid-South Wrestling* and *Power Pro Wrestling*. DiBiase, a second-generation grappler, matched well against Duggan, and the two locked up all over the region in early 1985. Mid-South's top singles title, the North American belt, passed from Brad Armstrong to DiBiase and then to Terry Taylor in March. In the tag team ranks, DiBiase formed a memorable partnership with a three-year veteran of the pro mat, "Dr. Death" Steve Williams. A protégé of Watts, Williams was a dual-sport athlete from the University of Oklahoma, with All-American status in wrestling and football. On May 3, 1985, DiBiase and Williams dethroned speedsters Robert Gibson and Ricky Morton, better known as the Rock and Roll Express.

Before long, the Express and Taylor departed Mid-South for Crockett. Already having lost Junkyard Dog to the WWF, Watts was well acquainted with the movement of grapplers during a period of heavy competition. "The WWF is trying to steal my talent," he told the *Shreveport Times* in 1985, "and I'm trying to steal talent out of Atlanta or somewhere else. In other words, if a guy's a good wrestler, we all want him. We're competing with the others for the services of the top talent."[240] Watts was a realist and wasn't shy to borrow tactics that he saw working elsewhere. The WWF had popular music in its telecasts, and a music video created in Memphis had done a lot to prop up the Fabulous Ones. Mid-South followed suit, and in 1984–85, Watts broadcast videos using well-known songs for Magnum T.A., the Rock and Roll Express, and the Fantastics.

Jim Duggan, a favorite in Wattsland, got in on the action as well, doing a country music gig with singer John Anderson at a venue in Tulsa in February 1985. "The profile of the wrestling public and the country music public is very similar," explained Jim Ross, the director of marketing for Mid-South, to the *Tulsa World*. "If you asked someone five or 10 years ago to give you a description of a person who liked country music, they probably would have said a male, 25 to 54 years old, a blue-collar worker in a middle to low income group. Those demographics were exactly the same for wrestling fans then. Now, the profile of the country music fan has changed. The audience got a little younger, thanks to people like Alabama, Exile, and Hank Williams Jr., whose main audiences are from 18 to 34. Now, we're looking at the very same growth in wrestling."[241] The country music and wrestling pairing was seen in several major promotions the following year.

Juggling the turnover of talent was sometimes exhausting, but Watts kept his momentum. He replaced his losses and pushed the right guys at the right time. Butch Reed, Dutch Mantell, Hercules Hernandez, and the Guerreros were Mid-South regulars, and Bill Dundee's booking kept things fresh. One of the literally hottest angles had Duggan in front of a fireball thrown by manager Skandor Akbar, putting the hero out of commission for weeks. The tensions increased after an inconclusive bout between Duggan and Kamala at the Superdome on June 1 and dominated the summer. Outgunned by Akbar's minions, Duggan received the support of Watts himself, who came out of retirement to even the odds. The Nightmare, a 6-foot-4, 275-pound masked man (known outside of the ring as Randy Colley) wore the North American belt between the reigns of Taylor and Dick Murdoch, and was managed first by Eddie Gilbert and then by Oliver Humperdink. Previously, Colley had used the gimmick "Moondog Rex" in Memphis and the WWF.

Dipping into the celebrity well, Watts imported the famed Muhammad Ali, coming off his appearance at WrestleMania, for the June 1, 1985, Superdome extravaganza. Ali acted as a second for the Snowman in his match against Jake Roberts, and delivered a timely punch that cost Jake the bout. In the war against the WWF, Mid-South was facing an invasion in Oklahoma City and Houston, but was far out ahead, drawing 7,000-plus compared to the WWF's 1,500. In some cases, McMahon was luring less than 1,000 people and, when possible, Watts ran head to head to further diminish turnout for his opponents. Watts called 1985 a "difficult year" in an article with the *Shreveport Times*, and cited McMahon's attempts to "monopolize wrestling." "[McMahon was] helping to add saturation to television," Watts explained. "The people in Shreveport can now watch probably 12 hours a week. It's just like football. It's getting to be much harder to entice them with a live gate."[242] Despite losing WTBS, and failing to land a valuable cable spot on ESPN, Mid-South was in a "constant growth pattern," and TV ratings were outstanding. There was a huge opportunity to follow the WWF and World Class further into syndication, and seriously consider expansion.

Ron Fuller, head of the Southeast territory, was exploring the same thing. With a loyal bunch of wrestlers, an entertaining TV product, and the backing of fans in Alabama and Florida, Fuller was in a good spot, at least for the time being. Through the first half of 1985, he outdrew the WWF in Birmingham, but Fuller understood the changing landscape and wanted to protect his business at all costs. That meant upgrading his local television presentation, and he pulled his regular tapings from the WTVY-4 studios and moved them to the much larger Boutwell Auditorium in Birmingham. Gordon Solie served as host. In June 1985, Fuller changed his promotion's name from the regional Southeastern Championship Wrestling to the broader Continental Championship Wrestling. The move gave him better positioning if and when he was ready to expand outside his regular circuit. His promotion already had a "Continental" heavyweight championship, and over a three-month period between June and September 1985, the belt switched eight times. Jody Hamilton, under the guise of the Flame, became a four-time title-holder during that stretch, and won the belt from Bob Armstrong, Lord Humongous, and Tommy Rich. Other regional stars were Austin Idol, the Nightmares (Ken Wayne and Danny Davis), Porkchop Cash, Bill Ash, Steve Armstrong, and Johnny Rich. Notably, this promotion had a good working relationship with All-South Wrestling of Georgia, a fairly new indie run by Ann Gunkel and booked by Jody Hamilton.[243]

Gunkel wasn't the only promoter attempting a comeback. Up in Michigan, Edward Farhat, a.k.a. the Sheik, was resuming operations nearly four years after his Big Time Wrestling group had fizzled out. He made an appearance at Detroit's Leland Hotel and beat Fred Curry before 400 fans in mid-1985 and got some favorable print in the *Detroit Free Press*. His wife, Joyce Fleser Farhat, was quoted in the story (though not acknowledged as his wife), saying the 43-year-old was returning to the mat because "a lot of people [were] trying to claim his title," referencing his long-running reign as United States champion.[244] The Sheik was really 59, and his interest in reviving Detroit under the NWA banner proved impossible because of Vince McMahon's stranglehold. It was no secret that the Detroit–Toronto area was the WWF's strongest-drawing region outside the Northeast and southern California.

The WWF packed Detroit's Cobo Hall from pillar to post on January 12, 1985, selling the joint out for the first time since the Sheik's heyday, and without Hulk Hogan. In fact, the WWF withheld Hogan from Detroit for eight months that year and built incredible anticipation for his eventual arrival. Over the course of five days in August, the promotion drew more than 50,000 fans for two shows in the Detroit area, with Hogan at the top of the bill for each. The first, on August 23 at Joe Louis Arena, drew nearly 21,000, and Hogan teamed with Ricky Steamboat to beat Don Muraco and Mr. Fuji. That number was topped on August 28, when 30,000 people at the Michigan State Fairgrounds saw Hogan beat Greg Valentine in defense of his WWF championship. The numbers were astonishing, and while a 1985 show headlined by the Sheik was good for nostalgia, the WWF was the only real game in town.

Indianapolis was another old-time territorial city up for grabs, and McMahon had turned the tables there too. The local promotion of Dick the Bruiser was a shell of its former existence and, though Dick the Bruiser was a folk hero in and around Indiana, young wrestling fans were looking for something different from the grappling their parents had watched in the 1960s and '70s. Bruiser was a symbolic figure of the territories, and his matches in 1985 were a throwback to a bygone era. But when it came to supporting a wrestling promotion, fans in Indianapolis were excited to see the cast and characters of the WWF. On January 19, 1985, McMahon's group debuted at the Expo Center to just under 7,000 spectators. Over at the Convention Center, that same night, Bruiser and his crew performed before fewer than 1,000. The following month, the WWF sold out their building, and the WWA sold about 250 tickets.

Within a matter of months, Bruiser downgraded his regular venue in Indianapolis to a stage at the Vogue nightclub, beginning on May 16, 1985. Vogue owner John Ross told the *Indianapolis Star*, "Everybody's talking about [wrestling], so we thought we'd give it a try."[245] But wrestling's popularity didn't trickle down to the WWA, and before the summer ended, Bruiser dropped his monthly programs in Indianapolis. He didn't completely fold up his tent, however, and continued running spot shows in places like Kokomo and Springfield. On August 17, Bruiser headlined a free wrestling show at Trader Bud's North Hills Chrysler-Plymouth in the Pittsburgh area, and the advertisement told fans to bring their "lawn chairs." The run of the WWA, as it was known, was truly over.

Joe Blanchard, head of the Southwest promotion in San Antonio, also neared the end of his run. The constant battle to obtain and keep star-quality wrestlers was one of his biggest problems, and crowds fluctuated throughout 1984 and '85. But things were getting worse, and his decision to sell out was being made for him. "You've either got to be big or little," he told the *Los Angeles Times.* "You can't be in the middle. And we can't compete with the big three who have that kind of money to provide first-class shows." Blanchard encouraged his son Tully, now a star for Jim Crockett, to leave San Antonio and get rich elsewhere. "He should get syndicated and go the route," Blanchard continued. "Big tours, big arenas, big promotions. He's looking at a shot at making $1,000 a night. Why, I can't afford to hire my own kid. Maybe if I could guarantee him $4,000 a week for three years."[246] In April 1985, he liquidated his interest in Southwest Championship Wrestling, selling to his former partner Fred Behrend.[247] Now more of an independent group than an official territory, the San Antonio promotion experienced several name changes. It was first dubbed Lone Star Wrestling, then Texas All-Star Wrestling, and finally, USA All-Star Wrestling. Behrend managed to increase attendance with Chavo Guerrero, Nick Kiniski, Rick McCord, and a young Shawn Michaels, among others, and highlighted a hot feud between Bruiser Brody and Mark Lewin. The USA heavyweight crown, designated the primary singles championship, was held by Guerrero, Ted DiBiase, and Big Bubba in 1985. An understanding was reached with World Class that kept the promotions from running against each other, and put an end to the destructive war in San Antonio. That was good news for World Class boss Jack Adkisson, as he had bigger things on his mind.

Syndication for the World Class TV show was going well, and the Continental Broadcasting Network, the promotion's syndicator, had the show in New York, Chicago, and Los Angeles — the top three markets in the U.S. At its height, the telecast was broadcast on two stations in Los Angeles (KCOP-13 and KDOC-56) and featured on the MSG cable network in New York. The in-ring work of Chris Adams, Gino Hernandez, and the Midnight Express were ratings grabbers, and interviews by Jim Cornette and Michael Hayes were must-see. At the second annual David Von Erich Memorial Parade of Champions on May 5, 1985, NWA champion Ric Flair and Kevin Von Erich battled to a double count-out, and Kerry Von Erich went over One Man Gang. Over 25,000 fans were in attendance, for a gate of $250,000, and this show, combined with weekly sellouts of the Sportatorium, proved that World Class was in perfect form.

The TV ratings in many cities were off the charts, so much so that in places like Boston, live shows were the logical next step. On June 1, 1985, Adkisson's tribe worked Lynn, Massachusetts, 11 miles outside of Boston, and attracted 8,000 people in a huge success. From August 3 to August 7, 1985, World Class staged five programs in Tel Aviv, Israel, and on the final night, Kevin Von Erich beat Gino Hernandez for the inaugural Middle East championship. The tour was audacious for an American wrestling promoter, but Adkisson took the risk and cleaned up nicely at the gate.[248] The matches in Israel were costly, though. A hard canvas at Tel Aviv Stadium put a beating on the troupe, and an injury to Mike Von Erich's shoulder required surgery.

Outside of the ring, Adkisson inked an important six-figure deal with Antonio Inoki to supply American talent to New Japan.[249] This was the same agreement Inoki used to have with Vince McMahon, but for about half the price, at a reported $200,000.[250] Additionally, World Class was in the running for an ESPN cable timeslot, which would only broaden the company's exposure. The WWF was a complete nonentity in Dallas. As proof of that fact, three days before the Parade of Champions event at Texas Stadium on May 5, a WWF show held at the Convention Center drew a paltry 180 fans. It was embarrassing, but Adkisson's office took the high road in the media when discussing the wrestling war. "Some of the promoters across the country are really pushing, but we've been trying to stay away from the 'let's get him' attitude," World Class booker Ken Mantell explained. "We say the man with the best product is going to survive."[251]

The WWF struggled in Jerry Jarrett's territory as well, and Vince McMahon decided to stay away from Memphis completely in 1985. But he ran Louisville, Lexington, Nashville, and Chattanooga, and crowds ranged from 350 to 2,500. Jarrett maintained the highest local ratings for a wrestling

TV program in the country and was near untouchable in head-to-head competition. The famous Jerry Lawler–Randy Savage feud reignited in early 1985, and lasted several months, culminating in a loser-leaves-town championship match on June 3, 1985. That night in Memphis, Lawler captured his 40th Southern title and sent Savage packing. But Savage already had a job lined up, and made his WWF debut two weeks later at a Poughkeepsie taping.[252] The following month, his wife Elizabeth joined him as his valet-manager. Savage was a huge acquisition for McMahon, and there was no question he was going to make a big impact on the promotion.

In the Pacific Northwest, Don Owen wasn't as comfortable as Adkisson and Jarrett. He was stressed by the wrestling war, telling a reporter in May 1985, "In the last six months I've been suffering. I'm down as bad as I've been in 20 years."[253] But on May 21, 1985, he enjoyed a once-in-a-lifetime wrestling event at the Memorial Coliseum in Portland when more than 12,000 fans turned out to celebrate his family's 60th anniversary in sports promotions. It didn't hurt that Owen had booked a superstar lineup, including NWA world champion Ric Flair, AWA world champion Rick Martel, the Road Warriors, and Sgt. Slaughter. Roddy Piper, who was on break from his WWF schedule to be with his pregnant wife, also made an appearance in tribute to Owen.

The heavily cheered Piper went over Buddy Rose in his bout, and it was noteworthy that Rose had also been a participant at WrestleMania under a hood as the Executioner. Flair wrestled Billy Jack Haynes to a 45-minute draw, and Martel beat Mike Miller. The gate was more than $100,000, and the 73-year-old Owen was ecstatic. "Frankly," he told a reporter for the Associated Press, "I never thought it would be possible. We darn near got a full house."[254] Two days before the event, the *Portland Oregonian* ran a lengthy piece on the longtime promoter, and the journalist indicated that Owen was becoming "old, cranky, and senile" and "getting crustier by the minute." But Owen was a "fighter" at heart, and would rather relent to bankruptcy than give in to a rival. "I've always been an independent sort of cuss," Owen explained. "I don't bother anyone. I've never tried to take over a town like 'New York' is doing. They're trying to kill us off. Well, they're going to have more trouble with me. I own my own building. It took me 14 years to pay for it, including 12 years without a vacation. I'm not going to back off from those . . ." The rest was left up to the reader's imagination. Despite rumors that Owen was going to sell out soon, perhaps to Verne Gagne, he remained active and was a steadfast member of the NWA. "I have the respect of every wrestler who ever worked out here," he said. "I've been honest with everyone. I've paid the highest percentage for the talent. I've treated everyone fair."[255] Owen was a top-shelf promoter, but his honesty wasn't in question. It was all about patronage, and whether the fans of Portland were ready to jump on the WWF bandwagon remained to be seen. Only time would tell.

CHAPTER FOURTEEN

YEAR OF THE SUPERSHOW

In the 1980s, wrestling fans enjoyed a diverse array of in-ring performers. There were high-fliers, sound technicians, rowdy personalities, smug heels, and smiling fan favorites. Colorful gimmicks were everywhere, and promoters did all in their power to get their talent "over" with audiences. Things hadn't really changed all that much, though, as promoters throughout history had fashioned such characters, from French and Swedish Angeles to the Elephant Boy, the Blimp, and boisterous loud-mouths like the original "Nature Boy" Buddy Rogers. In 1985, Hulk Hogan was the sport's poster boy, recognizable worldwide thanks to the exhaustive WWF marketing machine, but pro wrestling still had its off-the-wall gimmicks, behemoths, and monsters.

In Florida, Kevin Sullivan was portraying a Devil worshiper with a pack of disciples, the Army of Darkness, which included the Purple Haze, the Lock, Maya Singh, and his wife, Nancy, as the Fallen Angel. Longtime Dallas-area manager Gary Hart maintained at least one or two monsters in his stable, and few were scarier than the 6-foot, 330-pound Abdullah the Butcher or the 6-foot-8, 400-pound One Man Gang. Of all the unusual characters in wrestling, one man stood above them all, and he was Bruiser Brody. Originally from Michigan, Brody played football at West Texas State and became a wrestler under the tutelage of Jack Adkisson. Brody was better than 6-foot-6 and north of 270 pounds with a scraggly beard, wild eyes, and an unpredictable disposition. In and around the ring, he was an exceptional performer, and left his mark all over the world. Outside the squared circle, Brody was an unyielding free-thinker and incredibly protective of his character's reputation, refusing to put over other wrestlers even when called upon to do so. As a result, he was pretty much always quarrelling with one promoter or another, and had no qualms about walking away from a territory if he felt wronged. Brody's behavior was usually overlooked because he was an exceptional box-office draw. He was an Andre the Giant–level attraction, working big houses from New York to Tokyo against everyone from Bruno Sammartino to Giant Baba. In 1984 and into '85, he was working the AWA circuit, and his relationship with Verne Gagne ran hot or cold depending on the week.

After pulling double duty in Chicago (afternoon) and St. Paul (evening) on January 13, 1985, Brody jumped from the AWA right in the midst of an ongoing feud with "Crusher" Jerry Blackwell, leaving a string of nonappearances through January and February. Two months later, Brody walked out on Giant Baba as well and signed with Antonio Inoki's New Japan. That decision was made after Brody found out that Baba was paying the Road Warriors the same money he was getting, even though it was the "Roadies" first Japanese tour, while Brody had been paying his dues for years.[256]

Brody's departure was jarring, but the AWA was used to the turnover in talent. Elsewhere in the AWA, Verne Gagne was working overtime to keep his central cities strong against the WWF. On the night of WrestleMania, he hurt Vince McMahon's CCTV aspirations in Chicago by running a live show with 9,600 spectators. A few weeks later, on April 27–28, the AWA and WWF staged events within a day of each other in that same city, and the AWA held a 15,000-to-2,700 advantage. The week prior, the numbers were 12,000 to 7,000 in the Twin Cities with the AWA on top, and Gagne himself came out of retirement for a special tag team bout on that card. The 59-year-old local celebrity thrilled the St. Paul crowd by teaming with his son Greg to beat Nick Bockwinkel and Mr. Saito. McMahon put on his biggest seller in Minneapolis, Hulk Hogan versus Jesse Ventura, and got a good turnout. Hogan took the victory by count-out.

Salt Lake City only saw the WWF once in 1985, on January 14, and attracted about 3,500 people. The rest of the year, Gagne's AWA operated uncontested, and his attendance peaked at 10,455 on May 10, 1985, dropped to 1,400 in July, but went back up in November, only to seriously fall once again in December. The turbulence of fan interest was jolting, and was likely a barometer of how well Gagne's TV show was selling the various storylines. Over in Denver, there was a fight for supremacy, and the closed-circuit sales for WrestleMania were surprisingly high. Attendance for WWF programs grew from 5,000 in May to 10,000 on November 27, 1985. In comparison, the November AWA show 12 days before drew 2,500 less. Had the instability in Salt Lake and the WWF's growing popularity in Denver been Gagne's only concerns, things wouldn't have seemed so bad. But the problems multiplied in 1985, starting with the AWA losing one of its most important buildings to McMahon's promotion.

On June 10, 1985, the WWF assumed control of the Cow Palace in San Francisco, the AWA's premier Bay Area venue since 1982. The move pushed Gagne out of northern California, and although he immediately sought to return, it was a damaging turn of events. In suburban Chicago, officials at the Rosemont Horizon rescinded whatever exclusivity Gagne had at the building and gave dates to McMahon, thus splitting bookings between the AWA and WWF. It was interesting because two months before the WWF's Rosemont debut, the general manager of the facility, Paul Johnson, talked about "wrestling's demise" with a reporter for the *Chicago Tribune*: "When [pro wrestling] made the cover of *Sports Illustrated*, when it became yuppified, I knew it was in trouble," said Johnson, referencing Hulk Hogan's famous April 29, 1985, cover.[257]

Personal opinions aside, the WWF's success was indisputable, and made a huge impact in its debut at the Rosemont Horizon on August 31. The WWF sold out the arena (18,211), and Hogan beat Nikolai Volkoff in the main event. The last time Gagne drew a Chicago crowd that large had been in November 1984, nine months earlier. McMahon maintained his advantage in Chicago through the end of the 1985, drawing better than the AWA over its next three cards. This was Gagne's fourth core city to either waver or fall completely (the other three were San Francisco, Salt Lake City, and Denver). Despite all of his progress in the Northeast and the positive changes to his TV setup, he was seeing a genuine deterioration of his original circuit. The biggest indication of his decline was the dipping attendance in St. Paul.

Gagne's June 9, 1985, show drew an abysmal 1,500 fans, whereas the WWF had 5,000 on June 1 and 6,000 on June 30 in Minneapolis. Gagne outdrew McMahon in October (3,000 to 2,600), and the two promotions went head to head on Thanksgiving, November 28, 1985. An estimated 27,000 people went to wrestling matches that holiday, and the breakdown was 15,000 at the Met Center and 12,000 at the Civic Center. The winner was Vince McMahon and the WWF with former AWA stars Hulk Hogan, Jesse Ventura, and Jim Brunzell. Mr. T made a special appearance as well, in Hogan's corner, and Paul Orndorff defeated Roddy Piper by disqualification. AWA fans saw the Road Warriors beat Michael Hayes and Buddy Roberts, and 27-year-old up-and-comer Scott Hall won a battle royal.

Talent wasn't a problem in Gagne's universe in 1985. The Road Warriors and Freebirds were two of the hottest teams in the business, and rarely failed to draw at the box office. The heavyweight champion of the AWA, classic good guy Rick Martel, was a conditioned athlete with all the hallmarks of a wrestling idol. He had ring awareness and ability, but he lacked the charisma of Hogan or Ric Flair. Robert Wolf of the *Chicago Tribune* referred to him as "Mr. Bland." Wolf added, "Martel lacks a heel's aura of vitality."[258] Also in Gagne's talent pool were Jim Garvin, Butch Reed, Larry Zbyszko, Nick Bockwinkel, and Curt Hennig. In September, Stan Hansen, the man known for breaking Bruno Sammartino's neck in 1976, joined the promotion and was an immediate challenger for Martel's belt.

On August 27, 1985, Gagne ran a special benefit show in Boston at Matthews Arena (Northeastern University) for the Muscular Dystrophy Association. "Wrestling for a Cure," as the event was billed, featured six matches and was broadcast live on WCVB-5.[259] Martel wrestled Bockwinkel to a draw, Bob Backlund beat Larry Zbyszko by DQ, and the Road Warriors topped the Irwin Brothers. The charity performance took in an estimated $50,000 in donations and scored a 10.0 rating and 17 share on TV.[260] August 27 was also the day the Minnesota-based promotion made its debut on national cable television. Gagne had landed placement on ESPN, offered as part of basic cable around the country, elevating the organization to compete with the WWF on USA and Jim Crockett Promotions on WTBS.

The cable station, which had selected Gagne's over several other outfits, packaged *AWA Championship Wrestling* into a Tuesday night block with Roller Derby. "We're pure as driven snow on the other six days, but we're gonna have fun on Tuesdays," explained Loren Matthews, director of programming for ESPN. "Personally, I think we should have added wrestling before now. The ratings speak for themselves. The WWF was the first to get a national cable outlet, and frankly they had the intelligence to promote their product. I believe the AWA compares very favorably to the WWF and we will give them their first national outlet."[261] ESPN was apparently confident in Gagne's product, and scheduled it against USA's *Prime-Time Wrestling* at 8:00 p.m. Considering all of Gagne's recent struggles, winning the timeslot would be difficult, but *AWA Championship Wrestling* became one of ESPN's highest-rated shows.

On September 28, the AWA held the massive SuperClash '85 show at Comiskey Park in Chicago featuring more than a dozen current, former, and future world heavyweight champions including AWA titleholder Rick Martel and NWA kingpin Ric Flair. Among the others on the card were Kerry Von Erich, the Road Warriors, Sgt. Slaughter, the Freebirds, Ivan and Nikita Koloff, and Giant Baba. Nearly 21,000 enthusiasts were in attendance, but Gagne and co-promoter Jim Crockett managed to end what should have been a triumphant night in a quarrel. Their disagreement reportedly stemmed from a disparity in the gate figures, with Gagne saying it was just over $200,000 and Crockett putting it near $280,000.[262] The dispute was ultimately smoothed over, and combined JCP–AWA events continued through the end of the year. In fact, at the joint Meadowlands program on December 29, Martel dropped his AWA world title to Stan Hansen.

1985 was treating Jim Crockett pretty well as JCP transitioned from a regional group to a national promotion, visiting New York, New Jersey, Pennsylvania, Ohio, and Michigan. On June 29, he ran a show at the

Olympic Auditorium in Los Angeles, drawing slightly less than 2,000 fans, with Flair, Magnum T.A., Dusty Rhodes, Tully Blanchard, Manny Fernandez, Krusher Khruschev, and a crew of locals. Ten days later, on July 9, the Rock and Roll Express made their JCP debut as regulars, and captured the NWA world tag team title from Khruschev and Ivan Koloff in Shelby, North Carolina.[263] Ricky Morton and Robert Gibson were electrifying performers, and their popularity as teen idols tore down the house throughout the Carolinas and across Crockett's circuit. They helped the box office take greatly, and with Rhodes still churning out bankable angles, JCP was, overall, a healthy promotion.

In August 1985, Crockett treated as many as 18 of his top grapplers to an all-expenses-paid vacation to Las Vegas, a trip that was made in conjunction with the NWA's annual convention.[264] The meeting at the Dunes Hotel was key to the future of the organization, and, in keeping with the changing times, it was clear that some procedural things needed to be refined a bit. At the center of all issues was the heavyweight champion Ric Flair, and how he was booked. In years past, the world titleholder's schedule had been arranged in more or less an even fashion, and every dues-paying affiliate received dates. Depending on the size of the territory, the champion made upwards of five appearances in a particular region before heading to the next. But in the new marketplace, Crockett needed Flair more for his own ventures, particularly as he pushed into new cities and WWF strongholds.

But Crockett wasn't only selling his own product for selfish reasons. He was promoting the NWA brand, marketing the stars of the Alliance, and carrying the largest burden of all members because of his growing role on the national stage. Sportswriters who didn't know any better blatantly called JCP the "NWA," even though the NWA was never a single promotion. The NWA was always a union of offices, and referring to Jim Crockett Promotions as "the NWA" was simply wrong. Writers didn't care. They needed a three letter acronym, and since Flair was the NWA world heavyweight champion, it all seemed to make sense. At the NWA convention, the members of the board of directors retained their voice but conceded more and more power to Crockett, since his group was the face of the Alliance. Crockett was in the best position to fight the WWF, and affiliates gave him the resources he needed to win the wrestling war. There were going to be repercussions, though. The loss of dates on the world champion would hurt the other territories financially, and Crockett was sympathetic. To lessen the anxiety of his contemporaries, he agreed to set aside two open dates for Flair each week, but changed the payment scale from a percentage of the box office to a flat fee.

There was another option for an NWA member to get dates on Flair, one that was more in tune with Crockett's national objectives. Crockett agreed to send Flair and half a card of well-known JCP wrestlers to a promoter for 50 percent of the gate, a deal which sounded good on the surface. The local promoter would get a hefty boost by featuring the various stars, and Crockett would pocket some serious coin. But there was also a downside to the concept. If regional fans were exposed to a combination of Flair, Dusty Rhodes, the Rock and Roll Express, Tully Blanchard, Magnum T.A., and the Koloffs, would they really be energized to see the local promoter's regular cast the following week? If the promoter had a group of upstarts, journeymen, and possibly one or two solid mid-level stars, their lineup wouldn't compare, and all subsequent programs in the territory would be disappointments.

And if that left the promoter in need of Crockett's wrestlers to sustain future business, who exactly was in the driver's seat? The door was then open for additional bookings and maybe eventually a buyout. In years past, when Flair would enter a territory alone, the local promoter picked the challenger and filled the rest of the card with his own roster. In contrast, Crockett was sending Flair with a ready-made challenger from his own WTBS angles. That meant there was no opportunity to build a regional grappler up through a highly competitive match with the NWA champ. Promoters also let Crockett set the ticket prices for his 50-50 combo shows, a stipulation they approved to ensure cooperation.[265] The interesting thing was that none of Crockett's pullback on the use of Flair and the proposal to split gates was received with lasting animosity. The members of the NWA needed Crockett more than ever, and were willing to compromise to keep things running smoothly. Jerry Jarrett, Ron Fuller, and Don Owen agreed to the 50-50 gate split, and Crockett supplied wrestlers for Lexington on September 5, Pensacola on September 15, Portland on September 23, and Memphis on September 30, 1985.[266] As expected, attendance for these shows was generally good, although Pensacola's 2,000 was a bust. To accommodate the demands of expansion, Crockett had to make cuts to his schedule in his home territory, and certain Mid-Atlantic towns that used to get more than one showing a month, saw a reduction. Also, he moved his regular WTBS studio tapings in Atlanta from Saturday to Sunday beginning on September 1, 1985, so his wrestlers could make the most of important Saturday night events on the road.

Headed toward Starrcade '85, booker Dusty Rhodes set up the main event for the annual extravaganza, and changed the direction of the promotion forever. On September 29, 1985, at the Omni in Atlanta, Ric Flair successfully defended his NWA championship against Nikita Koloff in a cage bout. Koloff then joined his uncle Ivan and Krusher Khruschev to pummel Flair, but Rhodes ran out to make a compassionate save. Ole and Arn Anderson, though, didn't see it as a friendly gesture and jumped Rhodes. Flair joined in and broke the American Dream's ankle, cementing his heel turn and establishing the headline attraction for Starrcade.[267] It was Flair and Rhodes once again, and on Thanksgiving, November 28, Starrcade took place in two cities, Atlanta and Greensboro. Closed-circuit TV ensured fans at both arenas didn't miss a second of action, and the matches were beamed to places like Charlotte and New Orleans as well. Both the Omni in Atlanta and the Coliseum in Greensboro sold out for a total gate of over $900,000. Rhodes pinned Flair in what appeared to be a title winning bid, but his victory became a disqualification win after officials acknowledged the interference of the Andersons. The Rock and Roll Express regained the world tag team belts from the Koloffs, and Magnum T.A. beat Tully Blanchard for the United States championship in an I-Quit cage bout. Once again, Starrcade was a winner.

A week later, Crockett filed a federal antitrust lawsuit against Titan Sports and Vince McMahon in Richmond, Virginia.[268] The suit claimed McMahon had conspired to push JCP out of the Richmond Coliseum and tried to get a local TV station to replace Crockett's syndicated show with one produced by the WWF. Officials at the Coliseum quickly rectified the situation by adding Crockett events to its 1986 calendar.

The WWF, incidentally, staged a special benefit in the heart of Crockett country, Charlotte, on December 16, 1985, and attracted 2,400 spectators.[269] The event was for the family of 30-year-old Rick McGraw, a talented and popular undercard performer who passed away on November 1. The wrestling world nearly suffered another tragedy in Dallas on September 29, 1985, when Mike Von Erich nearly died of toxic shock syndrome.[270] Von Erich acquired the bacterial infection following shoulder surgery, which he needed after the Middle East tour in August, and his body temperature rose to 107 degrees. For several days, he was listed in critical condition, but he slowly recovered, and doctors attributed his rebound to his superior athletic condition.[271] Kevin Von Erich told the Associated Press that a "miracle took place," and considering how touch and go things were, he appeared right.[272]

Before a big World Class program at the Cotton Bowl in Dallas on October 6, 1985, Kerry and Kevin Von Erich appeared alongside Mike for an interview at Baylor Hospital. They discussed what a fighter Mike was and indicated that he was going to make his return to pro wrestling, even if it took months to regain his physical health. Mike had lost upwards of 80 pounds, and there were concerns about brain damage from his extremely high fever. Mike would be at the Cotton Bowl to thank fans, in a move that some saw as exploiting his condition to sell tickets. More than 25,000 fans turned out to see the spectacle and not only witnessed Mike's return, but Kerry and Kevin's victory over Chris Adams and Gino Hernandez in a hair versus hair bout.[273]

Jack Adkisson introduced his "nephew" Lance Von Erich during the Cotton Bowl event, the "son" of Fritz's "brother" Waldo. Lance was no blood relation, and had competed as Ricky Vaughn in the Pacific Northwest in 1984–85. But with his son Mike out of action indefinitely, and Kerry and Kevin bruised and battered from a grueling schedule, Adkisson needed a new Von Erich to lessen the burden on the family. On October 28, Lance wrestled NWA champion Ric Flair to a no contest in what ended up being the Nature Boy's final showing for World Class. A week later, Rick Rude, coming off a successful tour of Florida, won the American heavyweight championship from Iceman Parsons in Fort Worth.

Aside from the Cotton Bowl event and holiday shows on Thanksgiving and Christmas at Reunion Arena, Adkisson was dealing with a downturn in fan enthusiasm. Attendance for weekly programs in Fort Worth dropped to under 500 late in the summer of 1985, and some of the matchups were less than intriguing. In December, the Von Erich–Freebirds conflict resumed, and Adkisson hoped there was still a little box-office magic left in their feud. Notably, for the first seven months of 1985, Adkisson had lent many of his top wrestlers, including his sons, to Bob Geigel in St. Louis. His involvement, however, was phased out after the July 12, 1985, program, and Geigel pulled in more resources from his Kansas City promotion, the AWA, and Jim Crockett. But despite these efforts, NWA-branded grappling in St. Louis was at its lowest point in recent memory. Crowds were hovering between 1,300 and 1,800, and it wasn't until Flair returned on August 2 that attendance reached 2,600. The Kiel Auditorium, a traditional NWA venue with a historic past, was routinely packed when Sam Muchnick presided over wrestling in St. Louis. Lou Thesz, Pat O'Connor, Gene Kiniski, and Harley Race each left it all on the mat for the respectful fans at the Kiel. In 1985, there was a lot of disappointment in St. Louis, and because the wrestling war was well into its second year, people were tired of the quarreling. The active operations of the St. Louis Wrestling Club and the WWF were too much for one city, and both sides were worse off than they had been in 1984. But the WWF was clearly winning the attendance battle between July and September 1985, and the Kiel management took notice. Finally, officials decided to break with Geigel and opted into an exclusive deal with Vince McMahon beginning on October 25.

Losing the Kiel was a deathblow to the St. Louis Wrestling Club, and Geigel and his partners were running on fumes. On November 29, 1985, they rented the more expensive (and much larger) St. Louis Arena for a combined show featuring mostly Jim Crockett talent. Only three wrestlers, Jerry Blackwell, Art Crews, and Tarzan Goto, were Geigel regulars, and in the main event, Ric Flair and Dusty Rhodes battled to an inconclusive double-disqualification finish, which would've been a big no-no during the Muchnick era. They drew 3,600, and across town at the Kiel, that same night, the WWF pulled in 4,300 people with Andre the Giant going over King Kong Bundy by DQ. The influence of Crockett in St. Louis was expected to remain at that high level, and there had been rumors since January that he was trying to leverage a buyout for full rights to the city.

Geigel was seriously considering a deal. Over in Kansas City, his crowds were routinely under 1,000, but occasionally 2,000 to 2,200 for bigger shows. The WWF was doing double that consistently.

Tulsa, Oklahoma, was a good four-hour drive southwest from Kansas City, and surprisingly, it was one of the few major wrestling metropolises that McMahon had yet to target. On September 21, 1985, he changed that by running a program at the Expo Square Pavilion with two old Mid-South stars, Junkyard Dog and Mr. Wrestling II, on the bill. But Bill Watts didn't have to worry yet, as only 1,200 people were interested in the WWF's product. The next night, Watts ran Tulsa, and 7,200 of his loyal customers saw a huge eight-man tag team main event, plus appearances by Kerry and Kevin Von Erich, Jake Roberts, and Butch Reed.[274]

The WWF made its debut in Portland, Oregon, the following month, on October 7, 1985, and brought a sizable headline attraction. On one side were Andre the Giant and Junkyard Dog, and on the other, Big John Studd and King Kong Bundy. Apparently, the ring held up under the massive weight, but the finish was not exactly satisfying to the 3,500 in attendance. The bout ended in a double DQ. Also on the card was Matt Borne, a perennial Pacific Northwest grappler, who drew with Lanny Poffo. Two WWF representatives, Red Bastien and Jesse Ventura, spoke with a journalist from the *Portland Oregonian* for an edition the next day. "All we expected tonight was three or four thousand fans and maybe $30,000," explained Bastien, a west coast agent for the WWF. "The history of the WWF is that we really don't do that well when we go into a place for the first time. It takes awhile for our people to be recognized. We have a product we think people want to see. It's proven to be a good product in other markets and I don't see why Portland has to be deprived." Ventura called his time wrestling for Don Owen early in his career "rookie wrestling, like the minor leagues in baseball." He went on to say: "I respect Don Owen, and I appreciate what he did for me just as I think he appreciates the money I made for him. But this is business. Personal feelings can't enter into business. I would hope that Don Owen would accept it as that. I heard he came out in the newspaper and told people not to come here tonight. I think it's kind of sad that he would stoop to that. Doesn't he think people are intelligent enough to decide for themselves whether they want to come or not? If it was me, I'd consider it an insult to my intelligence. We're not out to put anybody out of business. You got Burger King on one corner and McDonald's on another. We're just exploiting what society's made of, and that's capitalism."[275]

As a whole, 1985 was a memorable year for supershow spectaculars. There was WrestleMania, the Great American Bash, SuperClash, and Starrcade. An oft-forgotten all-star extravaganza occurred on August

3, 1985, at Aloha Stadium in Honolulu, Hawaii. Promoted as "A Hot Summer Night," the show featured 16 matches and 44 wrestlers from the NWA, WWF, and New Japan. In the main event world title match, Ric Flair retained his belt against Sivi Afi after a double DQ. Antonio Inoki wrestled Bruiser Brody to a double count-out. Andre the Giant teamed with Steve Collins and Angelo Mosca to beat Kevin Sullivan, Mark Lewin, and King Kong Bundy, while Magnum T.A. partnered with Dusty Rhodes to topple Nikita Koloff and Krusher Khruschev. The audience of 12,553 was treated to an international event, and promoter Lia Maivia scored a six-figure gate. Backstage, there was an extra confrontation, which only insiders were privy to. For reasons unknown, but perhaps relating to the booking of the event or payoffs, Jim Crockett got into a heated argument with Polynesian matchmaker Lars Anderson, and Anderson threw a drink in the promoter's face.[276]

Even when promoters were cooperating for a successful supershow, tempers were high. "A Hot Summer Night" was no different, and with Crockett fast becoming the NWA's lone power broker, the politics inside the Alliance were curiouser and curiouser.

CHAPTER FIFTEEN

THE WAR EXPANDS AGAIN

In a way, the pundits were right. The World Wrestling Federation had over-exposed itself and faced backlash in the days and weeks after WrestleMania. The network appearances, late-night interviews, and endless mainstream hype was beyond anything pro wrestling had ever seen, and fans in many markets were exhausted. While a decline in ticket sales after a highly antic-ipated show wasn't unusual, the massive wave of publicity hurt the WWF expansion in a number of battleground cities. Events in St. Louis, Miami, and Chicago were at half or below-half capacity and the Omni Coliseum in Atlanta, which sat 16,000, had about 900 spectators on April 28, 1985. Carver Arena in Peoria, Illinois, enjoyed two near-sellouts of 12,000 before WrestleMania, only to drop dramatically after the spectacle to only 1,200 on May 6, 1985.[277]

The WWF drew consistently in core cities like New York, Boston, and Philadelphia, but there was the occasional bump in the road. Not surprisingly, Hulk Hogan was often the difference between a great house and a mediocre or poor one. "People just idolize Hulk Hogan," explained Mike Weber, a media coordinator for the WWF. "One promoter told me he introduced his kids to Hulk Hogan and said they couldn't have been more impressed if they'd met Jesus Christ himself."[278] Two weeks after WrestleMania, Los Angeles and Oakland popped big for the WWF with estimated crowds of 12,000 to see Hogan wrestle Roddy Piper in singles bouts. But the promotion returned to the West Coast in May without Hogan, and attendance was cut in half. In July, the numbers improved to 14,000 in northern and southern California with Hogan back on top.

Any sign of a depressed fanbase completely disappeared by July and August 1985, and the WWF entered one of the most lucrative periods in its history. Vince McMahon scored extraordinary sellouts in Toronto, Tampa, Detroit, Chicago, and Los Angeles, and achieved additional 20,000-plus crowds in Montreal, Columbus, and Foxboro.[279] The Foxboro program, at Sullivan Stadium, attracted 23,000 for the inaugural King of the Ring, a 16-man tournament won by Don Muraco. The status of Montreal was also notable. Prior to August 1985, the city was run by the International Wrestling group in conjunction with the AWA. McMahon stepped in and bought IW's television time, and used Edouard Carpentier as a French-language commentator for the WWF's *Maple Leaf Wrestling*. IW was weakened and soon entered an agreement with McMahon to co-promote the Montreal Forum and the Colisée de Quebec in Quebec City.[280]

McMahon hoped Montreal would resemble all the success in Toronto rather than the disappointment of western Canada. After a costly purchase of the Calgary territory and staging exactly four shows, the WWF vacated the region because of lackluster support. The withdrawal included Edmonton and Vancouver as well, and paved the way for locally based Stampede Wrestling to make its return in the summer of 1985.[281] Although the Calgary situation went bust, McMahon picked up three incredible workers in the deal: Bret Hart, Dynamite Kid, and Davey Boy Smith. Bret was one of Stu Hart's 12 children, and he'd learned grappling from the ground up in the famous Dungeon. In 1985, 28-year-old Bret was a fundamentally strong competitor, but since he wasn't overly muscular or freakish in some way, he languished in prelim or mid-card roles before joining with brother-in-law Jim Neidhart as part of a heel tag team, the Hart Foundation, managed by Jimmy Hart.

Davey Boy Smith and Dynamite Kid were actually cousins from England, and refined their skills working for Stu Hart in Calgary. By 1984–85, they were internationally renowned, getting better by the match. Beginning in March 1985, the duo (soon to be known as the British Bulldogs) jumped onto the WWF main circuit and wowed audiences with their slick maneuvers and innovative techniques. As fan favorites, it was only natural that they'd feud with Hart and Neidhart, and that's exactly what happened. The four men were capable of putting on wrestling clinics, and were often the highlight of house shows. Many people didn't know, though, that Davey Boy had married Bret's sister Diana the October before, and these competitors were close inside the ring and out.

On the TV front, *Saturday Night's Main Event* on NBC was a major hit, and replaced reruns of *Saturday Night Live* four times between May 1985 and January 1986. Its debut episode on May 11, 1985, drew an 8.8 rating and a 26 share, the network's second highest of the season in that timeslot behind an *SNL* hosted by Eddie Murphy.[282] NBC executives were taken aback by the numbers, and behind producer Dick Ebersol, pushed for another broadcast on October 5 featuring the real in-ring wedding of wrestler Uncle Elmer to fiancée Joyce. The press ate the story up, printing reports and photos of the affair from coast to coast. "Rasslin' and a Polish wedding, both punctuated by rock music," the *Akron Beacon Journal* declared. "That's *Saturday Night's Main Event.*"[283] The *Allentown Morning Call* declared the program a "variety show with a lot of beefcake."[284] Fans embraced *SNME*, and although ratings fell to 6.8 for the third episode, it rose back to 10.4 for the fourth, on January 4, 1986.

While the Saturday night show appealed to adults and the late-night crowd, a Saturday morning animated program targeted children. *Hulk Hogan's Rock 'n' Wrestling* debuted on CBS on September 14, 1985, and featured the cartoon versions of Hogan, Roddy Piper, Junkyard Dog, and other WWF personalities. Kids were hooked by the various characters, and WWF memorabilia flew off the shelves at record pace. Smartly, Titan Sports was ready for the barrage, and had a plethora of products to offer, from lunch boxes to trading cards.[285] Action figures were especially popular. Hogan first appeared with his doll at the American International Toy Fair in New York in February 1985, and over the next year, LJN Toys sold an incredible four million units.[286]

In the talent department, the WWF experienced the normal comings and goings. Losses included the Brisco Brothers, Dick Murdoch, Adrian Adonis, Jimmy Snuka, and Barry Windham. Adonis jumped back to the WWF, as did Brian Blair in 1985, and among the newcomers were Hercules Hernandez, Cousin Luke, Cousin Junior, Corporal Kirchner, Ted Arcidi, and Dan Spivey. Kirchner was a real army veteran and assumed the promotion's patriotic voice in the aftermath of Sgt. Slaughter's departure. Late in the year, he feuded with Nikolai Volkoff, a supporter of the Soviet Union. Arcidi was a tremendous powerlifter, and Spivey was a 6-foot-8 protégé of Dusty Rhodes with only two years of pro experience. He assumed many of Windham's bookings, and teamed regularly with Mike Rotundo. Of all the fresh faces, Randy Savage and Terry Funk were the two biggest additions, and both were booked into high-profile matches against Hogan for the world title.

A former NWA champion, Funk was a living legend. He was personable, edgy, and a lot of fun to watch work the squared circle. In his debut, he pummeled WWF official Mel Phillips, and over a several month period, he feuded with Junkyard Dog. Despite being on the losing end of many of his bouts with JYD and Hogan, Funk still displayed a level of ring mastery and aptitude the WWF needed. Savage was a one-of-a-kind performer as well, and his madcap behavior captivated live crowds and TV audiences alike. He was always unpredictable, and he backed up his zany interviews with exceptional in-ring skill. On November 7, 1985, Savage advanced to the finals of the Wrestling Classic tournament in Chicago, the WWF's first widespread pay-per-view offering, but lost to Junkyard Dog by count-out.[287] At the end of December, Savage took a count-out win from Hogan before a sellout crowd at Madison Square Garden. For longtime WWF fans, the return of former two-time heavyweight champion Bruno Sammartino as a semi-active competitor was a nice treat during 1985. Appearing first as a tag team partner with his son, David, Bruno went on to feud with Roddy Piper, and their conflict resulted in sellouts in Pittsburgh and Boston in November 1985 and February 1986. Another former WWWF titleholder, Pedro Morales, was also back in the fold, and he helped lead the group's charge into his native Puerto Rico for the first time on October 19, 1985. The WWF added Hogan, Savage, and Cyndi Lauper, who was in Wendi Richter's corner, to the San Juan bill, but the promotion was at a great disadvantage going head to head with the local WWC outfit. The WWC outdrew the WWF 10,000 to 1,200.

December 1985 marked the two-year anniversary of Vince McMahon's St. Louis invasion and the beginning of the wrestling war. Since embarking on that unprecedented attempt to wrangle the profession into a WWF-controlled headlock, he'd experienced a profusion of growth, both personal and professional. In that time, McMahon had hustled for every gain his company experienced as the World Wrestling Federation became a household name. The WWF was syndicated to 160 stations as of January 1986, up from less than 50 in early 1984, and it was still actively hunting new markets.[288] McMahon set up an elaborate booth with a ring at the National Association of Television Program Executives (NATPE) in New Orleans from January 16 to 21, 1986.[289] In addition, he took out a full-page advertisement in the trade publication *Broadcasting Magazine*, and highlighted the accomplishments of the WWF. It touted the record ratings on MTV, the number-one rating in children's programming on CBS, and that *Saturday Night's Main Event* was "rated number 15 with men, 18 to 49, out of all network shows." In terms of syndication itself, the advertisement cited a "healthy 10.8 national NTI (Nielsen Television Index)," which was essentially a national ratings average.[290] The sales methods were successful, and the WWF added 30 new stations over the next three months.[291]

The revenue streams of Titan Sports were diversified, much more than any competitor. Show gates were supplemented by ad revenue, national TV sponsorship, merchandising, the sale of video cassettes through Coliseum Home Video (a few tapes had gone platinum), a top-selling album featuring wrestlers as vocalists, and a magazine with a circulation of 200,000. Adding the money derived from production for NBC and CBS as well, and Titan Sports was logging impressive annual revenue. McMahon bided his time after his great TV expansion of 1984–85, but it was obvious he needed to rework some of his early deals to better correspond with the current status and popularity of the WWF. Back when he was first fishing for stations in places like Los Angeles, Minneapolis, and Chicago, he was more than willing to pay weekly amounts to get his promotion exposure. But by 1986, the WWF was no longer an unknown with a questionable product. It was a proven entity with a verifiable track record, ratings history, and huge publicity. TV executives wanted to avoid renegotiations at all costs, but McMahon was shrewd and amended deals where he could. WWF president Frank Tunney gave an insightful quote to the *Financial Post* about McMahon in 1986, explaining how many people, regardless of their industry, folded up after being confronted by "restrictions." McMahon never did. "He had the guts to keep going," Tunney said, and McMahon's lengthy battle to operate in Louisiana is a perfect example of that.[292]

As mentioned earlier, for years, Louisiana only issued one booking permit, and Bill Watts was the customary licensee. The actions of the athletic commission in distributing the lone certification protected Watts from anyone trying to muscle in. But in a free-trade environment, exclusive state licensing agreements opened things up to potential antitrust complaints, and the WWF was headed in that direction. In the meantime, McMahon acquired local TV outlets to introduce its wrestlers to Louisiana fans. McMahon then piped WrestleMania I into New Orleans through the Cox Cable system, and drew 2,000 buys. Finally, in late August 1985, Titan Sports filed suit against the Louisiana Athletic Commission in the Orleans Parish Civil District Court.[293] On October 7, the commission met in New Orleans to discuss the legality of the "one booker" statute, and heard testimony for 90 minutes.[294] The conference was adjourned without a formal decision, but the suggestion of a monopoly in Louisiana rattled enough cages to get the law overturned. The WWF made its debut in Shreveport on February 27, in Baton Rouge on March 6, and at the Superdome in New Orleans on March 7, 1986. The Superdome show, headlined by Hogan–Iron Sheik and Junkyard Dog–Terry Funk, drew more than 12,000 fans. Surprisingly, Jake Roberts, who'd recently departed the Mid-South territory for the WWF, didn't appear, and was instead booked in Philadelphia that night.

Roberts was just another star in a succession of "name" grapplers to beat a path for either the WWF or Jim Crockett Promotions. Terry Taylor actually returned to Watts in late 1985, and joined Ted DiBiase and Steve Williams as the group's top fan favorites. Jim Duggan was the other major babyface, and on March 16, 1986, after a bit of trickery, he beat Buzz Sawyer for Dick Slater's North American championship in Oklahoma City. The region's top singles championship changing hands was pretty big news, but in the context of what else Bill Watts had going on at the time, it was relatively small potatoes. Following the efforts of Ron Fuller in changing the name of his localized promotion into a more national-sounding outfit, Watts dropped the "Mid-South" name and rebranded his organization the Universal Wrestling Federation (UWF). For Watts, regionalism was a thing of the past, and it was all about syndication and expansion.

Watts co-promoted an ambitious show at the Superdome on April 19 with Jim Crockett, billed as the Jim Crockett Sr. Memorial Cup Tag Team Tournament. Featuring 24 teams and 48 competitors from eight territories, the tourney garnered international attention, and Watts made his WTBS return to hype the card on Crockett's telecast. The event started on the afternoon of April 19, drawing 3,500 spectators, and then continued that evening with 13,000 fans for a total gate of $180,000.[295] In the finals, the Road Warriors went over Ronnie Garvin and Magnum T.A. Two singles matches were also staged. Ric Flair beat Dusty Rhodes by disqualification in defense of his NWA championship, and Jim Duggan defeated Dick Slater to retain the North American crown. Duggan's title was soon phased out, and Watts introduced a UWF heavyweight belt in a tournament on May 30, 1986, in Houston. Terry Gordy became the initial champ after winning over a badly busted open Duggan in the deciding match.

Watts made a lot of quick progress. He had already upgraded his TV presentation by moving his tapings from the Irish McNeil Sports for Boys Club in Shreveport to Oklahoma City's Myriad Convention Center and then to the Tulsa Convention Center. An arena setting was pivotal for big-time wrestling on the tube in 1986, and his syndication efforts were paying off too. His TV show debuted in St. Louis, Detroit, Chicago, Philadelphia, and parts of Texas, Missouri, and Kansas. The UWF even got into New York City on WWHT-68. Talent acquisitions were essential, and Watts picked up a roster of heel performers: the Freebirds, Jack Victory, One Man Gang, Kamala, and Skandor Akbar, followed by John Tatum and Missy Hyatt. The Freebirds were a huge addition, and aside from Gordy winning the UWF championship, Michael Hayes became an important color commentator alongside Jim Ross. After leaving Memphis, the neophyte Blade Runners, Sting and Rock, gained a spot on Watts's payroll and took Eddie Gilbert as their manager. Both were future Hall of Famers, as Sting would go on to capture multiple world championships in WCW and TNA. Rock (later known as the Ultimate Warrior) won both the Intercontinental and world titles in the WWF. But in 1986, they were raw and enthusiastic performers with plenty still to learn. Rick Steiner, a former amateur grappler at the University of Michigan and legit tough guy, was an up-and-comer for Watts as well.

The UWF expansion went forward without hesitation, and Watts easily pushed into two of Leroy McGuirk's old towns, Springfield and Joplin, Missouri, in May and June 1986. On June 6, Watts also went into Memphis, instigating a war against his old business associate Jerry Jarrett. Programs in West Texas, San Antonio, and Dallas were booked over the summer months, and local promoters were forced to cope with yet another imposing outside group.

Jack Adkisson was one of those promoters, and based on a series of unfortunate events, he was having a horrible 1986. Two real-world incidents were especially painful. In late January, one of his top performers, Gino Hernandez, was found dead of a drug overdose in his Dallas-area home.[296] About four months later, Adkisson's son Kerry suffered serious injuries from a motorcycle accident in Argyle, Texas, the worst being a shattered right ankle. It was so bad that Kerry's career was in jeopardy, and he endured hours of surgery to restore circulation to his foot. Only time would tell if he'd be able to return to wrestling. The death of Hernandez and the injury to Von Erich were devastating to World Class and seemed to turn back the many gains Adkisson had made in previous years. In February 1986, World Class left the National Wrestling Alliance. The departure, which cut Adkisson off from his old allies, was a long time coming, and had been rumored for months. At the Sportatorium, Adkisson painted over the symbolic NWA logo and declared Rick Rude, the current American titleholder, the WCCW world heavyweight champion.[297] World Class was now an indie organization, and Adkisson's strained relations with Watts and Crockett promised a war for Texas that he couldn't afford to lose. The defections of the Freebirds, One Man Gang, and booker Ken Mantell to the UWF hurt Adkisson, and disorder reigned in the front office.[298] Adkisson remained focused, and, during the last week of April

1986, World Class toured Israel for a second time and summer shows were planned for New Orleans, Philadelphia, Providence, and Chicago.

Despite the downturn, July 4, 1986, was a landmark day for the promotion. A big show was staged at Reunion Arena in Dallas, and more than 11,500 people saw Chris Adams dethrone Rude for the world title. In a riotous affair, Bruiser Brody and Abdullah the Butcher brawled to a double disqualification, and Buzz Sawyer, who jumped from the UWF to Dallas in June, won the Texas championship from Brian Adias. But the predominant interest of fans centered on the return of Mike Von Erich. Mike's battle back from near death the September before was nothing short of miraculous, and he teamed with Kevin and Lance to defeat Sawyer, Matt Borne, and Butch Reed in a six-man bout. Though still weakened from his illness, both mentally and physically, Mike received the loudest "pop" of the night.

The night was also important as it marked the introduction of World Class wrestling on the ESPN cable network. The show was in a coveted 8:00 p.m. timeslot, right before live boxing on Friday nights, and increased the promotion's nationwide exposure. Locally, in Texas, Adkisson maintained his territorial footprint, running about a dozen cities between regular stops and spot shows.

On July 27, the UWF, in association with Jim Crockett Promotions and the NWA, invaded Dallas for the first time. Considering the long relationship between the NWA and Adkisson, it was a surreal moment in wrestling history. But ironically, Adkisson had made his debut into pro wrestling in 1953 with an outlaw organization at odds with the Alliance, so it was fitting he was to end his career the same way.[299] Adkisson wasn't going to cave without a fight. Less than 15 miles away, east of Dallas in Mesquite, he held a rivaling show and declared it "fan appreciation night."

No matter how you looked at it, though, the UWF and NWA had superior talent, and drew a crowd of 7,500 at the Reunion Arena. In the co-main event, Bill Watts teamed with the Road Warriors to beat the Freebirds by disqualification, and newly crowned NWA world champion Dusty Rhodes defeated Ric Flair. Many in Dallas were surprised to learn that Rhodes had conquered the Nature Boy the night before in Greensboro during the finale of the Great American Bash tour. Others on the bill were Jim Duggan, Magnum T.A., the Rock and Roll Express, and the Midnight Express. Because of his vulnerable position in the talent fight, Adkisson used one of his secret weapons in promotion for his show. He touted the return of Kerry Von Erich, not in the ring, but just as a special appearance, and told enthusiasts they could take photos with him. Approximately 6,000 faithful Von Erich fans turned out to see Kerry, but instead of doing the promised photo op, he left the building early, leaving fans disappointed.[300] The promotional bad blood was at a peak, and Adkisson filed a lawsuit against Watts over their previous partnership in Oklahoma. The latter was served with papers when he arrived at the venue in Dallas on July 27.[301] The wrestlers who'd jumped from his promotion were also sued in a separate action for breach of contract.

As was par for the course, Watts and Crockett fell out of favor right about the same time as the Dallas program, and added the UWF to the list of enemy non-NWA entities active in the country.[302] In Memphis, Jerry Jarrett was a non-Alliance promoter on good terms with the organization in 1985, and benefited from joint shows with Crockett. But the tides had turned by 1986. With the UWF, Crockett and the NWA, and the WWF all coming to town, Memphis was one of the hottest battleground cities anywhere. From a successful run as a grappler and booker in Mid-South, Bill Dundee emerged back on the Memphis scene and feuded heavily with his perpetual nemesis, Jerry Lawler. On December 30, 1985, he shocked the territory by winning a loser-leaves-town bout over Lawler, sending the King packing. Three months later, Lawler made his triumphant return and drew big houses at the Mid-South Coliseum with Dutch Mantell against Dundee and Buddy Landel. He gained his revenge on Dundee in a heated cage match on April 7 and regained his Southern belt in the process. Away from the mat, Jarrett was layering his defense. He changed the name of his promotion from Continental Wrestling Association to Championship Wrestling Association, and to counter the UWF's incursion into Memphis in early June 1986, he lowered ticket prices.[303] On such occasions, he practically gave away his shows for $2 a pop, encouraging patronage and loyalty.

Jarrett held a free show on July 4 for Memphis fans celebrating Independence Day. His efforts coincided with the debut of Jim Crockett at the Liberty Bowl, a massive structure seating 60,000. If Crockett with his army of superstars was able to draw half that, Jarrett was in serious trouble. As it turned out, though, the people of Memphis were more interested in festivities and fireworks than WTBS wrestlers, and Crockett drew a mere 1,900. High ticket prices ($20, $50) were also responsible for the embarrassing turnout, and JCP had to reassess its strategy. The UWF's second program in Memphis drew half of its first, and Jarrett ran a unique bit of opposition at a local park. It was a softball doubleheader, and again, the populace proved its devotion to Lawler with the regular crew outdrawing the outsiders three to one.

In Florida, the local NWA affiliate was making the most of its relationship with Crockett, and was competitive against the WWF when Dusty Rhodes, Ric Flair, and other JCP stars were on the card. Without them, CWF was struggling, only drawing in the hundreds in formerly strong towns like Miami and Orlando. On September 2, 1985, a huge Battle of the Belts event in Tampa featured talent from the NWA and AWA and was syndicated in 15 markets.[304] In a two-of-three-falls match, Flair beat Wahoo McDaniel, and the AWA tag champions, the Road Warriors, brawled their way to a double count-out against Stan Hansen and Harley Race. A second Battle of the Belts followed on February 14 in Orlando, and Flair wrestled Barry Windham in a 40-minute classic ending in a double count-out, as did a match between McDaniel and Bruiser Brody. In another contest, 27-year-old Lex Luger beat Jesse Barr to capture the Southern championship.

A former pro football player from New York, Luger stood 6-foot-3 and weighed over 250 pounds. Learning the fundamentals of wrestling from famed coach Hiro Matsuda out of the Tampa office, the naturally charismatic Luger won the Southern belt for the first time from Wahoo McDaniel within weeks of his debut. His Battle of the Belts victory was his second reign, and he would carry the strap for the next five months before dropping a match to the Masked Superstar. But Luger's push continued, and he regained it a week later. Matsuda also mentored Japanese youngster Keiji Mutoh, who was but 23 years old and destined to be an international star. Mutoh competed as the White Ninja in the Florida territory, and gained plenty of experience. The son of Blackjack Mulligan, Kendall Windham, was just a skinny teenager when he went to the top in Florida, and he was a state heavyweight champion several times over.

Florida and every other territory was dealing with the World Wrestling Federation's mass marketing platform. When it came time for WrestleMania, everything stopped as if the WWF's tagline, "What the World Is Watching," was true. The second WrestleMania was more grandiose than the first, spread out over three live locations and featuring a lineup of celebrities, better CCTV venues, and expanded pay-per-view connectivity. On April 7, 1986, arena lights kicked on at the Nassau Coliseum in Uniondale, New York, the Rosemont Horizon outside Chicago, and at the Los Angeles Sports Arena for the action to begin. Hulk Hogan, as could be expected, was the main-event star, and he defeated his weighty rival, King Kong Bundy, in a cage match in Los Angeles. In Uniondale, Mr. T returned to defeat Roddy Piper by disqualification in a special boxing match, when the latter decided to bodyslam his opponent. A 20-man battle royal was the center of attention in Chicago, mostly because six current and former football players were participants, and all eyes were on the 335-pound "Refrigerator" William Perry, a popular defensive lineman for the Chicago Bears. Although Perry was dwarfed by the match's eventual winner, Andre the Giant, his appearance was national news. On the celebrity front, McMahon spared no expense. Ray Charles, Ozzy Osbourne, Tommy LaSorda, Ricky Schroder, Joe Frazier, Joan Rivers, Dick Butkis, Ed "Too Tall" Jones, Cathy Lee Crosby, and many others each had an on-camera role.

Attendance at the live shows didn't meet expectations, however. Chicago failed to sell out, seeing only half the attendance of an earlier WWF house show. Los Angeles was less than full too, but with increased ticket prices, the gates were satisfactory. Closed-circuit and pay-per-view buys could have been better, and counting the exorbitant costs to run the massive event, the WWF was fortunate to turn a profit. Journalists around the country, some of whom went to local CCTV showings, offered wide-ranging critiques. On one hand, the press loved the excitement, the ritzy atmosphere, and the varied matchups. On the other, they were unmoved by the action, annoyed by the celebrities, and cantankerous in their reporting. For McMahon, though, there was much to be savored. The WWF was back in the news, and WrestleMania was still the hottest ticket in the business.

CHAPTER SIXTEEN

GRAPPLING WITH TURBULENCE

With incredible size and magnetism, the Road Warriors were an extraordinary box-office attraction. They quickly rose from a mid-level regional position in Georgia to world class superstardom, and promoters were dying to add Hawk and Animal to their programs. Since both men were originally from Minnesota, it made sense for them to work for Verne Gagne, and the latter put the AWA world tag belts around their waists. But as Gagne's circuit deteriorated, the Road Warriors looked for better opportunities. They got a taste of bigger paydays in joint promotions with Jim Crockett in 1985, and the experiences opened their eyes to life away from the AWA. Toward the end of September 1985, they made three appearances with Crockett wrestlers in the Northwest, including in Portland and Seattle for promoter Don Owen.

On September 28, they lost a controversial match and their AWA belts to the Freebirds at Comiskey Park in Chicago, but a review of the finish saw the straps returned to the Warriors, much to the delight of fans. But in St. Paul the next day, there was no post-match review. Jim Garvin and Steve Regal beat them with outside help from the Freebirds to capture the AWA tag championship. The title switch was inevitable, and for the Warriors, it was exactly what they wanted. The money to be made wrestling for Crockett and overseas for All Japan Pro Wrestling was life changing, and for a time, just being free agents was quite suitable. After the first of the year, in 1986, they increased their bookings for Crockett in the Carolinas, Atlanta, and Philadelphia and did more TV to build up their stature in the promotion. And aside from a few trips back to Gagne's region to finish up their obligations there, that's how things remained.

The Road Warriors won the first annual Crockett Cup on April 19, 1986, and traveled to Minneapolis to help Gagne the next day. The AWA was staging its biggest event of the year, WrestleRock, and needed the Warriors on the bill to sell tickets. WrestleRock was the AWA's version of WrestleMania, and Gagne was also laying out a small fortune to give it a major-league feel.[305] He rented the humongous Metrodome Stadium and tried to land Minneapolis native Prince to perform during the show. But Prince was filming *Under the Cherry Moon* in France, so Gagne went with country singer Waylon Jennings, which seemed to contradict the WrestleRock theme.[306] The card featured 16 matches and 52 wrestlers and lasted more than six hours. An announcer declared it "the greatest event in professional wrestling history," and the media confirmed that neither WrestleMania had had that many bouts "in one location."[307]

Among the victors that night was Gagne himself over Sheik Adnan Al-Kaissie, as well as the Road Warriors, Giant Baba, Mike Rotundo and Barry Windham, and Nick Bockwinkel, who beat AWA world champion Stan Hansen by DQ. An estimated 22,000 spectators were on hand, and the gate was a little over $250,000, enough for the AWA to break even. All told, though, WrestleRock was "somewhat of a fizzle," according to *Minneapolis CityBusiness*. A few months later, Gagne told that paper, "Waylon wasn't right for our crowd. Only about 2,000 stayed around for his show. And I made a mistake in not having lower prices at the Metrodome for the kids."[308]

Gagne's was facing innumerable challenges, and his own front office was crumbling before his eyes. His partner and cohort for more than 25 years, Wally Karbo, severed ties to the company early in 1986, as did Blackjack Lanza, and in one fell swoop, Gagne lost two valuable assistants. He also lost his TV and arena rights in Winnipeg to the WWF, and it was believed that Lanza had a significant role in the transfer. As it reportedly happened, Lanza convinced CKND-TV station manager Don Brinton to drop the AWA telecast and replace it with the WWF's *Maple Leaf Wrestling*.[309] And since Brinton was also the AWA's local promoter, he simply shifted from Gagne's product to McMahon's at the Winnipeg Arena. Thus, the AWA was aced out, and the WWF moved in on March 17, 1986. The WWF snagged the AWA's TV time in Rockford as well, on WREX-13, and it cut Gagne off from another vital monthly stop.[310] The AWA was further weakened when Dennis Hilgart, an affiliate promoter in Wisconsin and Illinois since the 1960s, jumped to the WWF and helped McMahon gain a better foothold in Milwaukee. In Chicago, after drawing only 1,800 for his April 27 program at the Rosemont Horizon, Gagne downgraded to the smaller UIC Pavilion. Two months later, he lost his flagship station in Chicago (WCIU-26) and was forced way up the dial into a much less visible spot on WGBO-66.[311]

Gagne had some good young workers in 1986. Shawn Michaels, a standout from Texas, was teaming with Marty Jannetty as the Midnight Rockers, second-generation Curt Hennig was one-half of the tag champions with Scott Hall, and rotund Leon White was in his sophomore year as a pro grappler. White would later gain fame as Big Van Vader. In contrast, WWF castoffs Sgt. Slaughter and Jimmy Snuka were going through the motions, but carried name value and a certain amount of popularity. Nick Bockwinkel, at 51, was everlastingly consistent, and was still capable of going to the mat with anyone. More important to Gagne, Bockwinkel was trustworthy, and when it came time to move the AWA world title off Stan Hansen, he got the call. On June 29, 1986, in Denver, the plan was set in motion.[312] But Hansen refused to drop the belt, left the venue in a huff, and ended up taking the belt with him to Japan. With no other option, Gagne declared Bockwinkel champ by forfeit, and the latter began his fourth reign as AWA king.

The disparity between the AWA's success in having a national cable television program on ESPN and its stunningly bad box office attendance.

was unreal. Gagne's shows drew from the low hundreds on one end to a 2,000 maximum, with the exception of a few special programs. Despite the evident signs of collapse, Gagne was resilient, and kept trying to rebound. He went back into the Bay Area by landing a facility in Oakland, began working with Angelo Savoldi's Northeast-based International Championship Wrestling (ICW), and kickstarted a merchandising campaign geared toward kids. Similar to the LJN series of WWF action figures, Remco produced a line of AWA characters, plus a wrestling ring to go along with it, so children everywhere could play out their favorite matches in their living rooms.

Jim Crockett Promotions was also trying to get in on the act by releasing several branded action figures. Crockett told a reporter, "The licensing deals that are signed are in the five-to-six figure range, but I [won't give] you exact figures because I don't want to cause problems between my wrestlers. Ric Flair and Rock 'n' Roll Express dolls will be out by Christmas."[313] Merchandising was a logical step for JCP, now the second-strongest promotion in America. Added revenue streams were increasingly important, and Crockett was following the McMahon blueprint. He brought in top talent from other regions, expanded his TV network, and used cable to boost his promotion. But it is arguable that Crockett was ahead of McMahon in some ways too. His first Starrcade event, in 1983, was an innovative supershow, predating WrestleMania by 15 months. JCP was known for cultivating superior talent and carried the support of traditionalists over McMahon's product by far.

Upping its number of live programs and outdrawing the WWF in places like Philadelphia, JCP was on a roll. On February 7, 1986, Crockett staged a primetime special on WTBS, *Superstars on the Superstation*, and featured four big matches as decided by a fan vote. In the main event, Flair went over Ron Garvin, and the Jim Cornette–managed Midnight Express topped the Rock and Roll Express to capture the NWA world tag belts. Crockett got in on the celebrity craze by bringing in country music legend Willie Nelson, and his efforts to "go mainstream" were well timed. But expansion was the name of the game, and seeing that Crockett already had a presence in St. Louis, a complete takeover of that hallowed wrestling city was relatively easy. Things there were about as low as a promotion could get. Shareholder Harley Race was so discontented with the decline of business in St. Louis and the Central States that he bowed out completely, taking a personal loss of more than $500,000.[314] Verne Gagne didn't have the manpower to spare for St. Louis, and Bob Geigel was using a depleted crew in Kansas City. Neither could help the St. Louis cause, and the final co-sponsored SLWC–JCP show took place on February 8, 1986. Starting on March 2, it was all Crockett. Geigel retained a key role on WTBS telecasts because of his status as NWA president, and he continued to run the fragile Kansas City office.[315] House sizes in the Central States were stagnant, yet improved when Flair and other JCP wrestlers appeared. The Flair–Bruiser Brody feud was a short-term success, and Kansas City's Memorial Hall scored a rare sellout (2,800) on March 20, 1986, as Brody and Race teamed to beat Flair and Bob Brown in one of the promotion's last hurrahs. Across the border in Missouri, at the larger Municipal Auditorium, the WWF drew 6,000 that same night.

Crockett was committed to helping Geigel in his war against the WWF in Kansas City, and Geigel needed the assistance, but casual appearances by JCP stars weren't enough. On August 7, 1986, Geigel pulled in resources from Crockett and All Japan, but a headline bout between Flair and Dusty Rhodes drew only 1,000 people. It was an anguished result, and taking into consideration the UWF's recent debut in Kansas City, Geigel was ready to pull the plug. He came to an arrangement with Crockett, handing over active promotional rights to the territory, and as part of the deal, he kept a visible presence on TV and received a percentage of local gates.[316] As for Crockett, his idea for the once-thriving Central States territory was to keep the regional feel by organizing a secondary circuit made up of lower to mid-card JCP wrestlers and newcomers on the rise. And like he did with Geigel, he'd occasionally send his top stars to spike the box office. Booked by Bill Dundee, the territory would highlight Sam Houston, Denny Brown, the Italian Stallion, Mark Fleming, and Buddy Landel, among others, beginning on September 26.

The Central States were completely absorbed by JCP, and another old-time territory had succumbed to a national entity. In other parts of the country, Crockett invaded San Antonio, Albuquerque, Washington, D.C. (against the WWF), and Jacksonville, Florida (a neglected CWF town). Washington and Jacksonville were part of the exhaustive Great American Bash tour, which ran from July 1 to August 2, 1986, and included stops in

Philadelphia, Memphis, Charlotte, Cincinnati, Johnson City, and Atlanta. Attendance ranged from 1,900 in Memphis to 23,000 in Charlotte. High ticket prices hurt fan enthusiasm, but with a steep overhead, JCP wanted to ensure better box-office returns. Many stadiums were less than half full, and the revived country music gimmick fell flat once again. "We feel country music fans and wrestling fans are about the same," said Sandy Scott, a JCP event coordinator.[317] The AWA and UWF had believed the same thing, but it wasn't proving true. Nevertheless, Waylon Jennings, David Allen Coe, and George Jones were three of the musical performers at Bash programs around the country. The other major gimmick of the Bash was Ric Flair's successive string of NWA world title defenses, one for each night of the tour. He wrestled both the Road Warriors, Ricky Morton and Robert Gibson, Magnum T.A., and Nikita Koloff. On the 13th stop, in Greensboro on July 26, he was defeated by Dusty Rhodes in a cage bout and lost the championship. Flair regained the belt on August 9 in St. Louis. Rhodes, as booker for JCP, was a consistently strong creative force in 1986, and his well of ideas was seemingly endless.

That year, the famed Four Horsemen were born — Flair, Arn and Ole Anderson, Tully Blanchard, and manager J.J. Dillon. They wreaked a lot of havoc on Rhodes, the Rock and Roll Express, the Road Warriors, and any other wrestler who got in their way.[318] In May, Magnum T.A.'s rivalry with Nikita Koloff took a unique turn when Magnum, the baby-face, punched out NWA president Bob Geigel during a WTBS telecast. Geigel stripped Magnum of his U.S. title and announced a best-of-seven series for the belt, to be played out in July and August. Koloff ended up winning the classic series, four bouts to three. Another interesting scenario showcased Ricky Morton, weighing around 200 pounds, as a challenger to the 240-pound Flair. It was Morton's speed against the "dirtiest player in the game," and fans witnessed a number of good back-and-forth battles.

After an absence of more than a year, JCP yearned to return to Pittsburgh and wanted to rent the Civic Arena, the same venue the WWF used, but building officials remembered the egg the NWA laid at Three Rivers Stadium in May 1985. "They haven't been successful, obviously, so we wouldn't encourage them to come in here," explained Civic Arena marketing director Tom Rooney. "I can't speak for them, but I'm guessing they probably think the [Convention Center] was the reason they were not successful, and not the product. I would tend to disagree with that, because if we said we were going to do the Rolling Stones and we were going to do them on Mars, people would find a way to get there." In response, Sandy Scott told a reporter, "We're not worried about the past. We're very enthused about the future."[319] JCP didn't let up, filing a lawsuit to get into the building. Finally, Crockett secured a date, on October 24, 1986, and drew a crowd of 10,000 to the Arena.

Between August and December 1986, Crockett made incredible strides. On August 28, he returned to the Los Angeles area for the first time in more than a year and drew a crowd five times bigger than his June 1985 effort.[320] Shifting from the Olympic Auditorium to the Great Western Forum, a good-sized structure in Inglewood, Crockett's event drew 10,000 spectators, and Flair beat Rhodes by DQ in the main event. In an even bolder endeavor that sent shockwaves through the AWA, JCP went into Bloomington, Minnesota, on September 19 at the Met Center, and held a program in Verne Gagne's backyard.[321] Crockett and Gagne had silenced their cooperative efforts just a short time before, ending years of up-and-down business.[322]

But JCP entering Bloomington, and also Green Bay, Wisconsin, on September 18 was an aggressive move, and Crockett was now the one disregarding old territorial boundaries to press his expansion. On the whole, cooperation between promoters was at an all-time low. Pro Wrestling USA was a dead concept, and in many opinions, was doomed from day one. "Three years ago, I thought the promoters could get together and present a united front," Gagne told a reporter. "Unfortunately, we've gone our separate ways."[323] Demonstrating just how fractured things were, over the last nine months, Crockett had severed his agreements with Gagne, Bill Watts, Jerry Jarrett, and Jack Adkisson, and had already gone into the territories of three of them. JCP still was a member of the NWA, on good terms with Bob Geigel, Gary Juster, the Murnicks, Shohei Baba, Don Owen, Carlos Colon, Ron Fuller, and Hiro Matsuda and Duke Keomuka. For the NWA to stay cohesive, affiliates had conformed to Crockett's newly instituted booking policies. But how many more changes (and demands) would they agree to before the NWA was nothing but a liability? As it was, booking the world heavyweight champion had become a lot more difficult than in the past, and that in itself was a severe detriment. But it wasn't necessarily impossible to get help from Crockett in that regard. In 1986, Flair worked a few dates for Geigel, Owen, Fuller, Juster, the Murnicks, and Matsuda and Keomuka, plus went to Honolulu for Lia Maivia and Puerto Rico for Carlos Colon. But Flair's priority was always JCP cities.

In addition to Los Angeles and the Twin Cities, Crockett went into Kansas City, Wichita, and Omaha and added a regular stop in Washington at the D.C. Armory. Debuts in Chicago (December 14) and San Francisco (December 30) came before the end of the year, and JCP was definitely primed for bigger business in 1987.

Sadly, on October 14, in Charlotte, the blossoming career of 27-year-old Magnum T.A. ended when he suffered a broken neck in a car accident in Charlotte. The loss of a principal figure and popular idol was immeasurable, and JCP was weakened significantly. Magnum's in-ring rival Nikita Koloff turned fan favorite following the accident and helped revitalize the promotion, often teaming with Dusty Rhodes and going to war with the Four Horsemen. As a result of all the positive reaction he was receiving, Koloff was pushed into the main event of Starrcade against Ric Flair on November 27, 1986. Their bout, which ended in a double disqualification in 19 minutes, was staged in Atlanta before 14,000 spectators. On the Greensboro end of the show, in front of 16,000 fans, Tully Blanchard went over Dusty Rhodes for the world TV championship in a first-blood match. Another memorable contest in Atlanta was waged between the Road Warriors and the Midnight Express in a special scaffold match. The Warriors were victorious, and Express manager Jim Cornette delivered the most incredible bump of the night when he fell from the 25-foot scaffold to the mat below. His death-defying drop was taken at great personal risk, and he paid the price with a torn ACL in his right knee that required surgery. Starrcade, dubbed the "Night of the Skywalkers," was a success, and with live attendance and CCTV, the gate was nearly $1 million.

"Big" Bubba Rogers, Dick Murdoch, Brad Armstrong, and Rick Rude were talent acquisitions for JCP, and, in December 1986, Crockett picked up one of wrestling's top free agents, Barry Windham. Windham, it can be remembered, jumped from the Mid-Atlantic region to the WWF on no notice in 1984, but he was a box office draw, and booker Dusty Rhodes wanted him back. All things considered, it was a smart move. A growing segment of the audience had grown dissatisfied with Crockett's week-to-week productions, and was tired of never-ending feuds and lackluster TV shows. The arrival of Windham boosted interest in the immediate aftermath of Starrcade. But there was a guy in Florida with a little over a year's experience who was destined to make a national impact as well. He was Lex Luger, and Rhodes was watching his progression very closely.

Over in the UWF, owner Bill Watts was a busy man. He came out of retirement for two months of active competition in mid-1986, partnering with fan favorites Jim Duggan and Ted DiBiase against the Freebirds. His syndication network was growing impressively, and dozens and dozens of stations were signing on, in places such as Los Angeles, San Francisco, Minneapolis, and South Florida. But prime television spots were costly, and the UWF was racking up sizable weekly bills. He planned for a major live event at the Rosemont Horizon outside Chicago in October, but that show was abruptly canceled under strange circumstances. It was later alleged that an opposing promotion paid officials at the venue to call off the booking.[324] If true, it illustrated the kind of open hostilities in the grappling world, and fanned the warfare even more.

Watts wanted a presence in the Dallas–Fort Worth area, and within a two day span in October, he debuted his syndicated show there and introduced *Power Pro Wrestling* TV tapings from Fort Worth's Cowtown Coliseum. On November 9, at a *UWF Wrestling* taping in Tulsa, each of the company's three championships changed hands. One Man Gang won over Terry Gordy by forfeit to become the UWF world champion. (Gordy was injured in a car accident and unable to wrestle.) Leroy Brown and Bill Irwin won the tag straps from John Tatum and Jack Victory, and Savannah Jack captured the TV belt from Buddy Roberts.

Gifted English wrestler Chris Adams was a mainstay on the UWF circuit before going to jail for 90 days following a June 1986 assault. Just prior to showing up for Watts, Adams was actually a claimant to the heavyweight title in Dallas, but he walked on World Class, leaving Jack Adkisson to create a fictitious title switch from Adams to Black Bart. Adams missed the big Thanksgiving program at the Superdome in New Orleans on November 27, 1986, a show that drew 13,000 fans. Champion One Man Gang lost to Jim Duggan by disqualification but won a two-ring battle royal, while Steve Williams beat Michael Hayes in a cage. Former Blade Runner Sting was displaying much improvement, and his tag team with

Eddie Gilbert went a long way to round his sharp edges as a performer. The duo feuded with the Fantastics and held the UWF tag belts.

In keeping up with the new norms of pro wrestling, Watts offered many of his top stars guaranteed-money contracts to safeguard his promotion from future raids. Naturally, DiBiase, Williams, Gordy, and Duggan were signed, but in late 1986, when the promotion became cash-strapped, Watts found himself backed into a corner. The situation was compounded by a collapse of the oil industry, and in the South, people were losing their jobs left and right.[325] Attendance for UWF shows dropped dramatically. To alleviate some of his cash problems, Watts released several of his top acts from their contracts, Duggan among them. Duggan was a leading attraction in the UWF, and wasn't someone Watts's budding national organization could afford to lose.

Instability was also hitting Jack Adkisson hard in Dallas. His son Kerry Von Erich was still recovering from his horrific ankle injury, and an optimistic newspaper report in August 1986 suggested he'd be back training inside three months.[326] World Class needed him as soon as possible as weekly house shows were drawing meager crowds, sometimes less than 200 people. In looking for help, Adkisson landed George Scott, recently displaced from his job in the WWF, to book his promotion.[327] Rumor had it that it was some type of working relationship with Vince McMahon, but other than WWF regular Ricky Steamboat appearing on the October 12 Cotton Bowl bill, there was nothing to the speculation.

Adkisson picked up Bam Bam Bigelow, who went by Crusher Yurkov, George Wells (Master Gee), Tony Atlas, and Scott Casey. Bruiser Brody was a reliable face on World Class shows in 1986, and he engaged in a heavy feud with Gary Hart's charge, Abdullah the Butcher. On October 12 at the Cotton Bowl, Brody beat Abdullah in a cage bout, although he lost a loser-leaves-Texas rematch on Christmas night in Dallas. The Von Erichs were always in the thick of things, with Kevin going over Black Bart for the local world title at the Cotton Bowl in October, and Kevin and Mike feuding with Brian Adias and Al Madril. Adkisson returned to the ring himself as his alter-ego Fritz Von Erich to topple Abdullah the Butcher in a special claw-hold-versus-sleeper contest on November 27. Kerry was visible on TV too, and at one point, he was double-teamed by Adias and

Madril and, according to the storyline, suffered a setback in his recovery because of the beating he took.

The truth was Kerry was in no condition to wrestle anytime in late 1986 and early 1987. Plans for expansion outside of Texas were a pipe dream for World Class without Kerry and at least a few other recognizable stars. Behind the curtain, the promotion was in perpetual chaos, and George Scott was constantly butting heads with Gary Hart and David Manning, two of Adkisson's loyal assistants. Adkisson then invested an unknown amount of money to acquire the television contracts for San Antonio–based USA All-Star Wrestling, the last line to Joe Blanchard's old territory. USA was shutting down for good, and part of Adkisson's arrangement included future TV tapings at Gilley's Club in Pasadena, Texas, near Houston.

Montreal was the textbook image of a territory in turbulence. Following the deal made between Vince McMahon and International Wrestling, Dino Bravo, co-owner of the IW group, had certain expectations. He anticipated an upper-card berth on WWF programs north of the border, and he was sometimes given his proper due. But other times he was tossed into the middle of a card, and essentially dismissed. Bravo thought he was getting the respect he deserved when he was booked to wrestle Hulk Hogan at the Forum on January 13, 1986. For fans in Montreal, it was a dream match, but shortly before the card, WWF officials rebooked the show, pitting Hogan with Bob Orton and Bravo against Big John Studd. The deceptive marketing ploy was an immense disappointment to the 20,000 spectators in attendance, and to Bravo himself. It's believed the change was because of Bravo's popularity in Montreal, whereas Hogan was the WWF's customary hero. And they didn't want him shown up. Bravo quit the promotion and restarted International Wrestling in Montreal without the rights to the Forum, since the WWF had an exclusive contract. From Vince McMahon's point of view, Bravo's move was inconsequential. His promotion was drawing astronomical crowds in Montreal without his participation, notably a house of 23,000 on August 18. The WWF also brought aboard the Rougeau Brothers, Jacques and Raymond, two well-known Montreal grapplers. In October 1986, IW stars Bravo, Rick Martel, and Tom Zenk jumped to the WWF for full-time gigs, with Bravo as a heel managed by Johnny V and Martel and Zenk as a popular tag team known as the Can-Am Connection. The local Montreal office continued, but it was no longer the center of any kind of territory. It too had become a *bona fide* indie.

Looking at the Honolulu-based promotion of Lia Maivia, it was obvious she was trying to do a number of big things in 1986. Enhanced by a weekend timeslot on SCORE (Financial News Network), Polynesian Pro Wrestling was seen across the United States, and Maivia was exceedingly determined to pursue expansion. She invested tremendous sums of money rounding up stateside talent and venues in California, and then flew in her core wrestlers for shows in Los Angeles, San Luis Obispo, and San Jose. With booker Lars Anderson, Maivia crafted an ambitious plan to promote further in Calgary, Juneau, Seattle, and the Midwest in March and April 1986. The challenges for a stateside operation to expand in such a fashion were hard enough without first having to fly more than 2,500 miles to reach the U.S. coast. But Maivia charged ahead, and her California shows drew in the low hundreds with wrestlers such as Jerry Lawler, Kevin Sullivan, Tatsumi Fujinami, and Jimmy Snuka.

The financial losses were adding up, and an April program in San Jose only drew 25 paid spectators.[328] Her home crowds were not much better, and the office hoped to make up serious ground with its second annual Hot Summer Night at Aloha Stadium on August 9, 1986. With 20 matches, the event was an astonishing production, pulling together international wrestlers for yet another massive undertaking. Antonio Inoki, Bruiser Brody, the original Sheik, and phenomenon Keiji Mutoh were on the bill, but lack of interest and bad weather prevented the show from being a success. Only 1,900 people ventured to the stadium, more than 10,000 less than in 1985, and PPW was facing a real crisis. The $28,000 gate might have just covered rent on the venue, but very little else, and Maivia was left to pay the remainder of expenses out of pocket. On the heels of this, the Honolulu office closed Polynesian Pro Wrestling and incorporated World Pacific Wrestling, a new entity with new ideas. Maivia and her partners, Lars Anderson (Larry Heiniemi) and Ati So'o, moved their regular shows from the Blaisdell Arena to the Ilikai Hotel and put less emphasis on expansion. Two years later, Maivia and her cohorts were accused of extorting money and threatening harm on a rival promoter and endured a lengthy court process to clear their names.[329] In November 1989, they were acquitted of all charges.[330]

Like in Montreal, all traces of Hawaii as a wrestling territory vanished, but between small independents and the WWF, pro wrestling lived on. In fact, when the WWF debuted in Honolulu on July 10, 1986, an enthusiastic crowd of 5,000 turned out. As the *Honolulu Star-Bulletin* noted, the WWF were the "folks" who brought "entertainment wrestling," and a new era in Hawaiian grappling dawned.[331]

MANIFEST DESTINY

The myriad effects of wrestling's cable television success and national expansion altered the industry forever, and Vincent K. McMahon was the general in charge of the revolution. His bold maneuvering in the face of adversity was impressive, and McMahon's ambition had forced professional wrestling to evolve at light speed, in tune with technological advances and cultural shifts. Ultimately, every promoter was going to have to compromise to some extent when it came to cable TV and territorial boundaries. That is, if the old cooperatives were to remain in place. But McMahon cared little about the timeless cooperatives, and displayed the imagination and gall needed to turn the entire wrestling world upside down.

"When Vince took over from his father, he saw the Manifest Destiny which the WWF is approaching today," explained Basil DeVito, the vice-president of marketing of Titan Sports, to a reporter for the *Globe and Mail* in 1986. "It was in Vince's mind. It has been said that our best research is lodged firmly in Vince McMahon's gut."[332] Relying heavily on instincts, McMahon was delivering his vision to the masses, and he was arguably the hardest-working man in the industry. He wasn't afraid to take chances, nor was he fearful of spending money if the potential payoff made sense, whether it was in the short term or over the long haul. In most cases, exposure was his main concern, as was selling the World Wrestling Federation as a vehicle for family entertainment. The WWF wasn't about knock-down, drag-out professional wrestling anymore, and his dad's business philosophies were obsolete — well, most of them.

"There was too much emphasis on the sports element and not enough on entertainment in the old days," McMahon said to *Sports Illustrated* in 1991. "Now we call it sports entertainment. We don't want to de-emphasize the athleticism of wrestling; these are great athletes with great charisma. But in the WWF, entertainment is the key."[333] With the imagery of bigger-than-life characters and fantastical performances, the WWF was in a world all its own. The high-gloss television productions, well-crafted matches and interviews, and upscale live shows, each were the standard for professionalism, and elevated McMahon's promotion far above the competition. And by devising a range of popular characters, the WWF was geared particularly toward young people. That marketing strategy went hand in hand with the sales of merchandise, and a cartoon series on Saturday mornings. Altogether, the WWF appeared to be a wholesome environment perfect for people of all ages.

By changing the demographics, McMahon saw increased advertising opportunities and another huge revenue stream. For 30-second commercials during WWF programs in 1985, companies were doling out a whopping $30,000, and there was still room to grow.[334] The exciting, yet sanitized, product appealed to national advertisers like Dr. Pepper, Mars, Bic, and Gillette, and again, the old stereotypes about wrestling were no longer relevant. "Three years ago, there was a reluctance," explained John Howard, sales manager for Titan Sports in 1987. "Many advertisers found wrestling objectionable, even though they hadn't watched it in a long time. About two years ago, things started going our way. There's been an improvement of the product and the image of the WWF."[335]

The outside-the-ring troubles of Jimmy Snuka and the arrests of several of his stars for raucous behavior or driving-related offenses were the kind of negative publicity McMahon wanted to avoid. On top of that, wrestling in general was dealing with a sizable drug problem. Many well-known stars were hooked on cocaine. Steroids were also highly prevalent, but the media rarely touched on that subject. The WWF avoided it as well. But on the whole, McMahon ran a tight ship and controlled the comings and goings with precision. Of course, he surrounded himself with trusted allies who helped on the road. Blackjack Lanza, Chief Jay Strongbow, Gorilla Monsoon, and Pat Patterson were among McMahon's agents, the men responsible for corralling the talent, setting up match finishes, and collecting box-office percentages. Patterson was one of his go-to idea men, and Monsoon became a primary TV commentator. At the very top of Titan Sports, Vince had only one equal, and that was his wife, Linda.

When it came to business, McMahon could play hardball with the best, and he asserted control over his performers with stunning intensity. In 1985, he compelled 99 percent of his roster to sign two-year contracts.[336] In addition, he began trademarking his grapplers' names to ensure that characters developed on WWF telecasts were the property of his company. With venues, McMahon was more than happy to sign exclusive deals, which would keep his adversaries from utilizing the same buildings. But when that was not possible, he added stipulations to his arena contracts, blocking a rival group from using the venue 10 days prior and 10 days following a WWF show.

McMahon's strong-mindedness was an asset from the point of view of Titan Sports, but from an outside perspective, he was difficult to deal with at times. Two of his earliest agreements, made at the beginning of his national expansion, ended badly and resulted in lawsuits. The first was his arrangement with Mike LeBell of Los Angeles, established in October 1982, which gave way to the WWF's debut in southern California. It was an important step in the organization's growth, and LeBell was believed to have been well compensated. But somewhere along the line, there was a falling-out, and LeBell sued Titan for money he claimed he was owed.[337] Part of LeBell's problem was he had nothing in writing, only an oral agreement, and his legal action was dismissed.[338] George Cannon, McMahon's business partner in Detroit from 1983 to 1986, actually brought suit against Titan Sports over the Superstars of Wrestling trademark.[339] A court later determined that neither party owned the trademark and restored full rights to promoter Albert Patterson of Milwaukee.

As previously mentioned, George Scott had been bumped out of his position as booker a few months after WrestleMania II, and McMahon himself took on the role. Changes to personnel were abundant and, over the course of 1986, the WWF acquired Dory Funk Jr., Jesse Barr (Jimmy Jack Funk), Billy Jack Haynes, Dick Slater, Butch Reed, and Harley Race. The addition of two former NWA champions, Funk and Race, deepened the credibility of the promotion's roster by a wide margin. But McMahon liked to put his own spin on things, and gave both grapplers otherwise forgettable gimmicks. Dory was referred to as "Hoss," a play on his Texas heritage, and Race was known as the "King" after winning a July tournament in Foxboro. Race wore a crown and cape, and became just another performer on the wild and wooly WWF circuit. Tough guy Butch Reed dyed his hair blond and took Slick, a fellow Kansas City alumnus, as his manager.

The organization's eccentricity factor skyrocketed with the arrival of two unorthodox characters, Koko B. Ware and the Honky Tonk Man. Ware was a talented mid-card grappler from the UWF, known as the Birdman, and he went to the ring carrying his trusty bird, Frankie. As for Honky Tonk Man, he was pro wrestling's number-one Elvis impersonator, complete with the signature jumpsuits, the mutton chops, and a flashy guitar. For old-school fans who took wrestling very seriously, the influx of animals and goofy gimmicks solidified the WWF's full transition into a three-ring circus. But instead of clowns, McMahon had the Machines, a masked group of monstrous heroes consisting of Super, Giant, and Big Machine. Under the hoods, they were the Masked Superstar, Andre the Giant, and Blackjack Mulligan, respectively.

Roddy Piper took time off from his active schedule after WrestleMania and filmed the comedy *Body Slam*, a wrestling-themed movie also featuring the Tonga Kid, Captain Lou Albano, and cameos by Bruno Sammartino and Ric Flair. A few months later, Piper reemerged as a fan favorite at odds with flamboyant Adrian Adonis, and crowds were clearly in his corner. Paul Orndorff went in the other direction. Mr. Wonderful had been a babyface since 1985 and battled Piper and Bob Orton Jr. umpteen times. During a Poughkeepsie TV taping on June 24, 1986, Orndorff attacked his tag partner, Hulk Hogan, after winning a match against Big John Studd and King Kong Bundy by DQ. He subsequently took Bobby Heenan as his manager and entered a lengthy feud with Hogan, challenging for the WWF championship. There was immense interest in that feud, and houses popped across the country.

In Landover, Maryland, Hogan and Orndoff drew 20,000, another 18,000 in Chicago, and more than 11,000 in Minneapolis. The combination of that main event and a special Sam Muchnick tournament even sold out the Kiel Auditorium in St. Louis. Appropriately, Harley Race topped Ricky Steamboat in the tourney final for honors. But none of these crowds came close to the success of Hogan versus Orndorff in Toronto on August 28, 1986, at CNE Stadium. The Big Event, as it was called, was the culmination of an incredible promotional campaign, and the program was hyped on TV, radio, and in newspapers. Early reports predicted attendance around 40,000, which if realized, would be simply astonishing. The WWF managed to surpass that number with relative ease, and ended up with nearly 65,000 screaming patrons, a complete sellout of the venue, and an unbelievable C$1.1 million gate.[340]

On November 24, the WWF drew its second sellout in eight months at Madison Square Garden behind the strength of the Hogan-Orndorff feud, pitting them on opposite sides of a tag match. The unlikely combination of Hogan and Piper teamed to beat Orndorff and Race. For a time in 1986, McMahon ran a strong "A" lineup at the Garden and other major cities without Hogan, and gave the Hulkster time off to rest. And when the lucrative Orndorff feud was ready to set the business ablaze, he was in prime condition. Good thing, too, because McMahon booked the "Ugandan Giant" Kamala for Hogan next, and they did great business around the horn as well with big sellers in Chicago, Richfield, Toronto, and Oakland.

In one of the hottest angles of 1986, Intercontinental champion Randy Savage used a timekeeper's bell to "injure" the throat of Ricky Steamboat, putting him out of action. Interviews with Ricky's concerned wife, Bonnie, and doctors proclaiming him unfit to compete built the drama steadily until Steamboat made his return in January 1987. With two of the organization's top grapplers matching up, fans were promised a throwback-type wrestling match, an occurrence that definitely stood out on WWF cards. In December 1986, the Dynamite Kid, rated among the top five best pound-for-pound wrestlers in the world, suffered a devastating back injury during a bout in Hamilton, Ontario. One-half of the WWF tag champions at the time, Dynamite would be in no condition to wrestle anytime soon, but he showed amazing grit by presence alone on January 26, 1987, when partner Davey Boy Smith went through the motions in a title loss to the Hart Foundation.

To meet the demands of business and to stay ahead of his competition, Vince McMahon was constantly modifying and updating aspects of his empire. The offices of Titan Sports, with more than 70 full-time employees, relocated from Greenwich to Stamford, Connecticut, in September 1986.[341] That same month, their entire TV setup was revamped, with a new and improved *Superstars of Wrestling* syndicated show making its debut on September 6 and the inaugural *Wrestling Challenge* program starting the next day. As a result of these changes, *Championship Wrestling* and *All Star Wrestling*, both long-running telecasts, were no more.[342] The previous incarnation of *Superstars of Wrestling* was repackaged for affiliates and renamed *WWF Wrestling Spotlight*. McMahon halted the routine TV tapings in Poughkeepsie and Brantford and instead recorded three weeks of programs from various arenas around the country, naturally, every three weeks.[343] *Wrestling TNT* was also put to pasture by the USA Network.

The WWF wanted to end deals with stations in which they paid for their TV time. For example, since 1983, McMahon had been paying KHJ in Los Angeles for its Saturday morning timeslot. The fee was $2,500 a week when the deal originated, and undoubtedly went up each year. The advent of the FOX Network in October 1986 provided a new opportunity, and McMahon offered the standard barter deal, the "5/7 split," for placement on LA's KTTV-11. FOX agreed and added *Superstars of Wrestling* to its lineup on Saturday mornings at 10:00. For a couple of months at the end of 1986, McMahon had his shows running on both stations, but KHJ canceled the WWF program, and *Wrestling Challenge* became the WWF's primary telecast on KTTV. The market was covered by *Superstars of Wrestling* as well, at 11:00 a.m. on Saturdays from a station in San Diego (XETV-6).

WrestleMania III was right around the corner and was shaping up to be the biggest event in the sport's history. Andre the Giant, McMahon's "Eighth Wonder of the World," had recently returned to the promotion after filming *The Princess Bride* in Europe and would figure prominently on the bill. But his heel turn and challenge of Hulk Hogan for the WWF world title took a lot of his fans by surprise, even though much of the smart crowd knew it was coming. The shock on Hogan's face when Andre violently tore his shirt during a segment of "Piper's Pit" was palpable. Both wrestlers were considered unbeatable, only adding to the thrilling nature of the match. Randy Savage and Ricky Steamboat were slated to battle on the undercard, as were Roddy Piper and Adrian Adonis. Adding to the mystique of the program was the venue itself, the massive Pontiac Silverdome outside Detroit, with a seating capacity of 80,000 for football. But without the need of a field, there was the potential for more than 90,000 spectators and a possible world-record audience.

While Steamboat and Savage were expected to put on a clinic, the Hogan–Andre matchup was more about emotion and drama than fundamentals. Andre was past his prime, suffering from a bad back, and had wrestled only once since September. Hogan was versed at wrestling sizable foes and did a pretty standard routine, but Andre's condition limited everything. But the storytelling was the most important factor, and for WrestleMania to live up to the hype, Hogan and Andre had to deliver. On March 29, 1987, the legendary Aretha Franklin opened the show with "America the Beautiful" as a reported 93,173 fans looked on. Vince McMahon proved once again he knew what he was doing. The production values, sound, and commentary were top quality, and the finishes were sound. Piper went over Adonis, Harley Race beat Junkyard Dog, and the Honky Tonk Man defeated Jake Roberts.

The charismatic Jim Duggan, a transplant from the UWF, didn't have a regular spot on the card, but he still made an impact by interfering in the tag bout between the Iron Sheik and Nikolai Volkoff and the Killer Bees (B. Brian Blair and Jim Brunzell). His actions got the Bees disqualified, but his patriotic gimmick won over the crowd. Steamboat pinned Savage to capture the Intercontinental belt in the best match of the evening, and to this day, is fondly remembered as one of WrestleMania's greatest of all time. In the main event, Andre and Hogan carried the passion of the energized crowd. Just before the 12-minute mark, Hogan slammed his 500-pound opponent, landed his legdrop, and covered Andre for a successful pin. The scene was remarkable, and represented a symbolic passing of the torch from Andre to Hogan. The program wasn't perfect, but the enormity of the spectacle and the sheer awesomeness of Hogan and Andre displayed the extraordinary power of WrestleMania.

Taking into consideration the live gate, merchandise sales, closed-circuit, and pay-per-view, the extravaganza generated over $17 million.[344] Interestingly, the attendance of WrestleMania was later disputed, assessed at about 78,000, but the true significance lay in just how far out front in the wrestling war McMahon was by 1987.

Who was even close? Jim Crockett Promotions and the UWF were making progress expanding their syndication networks. But could either promotion draw 78,000 to a venue anywhere in the country? Could they draw even half that number? The UWF was losing ground in its base region, and house numbers at the usually reliable Superdome in New Orleans were sinking fast. The AWA and World Class were a tier below, and in the remaining "territories" (Florida, Alabama, Memphis, and Portland) business was topsy-turvy. And if they were struggling in their natural areas of operation, how were they a threat to McMahon?

They weren't, of course, but that didn't mean the war was over. There was ample room for talent stealing, pay-per-view squabbles, and quarrels over arena rights. After WrestleMania III, the WWF added Bill Eadie and Barry Darsow as Ax and Smash in the tag team Demolition, as well as Ken Patera and Bam Bam Bigelow. In May and June 1987, it grabbed five others while simultaneously hurting the UWF, JCP, and AWA. One Man Gang was a recent UWF world champion, having lost his claim to Big Bubba Rogers on April 19 in Oklahoma, and debuted in the WWF on May 12. Three days later, Ted DiBiase declared his WWF loyalty in Houston. After a May 22 program in Richmond, Rick Rude, holder of the NWA world tag team belts with Manny Fernandez, jumped ship and made his first appearance for the WWF in early June. Lastly, the Midnight Rockers (Marty Jannetty and Shawn Michaels), left the AWA and made their debut on June 3.

The Rockers didn't have much of a shelf life. In fact, they were gone before anyone knew they were even there, promptly fired after an incident away from the arena. But there was a much more visible out-of-the-ring episode, one that made national news and hurt the image of the WWF. On May 26, 1987, "Hawksaw" Jim Duggan and his wrestling nemesis, the

Iron Sheik, were driving together on the Garden State Parkway in New Jersey toward Asbury Park, where they had a show that night. They were stopped by a state trooper and found to have an open container of alcohol, a small amount of marijuana, and three grams of cocaine.[345] Both men were charged, and the WWF suspended them. Since Duggan was a good guy and the Sheik a rulebreaker, the situation was a public relations nightmare, and the media didn't let it slide. Wally Patrick of the *Asbury Park Press* wrote, "So forget about the allegations of alcohol and drugs. What were the Sheik and Hacksaw doing cruising down the Parkway together?"[346]

Regardless of Duggan's troubles up "north," he was still missed by Bill Watts and UWF fans. At a time of expansion for UWF, the losses of Duggan, One Man Gang, and finally Ted DiBiase were painstaking, and put a major crimp in its positive growth. Going into 1987, the Universal Wrestling Federation was syndicated in more than 80 markets and possessed a boast-worthy locker room of grapplers. With venues booked from Atlanta to Los Angeles, Watts was angling for his first national run. Ticket sales were good in Kansas City and Albuquerque in January and February in advance of the UWF's first West Coast swing, beginning on March 25 in San Bernardino. Watts smartly used Chavo Guerrero, an old Los Angeles favorite, in a primary role, and at the Olympic Auditorium on March 27, Guerrero won a Bunkhouse battle royal. In Stockton, Chavo also co-won a special I-Quit First Blood Battle Royal with Steve Williams. The California tour wasn't a bad first attempt, but Watts wasn't making enough money from his live shows to pay his expenses. Syndication costs alone were doing him in, and Watts was dropping $50,000 a week.[347] In April, he reached his breaking point and agreed to sell his entire operation to Jim Crockett Promotions for more than $4 million.[348] Watts was headed off for retirement.

Crockett's purchase gave him a ready-made product, established feuds, and a broad network of television stations. JCP was a greatly strengthened wrestling organization, and, on paper, was now better suited to engage the WWF in terms of manpower and exposure. Between the syndication packages of JCP and UWF, the company had nearly 200 stations, and aside from some overlap, Crockett was now in the same stratosphere as Vince McMahon, who was up and over the 200-station mark. The *UWF Wrestling* and *Power Pro Wrestling* telecasts were highly rated as well, which was a huge benefit to Crockett. Once finalized, on May 1, 1987, the deal all but guaranteed that the wrestling war was a two-promotion field down the stretch.

News of the sale was reported on May 6, 1987, and it was suggested that Crockett's purchase of the UWF gave "it more professional wrestling events per year than any promoter in the nation."[349] It was an impressive statement, if true, and seemingly shifted a lot of momentum in JCP's direction. All year, Crockett and booker Dusty Rhodes had been fostering a national circuit. Starting in January and continuing through April, they invaded Amarillo, Hammond, Waco, Houston, Boston, and Phoenix. On February 15, in conjunction with promoter Angelo Mosca, JCP returned to Toronto for the first time since June 1984, and staged a TV taping in Brantford, Ontario, the next day. Crockett was increasingly bold, and it was appropriate going into WWF strongholds. But JCP was also showing a certain amount of aggressiveness toward fellow NWA members. On January 16, 1987, JCP promoted a show in Hollywood, Florida, without CWF cooperation or approval.

Crockett held an additional unilateral program in Jacksonville on January 21. As a result, the Tampa office felt betrayed for two reasons. The first related to a promise Rhodes made on the way out the door from CWF to Crockett. According to the *Wrestling Observer*, Rhodes said he'd never run opposition, and the local office trusted him.[350] The second reason pertained to the National Wrestling Alliance and the adherence to specific territorial boundaries. Crockett and his Florida brethren, Hiro Matsuda and Duke Keomuka, had standing in the NWA and were privy to all rights and privileges. But considering the weakened state of the Alliance in 1987, what were those rights and privileges? Most sources were already referring to Crockett's promotion as the NWA, discounting the membership of every other dues-paying promoter. In a spiteful move, a CWF announcer told viewers that Ric Flair was refusing to defend his championship locally to make the NWA titleholder look bad.[351] Florida booker Kevin Sullivan then opened a back-channel line of communication to the Dallas office to discuss bringing WCCW world champion Kevin Von Erich to the region. Furthermore, there was speculation that the Florida office was going to band together with associates in Alabama, Kansas City, Portland, and possibly Dallas to form their own rival entity to JCP and the WWF.[352]

But before anything was decided, Rhodes and Crockett went to Tampa in mid-February and struck a deal. The terms were similar to the one JCP made with Bob Geigel for the Central States circuit. JCP would take over the territory, coordinate talent, and control television operations.[353] In exchange, Matsuda, Keomuka, and Mike Graham would receive an even split from live gates after Crockett collected a 10 percent booking fee.

At about the time Florida was being scooped up by JCP, Crockett was realizing the irreparable flaws in the Central States promotion. Four months had been devoted to the project, yet houses were still in the 200–300 range in Kansas City, with St. Joseph faring a little better on occasion. Unwilling to lose more money, Crockett withdrew his wrestlers in late February, and on March 6, 1987, Bob Geigel resumed active control of the territory. The purchase of the UWF and the arrangement in Florida more than made up for the loss of business in Kansas, Missouri, and Iowa, and JCP appeared to be on the right track.

On the talent front, Crockett imported one of wrestling's fastest rising stars, Lex Luger, from Florida, who didn't waste any time in joining the Four Horsemen. He formed a team with Tully Blanchard for the second annual Jim Crockett Sr. Memorial Cup Tag Tournament, held on April 10 and 11, 1987, in Baltimore. The tournament featured 24 teams, and only one was from a non-JCP entity — Giant Baba and Isao Takagi from All Japan. Luger and Blanchard were an unstoppable duo, defeating the MOD Squad, the Armstrongs, and Baba and Takagi before facing off with Dusty Rhodes and Nikita Koloff in the finals. Rhodes and Koloff, the undeniable heroes, beat Bill Dundee and the Barbarian, Rick Rude and Manny Fernandez, and the Midnight Express (now comprised of Bobby Eaton and Stan Lane) to reach the deciding bout. With the support of the courageous Magnum T.A., who attended the event, Rhodes and Koloff beat their foes in 17 minutes to win the $1 million prize. At the gate, the Crockett Cup failed to live up to expectations. The Baltimore Arena didn't sell out either night, and when contrasting production values to WrestleMania III, which took place days before, it was like comparing apples to oranges.

But JCP retained a gritty, old-school wrestling flavor adored by fans around the world — the antithesis of the bubblegum atmosphere created by the WWF. The promotions appealed to different audiences. JCP didn't strive to reach the same people who watched Saturday morning cartoons. Ric Flair's "Space Mountain" references, the gang mentality of the Four Horsemen, and the never-ending stream of bloody matches were geared toward adults. Crockett didn't have animal mascots, nor did he force-feed wild gimmicks to his loyal patrons. When Lex Luger made his debut, he did so as a former football player strongman, and not wearing an over-the-top superhero costume to build some imaginary mystique. The WWF created characters, and in 1987, with Honky Tonk Man, the hair-cutting Brutus Beefcake, and Koko B. Ware, they were becoming all the more exaggerated.

Longtime fans gravitated toward Crockett and his "NWA." But JCP had a number of challenges in its quest for supremacy, and raising production values on its larger-scale shows was crucial. There was also the question of whether Dusty Rhodes, in his position as booker, had overstayed his welcome on top of the promotion. Since 1984, Dusty had been a primary fan favorite and matchmaker, and his feuds with Ric Flair and Tully Blanchard were exhaustive. His Crockett Cup victory in April was another sign that "Dustymania" was there to stay. However, the overexposure of Rhodes was only part of the problem, and fans were tired of JCP's angles across the board.

Crockett trusted Rhodes and gave him the keys to the kingdom. But wasteful spending, repetitive angles, and a lack of foresight were gradually killing their business. The UWF situation, for example, was a possible game-changer, but from the jump Rhodes failed to hit the right notes. He missed an important opportunity for an interpromotion feud — akin to WCW versus the NWO, and instead pushed a mid-card JCP grappler, "Big" Bubba Rogers, as the UWF champion. As part of the UWF buyout, Crockett attained the lease for posh offices in Dallas, and he spent an exorbitant amount of money on a new plane to shuttle his wrestlers from date to date. To be a big-time player, big-time investments were needed, and Crockett demonstrated, time after time, he was all in. But so was Vince McMahon.

The real rivalry was just beginning.

CHAPTER EIGHTEEN

LOYALTY
VERSUS MONEY

The rapid downfall of the Universal Wrestling Federation represented the harsh business reality of pro wrestling in the 1980s, and a lot of people who were not privy to insider information didn't see it coming. After all, Bill Watts appeared to be highly successful. His television programs garnered above-average ratings with advertising rates high enough to add a significant revenue stream to his business. When it came to syndication, the UWF had placement on independent TV stations across North America, and seemed to cement its position as wrestling's third-leading organization behind the WWF and Jim Crockett Promotions. But behind the scenes, Watts's books were fried. Money was being lost hand over fist, and Watts, with few alternatives, sold out.

Unlike Watts, Verne Gagne hadn't buried himself in television debt by trying to mimic what the WWF had achieved in syndication. Instead, he was embroiled in a constant fight to retain what was left of his once-powerful AWA circuit. The same went for his talent and office staff. Gagne had been pillaged almost constantly since 1983, losing wrestlers, commentators, and valuable production crew, all of whom he'd devoted time and money to training and building up. Finally, Gagne threw his hands in the air and asked, "Why should I invest in wrestlers who go to work for other people?"[354] Seeing his current stars, along with AWA legends such as "Mad Dog" Vachon and the Crusher, head to the WWF was demoralizing. At the core, the departures damaged the credibility of the promotion, and Vince McMahon capitalized on it by running shows in Gagne's cities with ex-AWA grapplers up and down his cards. The reasoning for the exodus to the WWF was basically the same for everyone.

"My decision to leave the AWA was based strictly on economics," former AWA tag team champion Jim Brunzell explained. "I had stayed there too long, out of loyalty and friendship. When the WWF started taking over the country, AWA houses started to drop and the money got lower and lower. I went to Verne Gagne and asked for a guaranteed contract, so I could support my family. He told me I wasn't worth it." When asked about the comment, Gagne said, "I didn't offer Jim a guaranteed contract because nobody had one back then. But I never said he wasn't worth it. Jim is like a son to me." Brunzell credited Gagne with making him the wrestler that he was and freely admitted that the AWA had been good to him. According to Brunzell, after learning about his exit, Greg Gagne, his former tag team partner and Verne's son, asked him, "How could you do this after all we've done for you?"[355]

In a competitive marketplace, Gagne needed to match salaries, offer guaranteed contracts, and provide the kind of high-profile exposure wrestlers could get elsewhere. For veteran promoters, this stuff didn't come naturally. "Wrestling was never run on contracts but on handshakes," Gagne said. "This used to be fun. Now it's a business."[356]

The fact that the AWA was still on ESPN was a miracle, and offered hope for the future if Gagne made a few positive changes. A full upgrade of TV production quality was mandatory, even if he had to borrow ideas from McMahon or Crockett. Better lighting, improved camera work, and enhanced graphics were all necessary, and for some reason, Gagne was neglecting these fundamentals. His show's pacing needed help too. There was something to be gleaned from hooking viewers at the outset of a program and using creative techniques to keep their attention for a full hour. With finances stretched thin, Gagne needed additional revenue streams from international talent agreements, advertising sales, or merchandising. His Remco action figure deal "worked out quite well," but everything needed to be magnified for it to make a real impact.[357]

Gagne was beginning to think selling out was the logical option. In 1986, he allegedly placed a $3-million price tag on the AWA and was willing to negotiate with the man who had caused him plenty of sleepless nights, Vince McMahon. The dialogue between the two companies went on for weeks.[358] By the middle of the year, discussions ceased, though, and Gagne sought a potential buyer elsewhere. He remained firm on his price and the stipulation that his son Greg have a job with the new owners, and despite interest from at least one nonwrestling businessman, a deal couldn't be reached.

Gagne pushed on in 1986 and into '87, staging regular programs in his core cities of St. Paul, Chicago, Green Bay, Salt Lake City, Denver, and Milwaukee. ESPN TV tapings in Las Vegas were routine and popular, drawing over 2,000 on a regular basis at the Showboat Sports Pavilion. Holding on to the idea of expansion, Gagne also held shows in the Northeast with co-sponsorship from the ICW, went into Pittsburgh, and stopped at two locations in northern California in August 1986. Crowds were scarce until a few months later, on November 11, when the AWA and ICW ran a comparatively successful program in Palmetto, Florida, with 3,000 people in attendance. St. Paul on October 19 was a big disappointment (1,500), but Gagne drew 4,000 on Thanksgiving and 3,500 on Christmas at the Civic Center. For years, the Civic Center had been home to the AWA, and many important events were held there. In late 1986, Gagne was notified by arena officials that the WWF had signed an exclusive deal for the venue for 1987. The news left the AWA without a Twin Cities facility.

It was akin to the WWF losing Madison Square Garden. Instead of buying the AWA, McMahon was content with taking over Gagne's assets a little at a time. According to an article in the *Minneapolis Star Tribune*, McMahon was paying the Civic Center $10,000 per event for exclusivity, and writer Sid Hartman noted that Gagne's success "had supported the

Civic Center for many years when it was empty most of the time."[359] And in a repeating pattern, Gagne was on the losing end of the loyalty versus money argument, as he had been for most of the past three years.

Around the same time, Gagne was feeling the pressure from Curt Hennig, a talented 28-year-old grappler from just outside Minneapolis and the son of longtime AWA mainstay Larry Hennig. In late 1986, he was fielding offers from the WWF, and it was up to Gagne to aggressively fight to keep him in the promotion. Gagne did, and Hennig agreed to a $2,000-a-week guarantee and a run with the AWA world title.

After renting the costly Met Center in Bloomington for a January 1987 show, and attracting but 950 fans, Gagne entered into a lease for the old Minneapolis Auditorium, where he'd made his pro wrestling debut back in 1949. The AWA's return to the Auditorium on March 1 was part of a successful three-day run beginning on February 27 in Salt Lake City, a show that drew over 6,500 patrons. On February 28, Gagne ran the Cow Palace in San Francisco for the first time since 1985, and enthusiasts must have missed the AWA tradition as an estimated 9,000 people were on hand to see Jimmy Snuka win an 18-man battle royal. It was the largest AWA crowd since June of 1986, bringing in $104,000. Finally, on March 1 at the Minneapolis Auditorium, another 4,500 people were in attendance. Major feuds during this period included Hennig versus AWA champ Nick Bockwinkel, the Midnight Rockers against Buddy Rose and Doug Somers, and Colonel DeBeers against Jimmy Snuka.

On May 2, 1987, two-thirds fewer people were present at the Cow Palace for SuperClash II than the February 28 program. Nonetheless, Gagne went forward with the title switch between Hennig and Bockwinkel but was still cautious about Hennig. He booked a controversial finish, and the belt was held up after the bout in case Hennig pulled a double-cross and left for the WWF anyway. But Hennig was solid, and the AWA Championship Committee (Al DeRusha, Ed Francis, Jerry Jarrett, Larry Lisowski, Gene Reed, and Don Owen) declared him the rightful titleholder. Including Jarrett and Owen signaled Gagne's continued interest in promotional cooperation. The day before SuperClash, several AWA workers were in Eugene, Oregon, for a joint event with Owen at McArthur Court on the campus of the University of Oregon. The show drew 3,000 people, and Bockwinkel went over Hennig in the last match.

Gagne was angling to unite Memphis, Portland, Birmingham, and Kansas City — the four remaining territories — and act as a bridge between them. He was open to sending his AWA champions into the various cities, much like the NWA used to, and working together against the WWF and JCP. Jarrett was on board with the idea and had been booking Bockwinkel steadily since January 1987. (Jerry's son Jeff was named AWA's Rookie of the Year for 1986.) In April and May, Bockwinkel went into Kansas City twice for Bob Geigel's recently reopened office, and the Midnight Rockers appeared twice.

Gagne might have been grasping at straws with the co-op, but he was hustling to make the AWA work. It was rumored in May that he was close to landing a rich investor, perhaps even a lucrative arrangement with the Tribune Company of Chicago, giving him a spot on the cable outlet WGN.[360]

Such a deal wouldn't have been far-fetched. Gagne had a longstanding relationship with people at WGN, and as late as 1982, he'd discussed the possibility of a timeslot on the station. If the Tribune Company wanted into wrestling and put money behind Gagne to lure big-name talent to the AWA, it would have closed the gap between Gagne and McMahon and Crockett. But the idea never materialized, nor did a plan to operate a string of West Coast cities with Wahoo McDaniel as booker. But McDaniel did assume that role for Gagne's main AWA circuit beginning in June. By the summer of 1987, the promotion was again in dire straits, drawing 175 in Green Bay, 300 in Denver, and less than 900 in Minneapolis. Gagne pulled out of Chicago entirely. He made the same decision about Denver before the end of the year. Tommy Rich and Adrian Adonis were added to the roster, and Greg Gagne was feverishly chasing Curt Hennig's championship, but attendance wouldn't budge.

Memphis was an important cog in the AWA machine in 1987, and Jerry Jarrett had a tremendously loyal audience. Of course, a lot of it had to do with the sustained popularity of Jerry Lawler. During the second half of 1986, the central plotline of CWA action was Lawler's feuds with Bam Bam Bigelow and Big Bubba, and the King ended the year in a fiery war with ex-partner Tommy Rich. On February 16, 1987, Lawler teamed with Nick Bockwinkel to beat Rich and Austin Idol by DQ before a crowd of 9,000 at the Mid-South Coliseum. The latter duo was defeated by Lawler and Bigelow three weeks later in Memphis as 8,000 looked on. On April 27, 1987, in what was billed as the "Match of the Century," Lawler and Idol battled in a hair versus hair cage bout and the intensity of their rivalry captivated fans well beyond the normal standards.[361] In fact, after Rich interfered and Lawler was not only defeated, but shaved bald, irate spectators tried to climb the cage to attack the heel duo.[362]

The heat generated was off the charts, and the feud continued through June, when Lawler and partner Bill Dundee got their revenge in a scaffold match. As part of the joint AWA–CWA Super Tour '87 campaign, Memphis imported many recognizable stars. On July 27, Lawler beat Nick Bockwinkel, and Curt Hennig successfully retained his AWA belt with a little outside interference from a disguised Brickhouse Brown. Lawler and Dundee became two-time AWA world tag team champions during the month of October, first defeating Soldat Ustinov and Doug Somers and then Hector Guerrero and Dr. D (Carl Styles), both times in Memphis. They dropped the straps before the month concluded, losing to the Original Midnight Express (Dennis Condrey and Randy Rose) at a TV taping in Whitewater, Wisconsin, on October 30.

Notably, Jerry Jarrett's involvement with the AWA took a more serious tone when he entered negotiations to purchase the promotion outright. With check in hand, he went to Minnesota and reached a preliminary agreement with Verne Gagne to assume control of the organization. There was one stumbling block, and that had to do with Greg Gagne's future status with Jarrett's AWA, and whether he'd be guaranteed a job. Jarrett didn't see a position for him behind the scenes, and both parties walked away from the table without a deal.[363]

On the war front, Memphis was invaded by the WWF on September 11, 1986, and by Crockett's UWF on September 11, 1987. The WWF attracted a surprising 5,000 people, but eight months later, only 700 were interested in its return effort. As for Crockett, he drew 4,000 but didn't schedule a return program in 1987, or in 1988. While Memphis was generally off-limits to any promotion other than Jarrett's CWA, the WWF was making good elsewhere in the territory. It sold out the Louisville Gardens for a television taping on June 24, 1987, and crowds jumped to 10,000 in Nashville by September.

Down in Dallas, rebuilding was proving to be a considerable problem, and booker George Scott was striving to broaden the grappling pool. "The local talent cannot be one-sided, not just the Von Erichs, but the best, the finest competitors we can find in the business," he told a reporter in late 1986. "Nobody can touch the all-American personality and ability of the Von Erichs, but a variety of personalities create more fan interest, and right now we have a waiting list of 15 guys who want to come to World Class Championship Wrestling. We'll pick the best talent and not worry about those things going on around us. It's like that old saying, 'Can't worry about those things you can't control.'"[364] The challenge of having to constantly work through unforeseen, real-world issues was beyond the comprehension of any wrestling promotion. David's death, Mike's illness, and Kerry's accident were crippling to a once-thriving enterprise. These things were well beyond all control.

In spite of it all, Jack Adkisson was trying his hardest to keep his promotion afloat. Bruiser Brody replaced Scott as booker in early 1987, and a limping Kerry Von Erich made his homecoming on February 2 in Fort Worth. Adkisson was feeling the heat from the UWF's invasion into Dallas–Fort Worth and signed off on Kerry's premature return, hoping that his son was ready to go. A supportive and joyous crowd of 2,600 were excited to see Kerry back, and Von Erich defeated his old friend Brian Adias by pinfall. In the process, he re-broke his ankle. It was the worst-case scenario, and because so little blood was circulating into his foot, his chances of a full recovery were exceedingly slim. The pressure on Kerry was extraordinary, and he was considered sort of a white knight for the World Class promotion. Adkisson needed him back on the mat in tip-top condition if Dallas was going to rebound.

But doctors were limited in their ability to help Kerry. In mid-1987, doctors opted to fuse his ankle, a surgery that would leave his foot in a permanent walking position.[365] The operation limited his movement and only served to hamper his return to wrestling. He soon went under the knife again to have his right foot amputated. With prosthesis, he'd have better mobility, though there was always a risk of losing the artificial limb during a match. The importance of Kerry's return as a main-event star was made even more dramatic, following the suicide death of Mike Von Erich on April 12, 1987. The 23-year-old was depressed and despondent following a recent string of out-of-the-ring incidents, including an arrest, and he was believed to never have recovered completely from his 1985 battle with toxic shock syndrome. The Von Erichs and tragedy were becoming synonymous.

A deal that had been brewing even before Mike's death promised some good news for the family and the future of World Class. Adkisson signed with Bright Sports Marketing, headed by multi-millionaire Harvey "Bum" Bright, co-owner of the Dallas Cowboys football team. A plan was established to refresh all aspects of World Class, from the technical side of their TV programs to the way the Von Erichs were publicized. In an article in *D Magazine*, writer Kit Bauman explained that the World Class television show was going to feature "souped-up graphics and high-tech production techniques — things not normally associated with pro wrestling."[366] Lee Martin Productions took charge of the promotion's telecast and didn't waste time upgrading the music, the opening sequence, and its graphics.[367]

The fourth annual Von Erich Memorial Parade of Champions on May 3, 1987, took on an elevated significance after Mike's death, and Kevin was the only Von Erich to wrestle on the card. He went to a double count-out with Nord the Barbarian in front of a disappointing 5,900 spectators. Eight days later, Kevin passed out during an eight-man tag team bout in Fort Worth, and fellow wrestler Tommy Rogers revived him with CPR. The situation came a little too close to yet another heartbreak for the Adkisson family.

Heading into the summer months, World Class was going to try expanding again, but this time around, the Bum Bright outfit was shouldering much of the financial burden. A tentative schedule was arranged for shows in Boston, Chicago, and south Florida, but then the scale of the tour was greatly reduced. The promotion did venture to Hollywood, Florida, where both the WWF and JCP had promoted previously, and drew about 1,500 fans on November 21.

Kerry Von Erich officially returned to the ring for that Hollywood show, teaming with Kevin to topple Brian Adias and the Iron Sheik. Kerry had actually already performed in a live workout with three foes in Dallas at the Cotton Bowl a few weeks earlier, on October 17. The following month, on Thanksgiving, Kerry defeated Adias, Al Perez, and the Thing in separate contests, displaying improved coordination and speed. He seemed to be on his way to regaining his form, and all mention of his prosthesis was kept secret from the public. Fans were more than happy to welcome him back to the day-to-day mayhem of pro wrestling. Also on Thanksgiving night, there was a bombshell backstage, as Jack Adkisson informed a reporter for *D Magazine* that he intended to sell his interest in World Class and retire, telling him: "I'm just tired."[368]

The 58-year-old was worn out by the trials and tribulations of wrestling and the emotional roller coaster his family had been on. "It was simply the right deal at the right time," said a spokesman for Adkisson. "It was a simple business deal that doesn't represent any great philosophical [change]. He's still involved in wrestling in that he'll be managing his boys' (careers)."[369] In his place at the helm of World Class would be his former booker Ken Mantell and his sons Kerry and Kevin. With Kerry on the circuit once again, there was a fighting chance for the promotion in 1988.[370] Fans of the Von Erichs wanted to see their heroes in good wrestling action and hoped the family's misfortunes were behind them.

The Southeast franchise, Continental Championship Wrestling, was one of the last vestiges of the old territorial system. Throughout 1986, owner Ron Fuller kept his promotion strong with clever angles and skilled wrestlers like Brad Armstrong, Wendell Cooley, Tom Prichard, and Kevin Sullivan. Armstrong became a four-time Continental titleholder that year with victories over Robert Fuller and Jerry Stubbs, and between July 1985 and April 1987, Adrian Street held the Southeast heavyweight belt on six occasions. NWA world heavyweight titlist Ric Flair made four appearances in Birmingham for Fuller in April, May, June, and September of '86. The Bullet (Bob Armstrong) was his opponent in three of those shows, with Cooley his rival in the fourth. Attendance fluctuated from 2,000 to 6,000 at the Boutwell Auditorium in Birmingham, and CCW continued TV operations from that same venue. By the end of 1986, Fuller put less emphasis on the southern part of his territory, foregoing events in Dothan and Pensacola, and was frequently operating in Knoxville.

Fuller faced opposition from the WWF twice in Birmingham, on September 10 and November 16, 1986, and then the UWF charged into Pensacola on November 19. Fuller flexed his muscle in defense of Pensacola and went head to head, but drew only 350 compared to the UWF's 3,000. Interestingly, a few months before, on August 8, yet another adversarial group had challenged Fuller, this one an independent promotion headed by Austin Idol. The Bama Bash, as it was called, featured a unique mixture of grapplers, including Jerry Lawler, Road Warrior Animal, Paul Ellering, Abdullah the Butcher, and Stan Hansen, and lured 5,000 spectators in Birmingham. But Fuller expected the WWF, the then Bill Watts–owned UWF, and scrappy indie organizations to invade his region. What he didn't anticipate was fellow NWA member Jim Crockett doing it too.

On March 4, 1987, Fuller watched as JCP staged a show in Birmingham with Dusty Rhodes, Tully Blanchard, and the regular crew. Ex-CCW booker Bob Armstrong was part of the card, having joined Crockett in February. His son Brad was on the bill too, but the Armstrongs and the WTBS firepower didn't help push attendance over 750. Two months later, Fuller withdrew from the NWA and entered into a loose affiliation with the AWA, bringing in Nick Bockwinkel for two shots in June. Fuller also mapped out an expansion plan of his own, hitting Henderson's Arena outside Atlanta plus shows in Albany and Marietta, Georgia. He increased the number of spot shows in Alabama and Mississippi as well.

"Dirty" Dutch Mantell was an effective heel for Fuller in 1987 and he had a lengthy feud with Wendell Cooley. Bob Armstrong ultimately returned to CCW as the Bullet, and Marty Jannetty and Shawn Michaels (Midnight Rockers) spent nearly two months with the group from August to October 1987. Despite his best efforts to keep things fresh, Fuller's attendance dwindled and reports surfaced that Continental was on the market. Was CCW going the way of Florida and UWF?

Portland was in the same boat. Confronted by lackluster audiences, Don Owen had been gradually scaling back his promotion until withdrawing from Washington state entirely in 1986. As he restricted his circuit to the I-5 corridor in western Oregon, Owen was under the gun, and seriously considered selling the company that had been in his family's name for decades. Many of his problems were caused by misreading the direction of pro wrestling in the early to mid-1980s, and failing to change with the times. His television show and live events were amateurish in the eyes of casual viewers, while longtime fans appreciated the rough around the edges "territorial feel." But even loyalists had their limits. The downgrade of talent in the area depressed people who could remember the kind of grappling Owen used to deliver.

Getting star wrestlers from Jim Crockett was a temporary and expensive fix, and cooperation between Owen and JCP ceased around May

1986. That was right around the same time Billy Jack Haynes jumped from the Pacific Northwest promotion to the WWF, a big loss. On September 23, 1986, Owen brought in AWA world champion Nick Bockwinkel and Curt Hennig and booked the Road Warriors and Bruiser Brody for a big Coliseum show in Portland, but the spectacle drew only 2,000. Vince McMahon exploited the weaknesses in the Northwest territory, and the WWF assumed a dominant share of the market in 1986, running regular programs in Portland, Spokane, and Tacoma. On June 17, the WWF drew an amazing 23,000 fans to the Tacoma Dome with a Hulk Hogan–Big John Studd main event. In comparison, a 3,000-person house for Owen was considered impressive. Needless to say, the WWF was now on a strikingly different level.

Citing an oversaturation of wrestling on TV, Owen complained to the Oregon Boxing and Wrestling Commission but received little help in return. Associate promoter Sandy Barr pleaded their case to the *Portland Oregonian*, saying, "There's just too much wrestling on TV, for free. It's killing us. People wouldn't go across the street to watch Jesus Christ wrestle Oral Roberts."[371] Gates in Salem, Oregon, for example, fell from $65,300 in 1983–84 to $38,818 in 1985–86.

On May 1, 1987, Owen booked Bockwinkel and Hennig again in Eugene, and the duo battled to a double count-out. The Midnight Rockers were also on the bill, going up against Mike Miller and Rip Oliver and taking a victory. That same month, Roddy Piper turned up during a telecast of Owen's Portland show to do commentary as a favor to his old boss. It was relatively brief, but Hot Rod's appearance was exciting to area enthusiasts. Later in the year, booker Rip Oliver left the promotion for the WWF and was replaced by Len Denton, known in the ring as the Grappler. With diminished stature, a heavily reduced circuit, and few prospects for a real transformation, the Portland franchise was a few short steps away from financial collapse. But the 75-year-old Owen was a survivor and wasn't yet throwing in the towel. It was clear, however, that the Portland "territory" of old was practically extinct.

The Central States was another dilapidated territory. After Crockett withdrew his talent, Bob Geigel returned in March 1987 and pulled in wrestlers from across the area. "Bulldog" Bob Brown was a familiar face, and Geigel even came out of retirement for matches against Rip Rogers that summer. The AWA champion Nick Bockwinkel was booked into Kansas City, but crowds were rarely large enough for Geigel to break even. The Memorial Hall in Kansas City was seeing 150 to 350 people a night, and grew to 600 when Bruiser Brody made his return in late May. Much like the situation in the northwest, the WWF had a sizable advantage, attracting more than 8,000 for a Kansas City show on July 12, 1987. Geigel was in no position to compete. He certainly couldn't afford to pay superstar wages or arrange cable television and merchandising deals. But he carried on, and in October 1987, he withdrew from the National Wrestling Alliance, the organization he'd led as president for years. His departure was significant to the NWA insofar as tradition and leadership were concerned, but in the realm of the new Alliance, under Crockett's management, it was inconsequential. Of all the pioneering territories involved in the NWA, only Crockett and Don Owen were left, and membership was down to less than 10. The vanishing importance of the NWA coalition was a sign of the times, and it wasn't all thanks to Vince McMahon. In many ways the NWA had defeated itself, and members had forgotten why the Alliance was valuable. For many pundits and fans, JCP was now the "NWA," and that was fine when looking at the organization in its simplest terms. But the real National Wrestling Alliance, the one formed in 1948, was gone forever.

CHAPTER NINETEEN

A BRUISING TRAGEDY

In pro wrestling, true visionaries have always been a rare breed. Throughout history, they were the innovators, the inspired geniuses who changed the landscape of the business and left an indelible mark that continued to reverberate well after they were gone. Vince McMahon's entire national campaign was the product of a farsighted and bold personality, and such a move required tremendous imagination. Along with his trusted associates, he fostered idea after idea, pushing past bumps in the road with unparalleled ambition. Jim Crockett and Dusty Rhodes were driven as well, and each had a hand in the skyrocketing growth of Jim Crockett Promotions. They were both visionaries, but Rhodes was the creative mastermind behind the company's success.

Starrcade, the Great American Bash, and countless other ideas were the product of his inventive mind. Though it was true he took heat from fans who felt he needed to step aside a bit from his top babyface role, Rhodes was still hugely valuable as JCP expanded nationwide. Dusty was a superstar, and while people in many of Crockett's regular towns had seen him battle Tully Blanchard and Ric Flair countless times, enthusiasts elsewhere were taking in these bouts for the first time live. As a booker, he was also criticized. Feuds were overly protracted, talent was stale, and there was gross overuse of the Dusty Finish, with one wrestler apparently winning only for the decision to be reversed later. But the truth be known, Rhodes's talent as a booker had taken JCP out of its safe Mid-Atlantic locale and given the company placement on the national stage.

By 1987, Crockett had invested a large sum of money to purchase the UWF. He'd worked a deal with the Florida office and bought a plane to cut down on escalating transportation costs. With the new acquisition and responsibilities came the need for better organization and, more specifically, a solid plan to manage the company's cash and assets. Enormous sums were already being spent to pay stations to air original JCP TV content, which was magnified by the addition of the UWF syndication network. It is conceivable that if Bill Watts owed $50,000 a week because of his TV deals, Crockett was on the hook for double that.[372] And for such a massive syndication venture to make sense, JCP needed to be using those stations to generate income, either through advertising or by promoting live shows. Since they weren't running events in 175-plus markets, advertising deals had to make up for their TV expenditures.

Despite its success, Jim Crockett Promotions was still a rather humble organization. Whereas the WWF had a staff of over 70, JCP had 14, most of whom were the original office personnel from the heyday of Crockett's regional operation.[373] JCP's Charlotte office organized live shows across the country, coordinated talent for both JCP and the UWF, and handled extensive publicity.[374] Then came the responsibilities tied to television syndication and advertising and keeping the company's books. The latter necessitated a team of experienced employees by itself, and without additional hires, the regular staff was overwhelmed.

Crockett improved his TV arrangement, devising a specialized syndication package, called the Wrestling Network, made up of all four of his programs: *NWA Pro*, *Worldwide Wrestling*, *UWF Wrestling*, and *Power Pro Wrestling*.[375] The Network operated out of the new Dallas office and created an umbrella over the telecasts with the goal of streamlining production and promoting the NWA and UWF together.[376] Because JCP and the UWF had targeted the same cities prior to the buyout, some markets were receiving programming from both JCP and the JCP-produced UWF. Now viewers would get a mix of content under the Wrestling Network banner. Taking a big load off his Charlotte staff, Crockett hired Time Sales International Ltd., a company based in Connecticut, to sell advertising.[377]

By June 1987, Crockett had lined up stations in 37 of the top 40 markets, and his syndication network blanketed 77 percent of the country. The WWF, in contrast, had more than 90 percent coverage. In an interview with *Television/Radio Age*, David Crockett, a JCP vice president and TV commentator for its weekend broadcast on WTBS, affirmed that their promotion was going to retain a "legitimate" approach to wrestling: "We're not going to have any snakes, alligators or chainsaws."[378] But as some TV station honchos knew, viewers wanted the shenanigans of Hulk Hogan, the colorful gimmicks, the animals, and the over-the-top characters, which always did good business for the WWF. In spite of the trends in wrestling, JCP refused to stray too far into the realm of Vince McMahon when it came to in-ring characters and personalities.

It didn't take long for the influence of Dusty Rhodes to alter UWF programming. His pal Magnum T.A. was installed as a commentator alongside Jim Ross, and slowly the focus shifted off actual UWF performers to Crockett mainstays. As a result, the UWF was treated as a secondary outfit, diminishing the importance of its wrestlers, titles, and live events. In Florida, Rhodes tried to maintain a group of wrestlers for local shows in Tampa, Orlando, and Miami, but fans weren't interested. They wanted to see the big guns of JCP, including Dusty himself, and not second-stringers. It was the same reason the Central States' experiment failed. With house show numbers falling, Rhodes initiated a series of cutbacks, limiting the number of monthly events. Instead of TV tapings every week, they scheduled two tapings per week for 26 weeks and cut legendary commentator Gordon Solie's salary in half. Solie had no choice but to quit. "Obviously, Championship Wrestling from Florida no longer exists," he told a reporter for the *Orlando Sentinel*.[379]

The anticipated Great American Bash series kicked off in Lakeland, Florida, on July 1, 1987. Ticket prices were lower than the year before, and

Crockett played it much safer when it came to renting large venues, essentially avoiding them with the exception of Memorial Stadium in Charlotte and the Orange Bowl in Miami.[380] Atlanta's Omni Coliseum was the site of the inaugural War Games contest on July 4, a brutal five-on-five battle inside a two-ring cage. The Four Horsemen (Ric Flair, Arn Anderson, Tully Blanchard, Lex Luger, and J.J. Dillon) were defeated by fan favorites Dusty Rhodes, Nikita Koloff, the Road Warriors, and Paul Ellering. Tour attendance was impressive in Landover, Maryland (15,000), Chicago (10,000), Charlotte (25,000), and Miami (16,000), and Crockett ran the second War Games at the Orange Bowl in the Bash finale on July 31. The Horsemen were again toppled when the War Machine (Ray Traylor/Big Bubba), a masked substitute for Dillon, gave up.

On July 11, two major championships changed hands in two different cities. Lex Luger, using a chair tossed to him by J.J. Dillon, beat Nikita Koloff inside a cage for the United States belt in Greensboro. Out in Oklahoma City, Steve Williams went over Big Bubba for the UWF heavyweight strap. It was notable that UWF grapplers appeared alongside JCP talent in cities throughout the tour. Terry Gordy, Eddie Gilbert, Chris Adams, Rick Steiner, and Sting were prominently featured in early to midcard roles, and they were reliably good. Only a few weeks before, Sting had turned fan favorite and was feuding with Steiner, his ex–tag partner. Williams, another babyface, was at war with Dick Murdoch and formed a tag team with Terry Gordy to lock horns with Murdoch and Gilbert. (The Williams–Gordy tandem gained international fame in the early 1990s.) As for Ric Flair, the NWA world champion, he was inching into a rivalry with "Hands of Stone" Ron Garvin.

Crockett was juggling a lot of different issues, but one of his principal responsibilities was signing and protecting his talent. The Road Warriors, Hawk and Animal, were two of his most popular attractions and had been approached by both the WWF and AWA. Retaining their services was a priority, and Crockett locked the wrestlers down with a big-money, guaranteed contract that would keep them in the company through 1990.[381] Following his purchase of the UWF, he missed the opportunity to land Ted DiBiase, who promptly joined the WWF and made his debut as the Million Dollar Man in early June 1987. Between June and September, JCP also saw five grapplers depart for other organizations: Rick Rude, Terry

Gordy, Buddy Roberts, Chris Adams, and Manny Fernandez. Michael Hayes, the remaining Freebird, inked a contract and later fashioned a new team with Jimmy Garvin.

Crockett and Rhodes returned the NWA brand to Detroit, an unambiguously pro-WWF city, on September 25, 1987.[382] They rented the Joe Louis Arena, a venue McMahon had occupied from 1984 until recently, when he'd moved to the Silverdome. In a promo piece in the *Detroit Free Press*, the differences between JCP and the WWF were once again front and center, and writer Joe Barrett explained that the "NWA-UWF" combination was "less glitzy and show-business oriented than the other guys." Promoter Gary Juster was optimistic about the event. He told the newspaper that "Detroit fans have been waiting a long time" for NWA wrestling, and the night of the program, 8,000 frenzied spectators were present at the arena to see Crockett's best and brightest.[383] And those in attendance were in for a treat. Rhodes booked Flair to lose the NWA world title, but the new champion wasn't Steve Williams in a unification match, nor was it heir apparent Barry Windham. The new titleholder was Ronnie Garvin.

The result was a major surprise, and strategically important. Without question, Garvin was inherently tough and carried good fan support. At 42 years of age, he was a battle-tested veteran, and had been embroiled in a feud with Flair since July. Their chemistry worked when it came to street fighting and seismic chest-chopping, and their battles garnered a lot of attention. But of all Flair's challengers, including Windham and Nikita Koloff, Garvin was not expected to win the belt. The shock of the moment, plus the fact that Flair was finally beaten, carried a lot of excitement. The booking philosophy behind the switch related to the promotion's upcoming Starrcade event, which was historically the biggest night of the year for JCP. Crockett and Rhodes wanted Flair to win a return match and regain the championship at that show, meaning Garvin's reign was destined to last 62 days. The idea, credited by some to Flair himself, was agreed upon by all parties, and the Detroit switch kicked the plan into motion.

Starrcade was a Thanksgiving tradition for JCP, and the 1987 spectacular marked the company's first foray into the world of pay-per-view, adding to the magnitude of the event. To that juncture, PPV had been dominated by the WWF, and for Crockett to be competitive, he had to cross that bridge. Vince McMahon didn't want to concede anything to his rival and went on the offensive to narrow JCP's chances for success. First, he scheduled a competing pay-per-view show for Thanksgiving, naming it the Survivor Series. Then he used his leverage as a leader in pro wrestling's pay-per-view field to get cable systems to reject Starrcade entirely, telling executives that if they went ahead and presented the JCP program, they wouldn't get the next WrestleMania. It was a harsh move and severely damaged Crockett's ability to land outlets. In fact, Starrcade was only available for PPV in 300,000 households, while McMahon offered the Survivor Series to seven million homes.[384]

In the lead up to Starrcade, JCP TV ratings fell dramatically, and house shows in Los Angeles, Atlanta, and Charlotte drew less than 2,000.[385] Greensboro on October 25, 1987, drew a trifle better with 3,500. In Dallas, poor advance ticket sales caused Crockett to cancel a program outright on October 15. Despite a quality roster of athletes, the current matchups were sour, and marketing Ronnie Garvin as the lead babyface and defending champion had its disadvantages, especially when compared with WWF titleholder Hulk Hogan. Altogether, it was a bad time to lose momentum, and the leaders of JCP crossed their fingers in hopes of a triumph on Thanksgiving night.

The WWF was just too strong. Built on the premise of teams vying in elimination matches, the Survivor Series was a loaded bill with 50 competitors in four bouts. In one of the contests, Randy Savage teamed with Jake Roberts, Jim Duggan (who returned to the promotion in September), Brutus Beefcake, and Ricky Steamboat to beat Honky Tonk Man, Harley Race, Hercules, Ron Bass, and Danny Davis. Savage, Roberts, and Steamboat were the survivors. Hulk Hogan partnered with Paul Orndorff, Don Muraco, Ken Patera, and Bam Bam Bigelow in the main event but took the loss against Andre the Giant, One Man Gang, King Kong Bundy, Butch Reed, and Rick Rude. Andre pinned Bigelow to become the sole survivor. Hogan, startlingly, was counted out three quarters into the battle and eliminated. The WWF racked up more than 400,000 in pay-per-view sales and sold out the 20,000-plus-seat Richfield Coliseum in Richfield, Ohio, turning the Survivor Series into an undeniable success.[386]

In Chicago, Starrcade was underwhelming. Ric Flair recaptured the NWA world heavyweight championship from Garvin, but the hometown favorites, the Road Warriors, were subjected to the infamous Dusty Finish in their bout with Arn Anderson and Tully Blanchard, disappointing viewers. Dusty Rhodes was victorious in his contest with Lex Luger and won the United States title. The show was balanced to a certain degree, and drew 8,000 patrons to the UIC Pavilion, but it was far from the financial bonanza Crockett needed. He offered the program to over 40 closed-circuit TV locations and reached in the neighborhood of 20,000 homes via pay-per-view.[387] Neither the fans nor the powers that be were happy with the results, and loyalists back in Greensboro were exceedingly displeased. Starrcade was their event, and had been so since 1983. Moving the show to Chicago was an effort to play ball with the WWF nationally, but Crockett estranged his most faithful fans in the process, and it was a slight that was would not be forgotten.

The economic reality of Starrcade, high-priced contracts with balloon payments at the end of each fiscal year, and expensive television deals was creating an untenable environment, and the future of Jim Crockett Promotions was in doubt. Company finances were strained further by exorbitant spending on transportation (jets and limousines) and the cost of maintaining two offices, in Charlotte and in Dallas.[388] With regard to the Universal Wrestling Federation, Crockett had committed millions of dollars to purchase the organization, but over the last four months of 1987, he ceased running exclusive house shows and TV tapings under that banner. At Starrcade, Nikita Koloff beat Terry Taylor to unify his world TV title with the latter's UWF television crown. But the world championship of Steve Williams and the tag team belts held by the Sheepherders were effectively retired in December 1987 when JCP completed a full-fledged merger of the two groups. The UWF was no more.[389]

As the year came to a close, JCP was treading water, and Rhodes was creating new angles in attempt to spark attendance. Lex Luger turned babyface and went to war with his Four Horsemen mates, and up-and-comer Sting received a push to match his growing popularity. Over in the WWF, Sting's former partner in the Blade Runners, James Hellwig, was off and running as the Ultimate Warrior and displaying a fierce enthusiasm that struck a chord with fans. His impressive power was exhibited each time he stepped through the ropes, especially as he put away foes with his gorilla press slam. Talent, on the whole, was never a problem for Vince McMahon. Newcomers Ted DiBiase, Rick Rude, Bam Bam Bigelow, and

One Man Gang were impact players, and before the end of the year, both Gang and DiBiase were facing off with Hulk Hogan for the WWF championship. Many old faces were on the circuit, including "Superstar" Billy Graham, Don Muraco, George Steele, and Hillbilly Jim, and the tag team division was robust, led by the Hart Foundation and Demolition.

In the months prior to the Survivor Series, Paul Orndorff became a fan favorite, as did Randy Savage, who entered into a lengthy feud with the Honky Tonk Man over the Intercontinental belt. Heels were aplenty, and Bobby Heenan created an imposing "Family" comprised of Andre the Giant, King Kong Bundy, Harley Race, Rick Rude, and the Islanders, the perfect foils for WWF heroes. Hulk Hogan remained the top banana, and although his *Rock 'n' Wrestling* cartoon was canceled in June 1987, it wasn't because his standing as the WWF's central protagonist had diminished. Kids were growing up with Hogan, and the aura of the Hulkster still cast its glow across North America. On August 28, 1987, he was a headline attraction in Houston during promoter Paul Boesch's retirement show at the Sam Houston Coliseum and defeated One Man Gang. Boesch aligned with the WWF after the sale of the UWF, and his retirement event was attended by luminaries from throughout the grappling world.

Vince McMahon was joined by Lou Thesz, Gene Kiniski, rival Verne Gagne, and 12,000 spectators in paying their respects to Boesch for his exceptional contributions to the sport. The "Living Legend" Bruno Sammartino appeared on the undercard and beat Hercules by count-out in his second-to-last pro match. The next night at the Baltimore Arena, he teamed with Hogan to conquer One Man Gang and King Kong Bundy. Bruno then retired from active wrestling, capping a career that began in 1959 and saw him reign as WWWF champion twice for a combined 11 years. After giving up his job as a commentator in March 1988, Sammartino became a vocal detractor of modern wrestling and condemned the gimmickry antics of McMahon and the WWF. He wasn't alone. His Pittsburgh neighbor Johnny Valiant, a former WWWF tag champion in the 1970s, told a journalist, "I think Vince McMahon must be inspired by Walt Disney these days. Wrestling was on top of the world for WrestleMania I. Then they started getting in guys who were half-baked entertainers instead of wrestlers."[390] Verne Gagne wholeheartedly agreed. "It makes me sick, makes me want to vomit," he said. "It's too far out, tongue in cheek, they look down on the sport. They make a mockery of the whole gol-dang thing."[391]

The AWA continued to be raked over the coals by the WWF. Co-holder of the AWA world tag championship Boris Zhukov left the promotion for McMahon's group, mid-reign, in late September 1987, and Gagne was forced to reteam Zhukov's partner, Soldat Ustinov, with Doug Somers. A short time later, one of Gagne's most valuable long-term commodities, Nick Bockwinkel, took a position in the WWF as a part-time TV commentator and occasional referee. On November 16, 1987, at the Meadowlands in East Rutherford, New Jersey, Bockwinkel participated in an old-timers battle royal with a handful of former AWA stars. Edouard Carpentier, Gene Kiniski, Ray Stevens, and the Crusher were also involved, and in the finals, Lou Thesz tossed Pat O'Connor over the top rope to score a win.

Gagne saw another champion defect to the WWF in 1987, a few months before Zhukov. Sherri Martel, a talented grappler from Alabama, was the current AWA women's champion when she walked out, leaving Gagne high and dry. On December 27, 1987, a Minneapolis-trained Madusa Miceli beat Candi Devine to capture the vacant AWA women's belt in Las Vegas. That same night, Greg Gagne beat Adrian Adonis by disqualification in the finals of a tournament to win the initial AWA International TV title, and the returning Midnight Rockers defeated the Original Midnight Express for the AWA world tag crown.

On February 4, 1988, Gagne presented his final offering at the Minneapolis Auditorium, which was scheduled to be demolished, and invited fans to "Celebrate 55 Years of Wrestling" at the venue. Only 1,700 people were in attendance for the special event, but they warmly received Dick the Bruiser, Leo Nomellini, Hard Boiled Haggerty, and the other AWA legends on hand. The real story of the night wasn't the small crowd, but the fact Gagne was being stripped of his prime facility in the Twin Cities. He couldn't afford the Met Center in Bloomington and was aced out at the St. Paul Civic Center. So, in addition to stopping his shows in San Francisco, Salt Lake City, Denver, Milwaukee, Green Bay, and Chicago, Gagne called a halt to regular action in his primary cities of Minneapolis–St. Paul. Historically, a promoter losing the nucleus of his operation was doomsday, but Gagne was a resourceful man who'd just signed a new contract with ESPN.[392] But, essentially, he was a promoter without a territory, and the AWA was confined to TV tapings in Las Vegas and live shows in small cities in Wisconsin and Minnesota. He still carried the important lineage of a Big Three promotion, but in terms of live events and territorial control, the AWA had become a glorified independent.

The ESPN coverage kept him in the ballgame. As far as his TV situation went, Gagne was doing pretty well, all things considered. His original syndicator, the New York–based Syndicast Services, severed ties in early 1987, and Gagne hired a veteran radio guy from Minneapolis, Gary Rawn, to help run his television setup. But ultimately, he landed with RJS Marketing Worldwide, which also oversaw the syndication of *Pro Wrestling This Week* by Joe Pedicino.[393] The All Star Wrestling Network was commonly in the top 15 in national syndication ratings, lagging behind the WWF and JCP. With his circuit practically devoid of major markets, Gagne placed an even greater emphasis on booking his heavyweight and tag team champions in friendly territories. Over the first six months of 1988, his grapplers appeared in Memphis 18 times with additional showings in Louisville, Nashville, and Evansville. And to mark Gagne's alliance with Jerry Jarrett, Jerry Lawler beat Curt Hennig on May 9 to capture the AWA world heavyweight title.

The Memphis region was fueled by the influx of AWA workers and a reliable world champion in the area was a boon to ticket sales. Jarrett received a few JCP castoffs as well, Terry Taylor and the Rock and Roll Express among them. But Eddie Gilbert's return was the big news. He attacked Lawler with a fireball on February 22, and their subsequent matches drew intense heat. A week before Lawler won the AWA belt, Memphis was besieged by wrestlers from Dallas as part of another talent-sharing deal struck by Jarrett. Michael Hayes, Chris Adams, and Buddy Roberts were on the bill with WCCW champion Iceman King Parsons battling Kerry Von Erich in the main event. (Parsons won by DQ.) Linking the CWA and AWA with World Class was a tactical move, and all three promotions had something to gain. Notably, though, because of the weakened state of Gagne's company, he was a lot more willing to share power in 1988 than he had been in 1985 or 1986, as demonstrated by putting the AWA belt on Lawler.

Jarrett's CWA might have been in the best position of the three organizations. His main city, Memphis, was drawing houses two to five times larger than Dallas and, unlike World Class and the AWA, Jarrett had retained some semblance of a legitimate territory, including several population centers of over 50,000. His top wrestler was the AWA world champion and, in March 1988, he gained a national cable outlet on the Financial News Network. Young talent was in abundance in Memphis as at various times, Shawn Michaels, Scott Steiner, and Cactus Jack (Mick Foley) were in the region. Steiner, the younger brother of JCP upstart Rick Steiner, won the Renegade Rampage tournament in Memphis in June, and teamed with Billy Joe Travis to capture the CWA tag title. Cactus Jack, a protégé of Dominic DeNucci in Pennsylvania, held the CWA tag championship with partner Gary Young before dropping a loser-leaves-town bout in November. Jeff Jarrett was also making headway as a professional and was exceedingly popular.

From a Dallas perspective, the working agreement with the CWA and AWA was a home run made simpler by Ken Mantell's positioning as co-owner. The problems between Gagne and Jack Adkisson were well recorded, and the two had nearly run opposition against each other a few years earlier. But Mantell was mending fences and strengthening bonds with associates across the country. He sent out missives to groups of all shapes and sizes, and extended his willingness to book World Class wrestlers on independent shows, regardless of their location.[394] In the ring, Mantell was also trying to turn things around. He reinitiated the old Freebirds–Von Erich feud on December 25, 1987, and did an injury angle with Fritz Von Erich, which meant Kerry and Kevin wanted revenge on Terry Gordy, Buddy Roberts, and their new partner, "Blackbird" King Parsons. Michael Hayes joined the Von Erichs in their quest, and matches were set up for months.

On May 8, 1988, at Texas Stadium, Kerry beat Parsons to capture the World Class world championship, and Kevin teamed with Bruiser Brody to beat Buddy Roberts and Solomon Grundy. Attendance was upwards of 7,000, the largest Parade of Champions crowd in two years, and regular crowds at the Sportatorium were way up from their terrific lows in 1987. Mantell's gains were noteworthy, but the Dallas office had limited financial resources and could only do so much. Additionally, the arrangement Adkisson made with Bum Bright ended without the promised success. The October 1988 edition of *Penthouse* described the hypocrisies, tragedies, and the overall downfall of the Von Erich family. It was a revealing portrait of pro wrestling's first family that traced the timeline of events between David's death in 1984 and Mike's suicide three years later. Included were all the dark details about the various arrests, the drug abuse, and the injuries suffered by the brothers, and it was an article the senior Adkisson hoped would never see the light of day. "We're better known now because we die," Adkisson told *D Magazine*.[395]

Unfortunately, there was much sadness yet to come. Tragedy was being felt throughout the wrestling world in 1988. On July 4, 33-year-old Adrian Adonis was killed in a car accident in eastern Canada. A former AWA and WWF tag champion, Adonis was generally underappreciated as a wrestler, and although his weight held him back at times, he was a solid performer on the mat. Pat Kelly and "Wildman" Dave McKigney also lost their lives in the wreck, and Pat Kelly's twin brother, Mike, was the sole survivor. Twelve days later in Puerto Rico, 42-year-old future Hall of Famer Bruiser Brody was stabbed in the locker room of Juan Ramon Loubriel Stadium in Bayamon by Jose Gonzales, a wrestler known as Invader I, and died the next morning, leaving his wife and young son behind.[396]

An international superstar, Brody was pro wrestling's number-one nonconformist, and after 15 years in the industry, he'd pretty much seen it all. He had brawled with the biggest names in the business, exchanged fisticuffs with fellow wrestlers behind the scenes, and walked away from promotions at the drop of a hat when he felt slighted by promoters. Insiders knew his stormy disposition all too well, just as his friends knew the depths of his heart and loyalty. Brody was a force of nature and a man some people figured was immortal. Without a doubt, he was one of the most important performers of wrestling's territorial era.

CHAPTER TWENTY

THE END
OF AN ERA

Professional wrestling's territorial system was in shambles by 1988, and the industry was being redefined by freewheeling capitalism. Jim Crockett and Vince McMahon were second- and third-generation promoters, respectively, and knew the hardships of wrestling. They had seen their fathers struggle with the complexities of running a territory, but their problems in 1988 were on a much grander scale — now it was all about television distribution, advertising, and pay-per-view. While "Big" Jim Crockett Sr. managed his Mid-Atlantic empire with impressive skill, his son was trying to gain footing all over the North American continent.

As these two powerhouses fought for placement in the national picture, the rest of pro wrestling dealt with the fallout of wrestling's swift evolution. Bob Geigel, Don Owen, and Verne Gagne, three venerable promoters, were barely hanging on. Though Gagne had made headway a few years earlier, the AWA of 1988 was dangerously close to bankruptcy. Geigel and Owen were hanging tight but were in a different league from JCP and the WWF. In fact, there was no organization in the United States even a close third, and the distance between McMahon and Crockett was substantial as well. The pecking order in pro wrestling had been established, and everyone was chasing the World Wrestling Federation.

The territorial system was a casualty of the wrestling boom. Initially created after World War II, synched up with the explosive growth of TV, the territories were embraced by fans wherever the sport was presented. At its height, wrestling had self-governing offices in 30 individual cities in the contiguous United States, with at least five others in Canada, one in Hawaii, and another in Mexico. For more than three decades, the system thrived, and enthusiasts enjoyed regionalized wrestling organized by a local promoter with original TV content taped in the same geographic area. Fans saw quality matches featuring talented wrestlers, and when one grappler had worn out his welcome, he left for another territory and was replaced by someone new. Touring NWA, AWA, and WWWF champions were a welcomed sight, and the connection to a much wider organization made the territory system even more special.

Just as kids were growing up with Hulk Hogan, millions of fans came of age during the halcyon days of the territories and mourned their loss. In the wake of an aggressive organization with national aspirations, promoters also hurt themselves in many cases by pushing over-the-hill local favorites and worn-out acts, while failing to protect valuable young talent. That's where McMahon did take advantage of his ill-equipped rivals, and the WWF scored top wrestlers from all over the map, starting with Hulk Hogan and continuing with Roddy Piper, Randy Savage, Jake Roberts, and Ted DiBiase. Without the stars he took in from outside regions, the WWF would have struggled to achieve a fraction of what it did.

Not counting the JCP-affiliated members, the NWA only had one stateside affiliate left in 1988, and that was Don Owen. There were other promotions still in existence with direct lineage to the old territories, including Ron Fuller in Birmingham, Bob Geigel in Kansas City, Jerry Jarrett in Memphis, and Ken Mantell and the Von Erichs in Dallas. These survivors were doing what needed to be done to maintain their operations, but insofar as current business went, there was very little to no correlation between their promotions in 1988 and those of their organizations during the heyday of the territorial system. In Alabama, Ron Fuller was actually looking for a way out and ended up selling the Continental Championship Wrestling promotion to TV magnate David Woods in late 1987, in a deal that took effect in February 1988. Woods was owner and president of WCOV-20 in Montgomery, and he assumed control of CCW's interests in Alabama and Florida. He changed the name of the promotion to the Continental Wrestling Federation and hired Eddie Gilbert away from Memphis to be his booker. Fuller then launched a Knoxville-based group, USA Championship Wrestling, which ran shows at the Knoxville Civic Coliseum, and the two organizations split talent. On April 1, 1988, the Mongolian Stomper (Archie Gouldie) beat the Bullet (Bob Armstrong) to capture the initial USA Championship Wrestling heavyweight crown. Naturally, the Bullet won the belt in a May rematch, and the popular strongman Doug Furnas won the title in a tournament two months later. However, the promotion ran into trouble and closed up in August, with remnants sold to Woods. The CWF, even with Dr. Tom Prichard, Wendell Cooley, Tony Anthony, and the Armstrongs, was unable to sustain business, and it folded in November 1989.

Smartly, though, in the midst of his run, Woods tried to solidify ties to other promoters in an attempt to open talent-sharing lanes. He attended a special meeting at the Dallas airport in June 1988 to discuss the possibilities of a wider cooperative with Jerry Jarrett, Ken Mantell, and others, but the conference didn't prove fruitful.[397]

Barry Owen was also at the meeting, representing his father. The Portland promotion had always relied on talent trading, a hallmark of the NWA. But with the limited member structure of the Alliance, there wasn't much left to share. During the May 7, 1988, edition of *World Championship Wrestling* on WTBS, commentators took a moment to "say hello" to Don Owen, putting him over as "one of the great, longtime promoters of the NWA."[398] In addition, they hyped a show he had that night at the Portland Sports Arena and wished him "all the best." The shoutout was timed to help Owen in his regional conflict with wrestler-turned-promoter Billy Jack Haynes, who was now operating in the vicinity under the Oregon Wrestling Federation banner. In further aid, Crockett agreed to stage a joint program with Owen in Seattle on August 3, 1988, and his top stars appeared in seven of the 10 bouts on the card, a rare combination effort by two active NWA members.[399] On September 20, Ric Flair returned to Portland by himself to face off with local grappler Top Gun (David Canal) on Owen's Night of the Champions. Flair was defeated by DQ but retained his NWA belt in front of just more than 1,000 fans. Owen also faced consistent problems with the Oregon Boxing and Wrestling Commission. Since its founding in 1987, the commission had imposed strict drug, health, and code enforcement for pro wrestling in the state, and was paying close attention to ensure the new regulations were being followed. In November 1988, Don Owen was indefinitely suspended by the commission for two infractions.[400] For one, he hadn't fully complied with orders to implement metal barriers along the path between the ring and backstage area for his shows. The other pertained to blood and the act of blading. The commission banned any such activity, and after a grappler "juiced" during the November 12 program, Owen was suspended. He was reinstated the next week, but the scrutiny on his promotion intensified. Another indie group, Pacific Coast Championship Wrestling also tried to jump-start their organization in 1988, and the promoter, Mel Saraceno, made it clear he had no animosity toward Owen. "I've been watching Don Owen productions for 30 years," he told the *Portland Oregonian*. "I have nothing but the utmost respect and admiration for him. I don't want to sound goofy about it, but I've sort of idolized him."[401]

Owen was steadfast in his ways and known for his fairness. But when his gates decreased, he had to lower payouts to his employees. To that point, he'd survived where 99 percent of his contemporaries had failed and made it into the 1990s as an active promoter. On December 28, 1991, his television outlet KPTV-12 canceled *Portland Wrestling* because of dismal ratings and inflated studio costs, and Owen's promotion had no TV outlet for the first time since the early 1950s. He told the *Oregonian*, "Economic bad times, that's all there is to it. Everybody's hurting right now. We go into these little towns and half the mills are closed. I'm just like everybody else, a victim of hard times."[402] Just before KPTV's decision, Owen had lost his primary sponsor, Tom Peterson's of Portland, a popular retailer of appliances, furniture, and electronics, which filed for bankruptcy protection in October 1991.

Between 1988 and '91, Owen put his Pacific Northwest heavyweight title belt around the waists of Tatsumi Fujinami, Scotty the Body (Scott

Levy), Brian Adams, Steve Doll, the Grappler, Carl Styles, and Rip Oliver, among others. Even Billy Jack Haynes returned to the PNW for a final reign as titleholder in 1991. On May 30, 1992, Owen announced his retirement, closing out his 60-plus years, involvement in wrestling at age 80. "To tell you the truth, when I got up to tell the people that after 68 years, I wouldn't be doing this anymore, my eyes filled up with tears," he admitted. "But there comes a time when you've got to pack your grip and quit."[403] Owen's promotion had lasted five months without TV and could have continued to struggle along. But he ended his career with dignity and accomplished one thing he'd always wanted. "When I quit," he had told a reporter in 1988, "I want to quit on my own."[404] And he did. Owen was the longest-running promoter and NWA member from the old territorial days to finally call it a career, and his decision marked the end of an era.

Central States promoter Bob Geigel didn't stick with the NWA as Owen did, severing his connection to the organization in late 1987. Subsequently, he founded the World Wrestling Alliance, an independent group headquartered in Kansas City. The WWA crowned an inaugural world heavyweight champion on January 23, 1988, and a local grappler, Mike George from St. Joseph, beat Dick Slater in a tournament final to become the first titleholder. Geigel took Ken Mantell up on his offer to collaborate and saw wrestlers from Dallas, including Kerry Von Erich and Chris Adams. On July 16, 1988, George and Von Erich wrestled to a double count-out in a title versus title bout. Despite the name talent, crowds remained less than impressive at the Memorial Hall in Kansas City.

Later in 1988, Geigel reestablished his working relationship with Verne Gagne, and brought in grapplers from the AWA as well. Shohei "Giant" Baba of All Japan coordinated an extraordinary television taping stacked with talent in Kansas City with Geigel on February 2, 1989. The Funk Brothers, the British Bulldogs, the Rock and Roll Express, Jumbo Tsuruta, Stan Hansen, Tiger Mask, and other international celebrities were on the card, but it flopped at the box office. Only 300 people were in attendance. Geigel was forced to cancel several succeeding programs because of lackluster interest, and he eventually shuttered the WWA for good. Upon retirement, he took a job at the Woodlands racetrack as a security guard and looked back upon his career with fondness. "It was great for a long time," Geigel told a reporter. "Quite a ride."[405]

The Memphis–World Class–AWA cooperative was seemingly a beneficial venture in 1988, and fans enjoyed a string of matches between AWA champion Jerry Lawler and WCCW titleholder Kerry Von Erich. Their feud was essential viewing in Memphis and Dallas, and patrons at the Mid-South Coliseum witnessed a classic 60-minute Broadway on July 25 and saw Lawler win the World Class championship on October 23. Kerry then regained that strap on November 4 in Dallas. During this heightened partnership, Jerry Jarrett's Memphis promotion was in a commanding position based on its strength. In fact, World Class was in much worse financial condition than anyone realized, and the company needed well over $100,000 to square its debt. The rent at the Sportatorium hadn't been paid in months, and Ken Mantell abruptly quit near the end of July, leaving World Class without an experienced leader. As good as Kevin and Kerry Von Erich were in the ring, they weren't businessmen who could administer the Dallas office.

Needing immediate help, the Von Erichs contacted Jarrett, and the Memphis promoter traveled to Dallas in an advisory capacity. He examined the company's "books," and devised a plan to save World Class by offering to invest his own capital and taking over day-to-day control of the business.[406] He'd become the majority shareholder with 60 percent interest, and Kerry and Kevin would split the remaining stock. The brothers agreed, and around October 1988, the deal was finalized. With Jarrett in charge and crucial help from Eric Embry and Frank Dusek in the World Class office, the Dallas promotion was completely revamped. The old-school Texas wrestling methodology was now being interwoven with Memphis philosophies.

Representatives from the CWA, AWA, and World Class met at the Hermitage Hotel in Nashville a few weeks before Jarrett's deal went through to announce a massive joint promotion, SuperClash III, scheduled for December 13 in Chicago. At the press conference (filmed in conjunction with an ESPN taping in Nashville on September 17) were Jarrett, Kerry Von Erich, Jerry Lawler, Verne Gagne, AWA president Stanley Blackburn, and several other dignitaries. SuperClash was touted as the "biggest event" in wrestling history, and the CWF, PWOW, "Japan," Don Owen, and Bob Geigel were also said to be on board. Gagne admitted that putting the program together had been extremely difficult, and he was no doubt being candid. Not only were the specifics of lining up the venue, obtaining cable systems for pay-per-view availability, and arranging the talent a challenge, but he had to reach a compromise with promoters over match finishes, particularly the main event between Lawler and Kerry. It was obvious their feud was already overcooked, but it was believed to be the most marketable bout they had to offer. The fact that it was a "title unification" match made the contest even more significant.

SuperClash, however, was an unmitigated disappointment. Fewer than 1,700 fans turned out to see the spectacular at the UIC Pavilion, and the PPV buy-rate was 0.5. The Lawler–Von Erich affair was memorable, but the finish was marred as referee Marty Miller halted the action because Kerry had suffered a cut near his eye and there was too much blood. Kerry had appeared to be on his way to victory, but Miller stopped the bout in concern for the wrestler's safety. Lawler became double champion, holding both the AWA and WCCW world title belts. But in the aftermath of the show, turmoil between Jarrett and Gagne caused an irreparable split, fracturing the CWA–AWA alliance forever. Takes on the dispute varied, depending on the source, and ranged from general mistrust to a failure to pay talent for SuperClash appearances. On January 20, 1989, Gagne officially stripped Lawler of the AWA world belt, but the King remained the unified world heavyweight titleholder in all regions controlled by Jarrett.

That title lineage continued when Jarrett created the United States Wrestling Association (USWA) later in 1989, encompassing both the now-defunct CWA and World Class. But World Class was revived in September 1990 by Kevin Von Erich after a falling-out with Jarrett, lasted a handful of months, and went out of business for good. Jarrett was more resilient, and despite losing Lawler to the WWF in late 1992, he survived as an independent promoter until 1997. Verne Gagne was not so fortunate. He crowned Larry Zbyszko, his son-in-law, AWA champion on February 7, 1989, and strived to rebuild with Scott Norton, Colonel DeBeers, Ken Patera, the Destruction Crew, and JCP castoff Nikita Koloff. A Team Challenge Series was fostered to stir interest, but was unpopular, and worked against Gagne more than helped him. Live shows were becoming less and less frequent, down to once or twice a month, and finally ceased in August 1990. Gagne filed for bankruptcy the following year. Everyone knew that professional wrestling had turned into a two-promotion race, and Vince McMahon wanted to put more distance between himself and Jim Crockett. McMahon was playing a ruthless game of hardball, and dug into his rival whenever the opportunity arose. Prior to big JCP shows in New York and Chicago, McMahon ran programs in the same cities with his top stars in an effort to draw attention. Just before SuperClash in Chicago, his company informed the Illinois State Athletic Commission about Kerry Von Erich's prosthetic in the hopes the latter would be blocked from performing. And in a nod to Dusty Rhodes, he named Ted DiBiase's manservant Virgil, which was Dusty's actual first name.

Despite his huge advantage in the wrestling war, McMahon refused to let up on his foes, and JCP had to fight for every gain. Crockett planned for his first shot at a national pay-per-view audience on January 24, 1988, with the Bunkhouse Stampede Final from the Nassau Coliseum in Uniondale, New York. McMahon reacted by scheduling a Royal Rumble that same night, presented live on the USA Network. While he might not have been able to deter JCP loyalists from ordering the PPV, McMahon might've convinced some middle-of-the-road fans to watch a free program on cable instead of coughing up money for one. Crockett still garnered a 3.5 buy-rate and roughly 200,000 homes, giving him a nice victory.[407] And Dusty Rhodes won the Bunkhouse Stampede to boot (literally). At Copps Coliseum in Hamilton, Ontario, "Hacksaw" Jim Duggan eliminated One Man Gang to win the Rumble. The show attracted an 8.2 rating and a 12 share, making it the highest-rated program in USA Network history.[408]

On February 5, 1988, the WWF took another gigantic step by putting on pro wrestling's first live primetime special in more than three decades on NBC. Presented from Indianapolis, *The Main Event* featured the long-awaited rematch between Hulk Hogan and Andre the Giant and drew an astonishing 15.1 rating (25 share), the highest rating in American wrestling history. Andre pinned Hogan to end Hulk's four-year reign as WWF champion and then sold the belt to Ted DiBiase. It was soon revealed that Earl Hebner, not the assigned Dave Hebner, refereed the match, and he had refused to acknowledge when Hogan kicked out of Andre's pin attempt. Fans were shocked at the turn of events, and Hogan responded by tossing Earl from the ring. WWF president Jack Tunney vacated the championship and put it up for the winner of a huge 14-man tournament at WrestleMania IV on March 27, 1988.

Crockett fought fire with fire and booked the first-ever Clash of the Champions for WTBS that same evening with a better lineup of matches. Crowd favorite Sting wrestled NWA champion Ric Flair to an impressive draw in the main event, and Lex Luger teamed with Barry Windham to capture the world tag belts from Arn Anderson and Tully Blanchard. The program achieved a 5.8 rating (12.6 share). Overall, there was no stopping WrestleMania from financial success, but JCP's wrestlers at the Clash out-performed their WWF counterparts, and scrutinizing viewers condemned many aspects of McMahon's card. The tournament itself was lacking, espe-cially considering that a blurb in *WWF Magazine* had referred to Randy Savage as the heavyweight champion, which kind of spoiled the action. Savage did end up the titleholder, going over Ted DiBiase with a big assist from Hulk Hogan. WrestleMania IV had 585,000 pay-per-view buys.

The Hogan–Andre rivalry extended into the summer and was the highlight attraction at WrestleFest on July 31, 1988, in Milwaukee, drawing more than 25,000 spectators. Hogan took a victory in a cage. A week later, the WWF offered its first program in Greensboro, in the heart of Crockett country, and Hogan beat Andre by disqualification before 3,600 people. On August 29, Hogan and Savage partnered up to beat Andre and DiBiase in the main event of SummerSlam, the promotion's second pay-per-view of 1988. Also, the Ultimate Warrior, fast becoming one of the top babyfaces in the company, pinned the Honky Tonk Man in 27 seconds to capture the Intercontinental championship. Again, the WWF had a financial windfall, thanks to pay-per-view sales (over 900,000 buys), but the show was panned by critics. In terms of talent, McMahon signed "Big" Bubba Rogers (renamed the Big Bossman), Bad News Allen (Brown), Curt Hennig (Mr. Perfect), and Terry Taylor (Red Rooster). The loss of Rogers, the Rock and Roll Express, and Michael Hayes didn't exactly help Jim Crockett and Dusty Rhodes in early 1988, but their focus was on resur-recting turnout. TV format, style, and production issues were addressed, and Jim Ross joined the WTBS commentary team. Ole Anderson made a surprise return to aid Lex Luger against the Horsemen, and Luger's reg-ular tag partner Barry Windham turned on him to join the exclusive heel group in April. Windham went on to win the United States title in a May tournament in Houston, giving the Horsemen a lock on the NWA world title (Flair), the world tag (Arn Anderson and Tully Blanchard), and the

U.S. strap (Windham). Luger found a new teammate in Sting, and the duo was victorious in the third Crockett Cup in April. Among the major feuds over the first part of 1988 were the Midnight Express–Fantastics, Road Warriors–Powers of Pain, and, of course, Luger–Windham.

On July 10, 1988, a Great American Bash pay-per-view was held in Baltimore at the Arena, and the "Match of the Century," Flair versus Luger, was the headliner.[409] As with Lawler–Von Erich at SuperClash, their match was stopped after 23 minutes when the Maryland State Athletic Commissioner deemed Luger's blood loss to be too significant for him to continue, and Flair was declared the winner. And just like at SuperClash, Luger appeared to be moments away from winning the bout via submission with Flair in his Torture Rack. Fans were cheated out of a clean finish yet again, and those in the audience let JCP officials hear their displeasure. In another contest, a three-level 10-man Tower of Doom battle occurred, and fan favorites the Road Warriors, Jimmy and Ronnie Garvin, and Steve Williams defeated Kevin Sullivan, Mike Rotundo, Ivan Koloff, Al Perez, and the Russian Assassin. Elsewhere on the Bash tour, which stretched from June 26 to August 7, a number of War Games matches took place around the country, from Charlotte to Inglewood, and the Horsemen were vanquished every time.

In recent years, the relationship between Jim Crockett Promotions and Turner Broadcasting System, owned by Atlanta's media mogul Ted Turner, had improved measurably. Turner Home Entertainment, a subsidiary of TBS, assumed marketing and distribution for JCP wrestling video cassettes, and in February 1988, it was announced that the company was joining forces with Crockett in the pay-per-view field as well.[410] The Great American Bash was their first joint effort, and Crockett extended his WTBS contract through 1994. During the spring of 1988, however, rumors about Turner purchasing JCP were revealed, and the *Charlotte Observer* mentioned the sale price "could be" in excess of $10 million.[411] This wasn't the first time Turner had expressed interest in JCP. In 1985, he was said to have been "involved" in some capacity with Crockett, and was perhaps looking at an ownership or partnership agreement, but the situation apparently never worked out.[412]

But with Crockett in financial jeopardy in 1988, Turner entering the picture was a very real possibility. Insiders shrugged off questions about negotiations, but serious talks went on for months as attorneys wrangled over the details. The fact was, JCP was being consumed by debt, and Crockett was desperately trying to stave off bankruptcy. His obligations to Bill Watts had only been partially paid, and he had taken out personal loans to meet payroll and other expenses. Blame for the condition of the company, in spite of good revenue, TV ratings, and a lineup of talented grapplers, was leveled in all directions, but mostly landed on the two men at the top of the pyramid: Jim Crockett and Dusty Rhodes. Company finances had been mismanaged, and the escalating crisis was largely ignored until there was no turning back. Crockett had to sell.

On Wednesday, November 2, 1988, the sale was announced, and Turner took over that same day.[413] Jack Petrik of TBS was installed as the president of the newly fashioned Universal Wrestling Corporation, the subsidiary of Turner's company that would handle all things pro wrestling. Crockett was kept on as vice president, and Rhodes retained his booker position, at least for the time being. The UWC attained all current contracts, including those of the wrestlers, TV syndication, and arenas, and it acquired the physical assets of JCP. "NWA programming has been a highly successful part of the Superstation's schedule for many years," Turner told the *Atlanta Journal-Constitution*. "With the formation of [the] Universal Wrestling Corp., TBS and Jim Crockett Promotions have combined resources to further expand the marketing efforts and scope of the NWA worldwide."[414] Crockett added, "The new company will insure that [JCP] wrestling continues to grow and venture into areas which will give it expanded recognition and awareness."[415]

Although some publications claimed Turner had bought the NWA, that was an incorrect statement. Turner only bought JCP, and the National Wrestling Alliance maintained its independence as a nonprofit Iowa corporation. The leaders of the UWC realized its conundrum in marketing NWA as an exclusive brand and changed the name to World Championship Wrestling (WCW).

The end of Jim Crockett Promotions was a remarkable moment in wrestling history. While JCP hadn't technically been a territory since it began to expand nationally, it was the most successful of the old groups outside of the WWF, and was an important symbol of opposition to Vince McMahon. And World Championship Wrestling would continue to give

McMahon a run for his money going into what would be a new phase of the wrestling war.

Back in 1985, Red Bastien, in noting the rise of Vince McMahon, had stated that "There [was] still room for the other guys."[416] That was a nice thought, but really, there wasn't much room at all among the heavyweights of the business. It was a two-horse race, and whatever room was left for the "other guys" was limited by the lack of star-caliber talent. But with the disintegration of the territorial system, room opened up for independent promotions across the wrestling landscape. Led by inventive and resourceful promoters, these organizations interjected new concentrations of creativity into their programs to earn the loyalty of local audiences. They had to generate their own stars, find their own television deals, and attempt to maintain a small geographic area in competition with the WWF and WCW and their far superior product. The indies had heart, though, and the wrestlers, officials, and promoters loved the business at its purest level.

The independents were a place for young grapplers to hone their craft before getting their shot in the Big Two — much as they'd done in years past when an up-and-comer would perform in regional outfits before getting his shot in New York or St. Louis. The number of regional independents grew exponentially in the mid-to-late 1980s, and many name performers ended up on the indie circuit looking for jobs. International Championship Wrestling, Deep South Championship Wrestling, Global, Florida Championship Wrestling, World Organization Wrestling, and Windy City Wrestling were just a handful of groups to garner attention in various parts of the country. "Since the WWF took off, there are also a lot of little groups coming out of the woodwork every day," said John Ort, publisher of *Wrestling Eye* magazine. "You don't have to like [the WWF], but they've done a lot for themselves — and the rest of the business indirectly, whether they've wanted to or not. McMahon is a genius in his own time. You've got [to] give the devil his due."[417]

Vince McMahon, without a doubt, meant different things to different people, and to his enemies, he was everything that was wrong with modern day pro wrestling. But to the people who appreciated his hard work and accomplishments, there was no shortage of praise. "I feel that Vince McMahon is [the] best thing that happened to our business," explained former IC champion Tito Santana. "There's nobody better than him."[418] Hall of Famer Fred Blassie said, "No one had the foresight this man had. He is the greatest promoter ever. He showed me there's nothing but money out there."[419] "He took [wrestling] out of the '50s and '60s and brought it into the '80s," said Jesse "The Body" Ventura in 1985.[420] Richard Glover, a senior vice-president of Titan Sports, told a reporter in early 1989 that "Vince McMahon was the first of the TV generation to move into a position of leadership in the business. [He] saw that TV could lead [wrestling] out of being a regional business into a national business. TV could serve as a support for the live events, but it could in and of itself open up new opportunities."[421] Verne Gagne had a front row seat for all of McMahon's maneuvering and, in 1989, was blunt in his opinion: "[McMahon] disrupted the whole industry and put some of the promoters out of business. It hasn't been good for the industry; it's been good for him but nobody else. If McMahon hadn't done it, Crockett would have."[422]

McMahon's ascension caused a lot of resentment. "Vince Sr. was a gentleman," said an anonymous promoter in 1985. "I didn't like everything he did, but I could live with it. But that Junior is different. He's dangerous. He goes around telling everybody what a marketing genius he is, but believe me, it's not marketing — it's money. His method is just to buy everyone else out."[423] That same year, the legendary Dick the Bruiser was asked about McMahon and the wrestling war. He answered simply, "It's a business, just a business."[424]

More motivated, more organized, and better equipped than the oldtimers, McMahon had invaded each territory one by one with aggressive business tactics and, over time, outgunned local promoters. And his opponents were not choir boys. More often than not they were hard-nosed former wrestlers who were not used to, or susceptible to, being pushed around.

Truth be told, some of his rival promoters were certainly unscrupulous. Jim Ross, while attending a mid-1980s wrestling conference, overheard angry promoters seriously discussing a plot to kill McMahon. Years later, McMahon told Playboy, "Some of it was probably bravado from a pseudo tough guy. Some of it was real."[425] Revolutionizing a business wasn't always popular, and McMahon had a pretty clear-minded perspective about it. In a 1991 interview in Sports Illustrated, he said, "Had my father known what I was going to do, he never would have sold his stock to me."[426]

But, as it turned out, McMahon did take over in 1982 and transformed the industry. With annual revenue of more than $100 million, a national touring circuit, 250-plus stations in his syndicated TV network, and an immense pay-per-view following, the World Wrestling Federation stood towering above the rest. The wrestling war continued, but the playing field was perceptibly different, and longtime fans had the choice to accept or reject what the sport had become. The territorial era in professional wrestling was officially over, and there was no way to turn back the clock.

ENDNOTES

CHAPTER 1

1   Gus Sonnenberg, a former football player, is credited with introducing the flying tackle in 1928–29. Joe Savoldi, another ex–gridiron star, popularized the flying dropkick in 1930.

2   The Trust was formed in 1933 by Jack Curley, Joe "Toots" Mondt, Ray Fabiani, Tom Packs, Paul Bowser, and Ed White, and the group fizzled out three years later.

3   By-Laws of National Wrestling Alliance, Article IX, p. 8, part of the Department of Justice case files, File No. 60-406-0, National Archive at College Park, Maryland.

4   Orville Brown was the first National Wrestling Alliance champion beginning in 1948 and was booked to face National Wrestling Association titleholder Lou Thesz in a unification match in November 1949. However, Brown suffered career-ending injuries in a car accident on November 1, 1949, and the match scheduled for later in the month was canceled. On November 27, Thesz was named the Alliance title-holder, recognized by all members.

5   Fred Kohler letters to Sam Muchnick, October 10, 1950, December 9, 1950, part of

the Department of Justice case files, File No. 60-406-0, National Archive at College Park, Maryland.

6   Eddie Quinn letter to Sam Muchnick, dated September 4, 1957. Jack Pfefer Collection at the University of Notre Dame, South Bend, Indiana.

7   Coverage in the *Dallas Morning News*, beginning January 6, 1953, and continuing into 1954.

8   The Heart of America Sports Attractions Inc. was founded in 1963 and was owned by George Simpson of Kansas City, Gust Karras of St. Joseph, Bob Geigel, and Pat O'Connor. The latter two were still active wrestlers at the time and their ownership was kept secret. Later, Harley Race became a partner.

9   Rogers suffered a broken arm and fractured ankle. His health status in 1963 has been heavily disputed, with some sources at the time claiming he'd suffered a heart attack.

10 The NWA first reached 39 members at the Santa Monica convention in September 1952. The 39 members included both Sam Avey and Leroy McGuirk in Tulsa.

CHAPTER 2

11 Capitol Wrestling Corporation Financial Statements (Unaudited) for the Years Ending September 30, 1979, and September 30, 1980, Leopold & Linowes, Certified Public Accountants, Washington, D.C., 20036.

12 Watson was a two-time world heavyweight champion, having captured the National Wrestling Association championship in February 1947, and the National Wrestling Alliance crown in March 1956.

13 Boesch had his local TV on channel 39, KHTV, and because of its success, the station paid production costs. *Wrestling Observer Newsletter*, April 21, 2003, p. 1.

14 *Boston Globe*, June 10, 1983.

15 *Des Moines Register*, November 7, 1983, p. 22.

16 *Boston Globe*, June 10, 1983.

17 *New Orleans Times-Picayune*, December 22, 1982, p. 40.

18 *Chicago Tribune*, March 13, 1994, p. 1.

19 *Toronto Star* journalist Greg Quill noted in a 1986 article that he was "warned" by a WWF official not to call McMahon "Vincent Jr." *Toronto Star*, August 22, 1986, p. D20.

20 Following Andre's injury and subsequent surgery, Jim Barnett sent a telegram out to fellow promoters, informing them of his location at Beth Israel Hospital in Boston. "He is expected to be out approximately 10 weeks," Barnett noted. "Suggest friends call him to cheer him up." Barnett, interestingly, said that Andre was "operated on today for a broken leg." Stu Hart Collection, Glenbow Museum, Calgary, Alberta, Canada.

21 *Yonkers Herald Statesman*, October 1, 1981, p. 8.

22 The McMahons moved to 3 Driftwood Lane in South Yarmouth. The Cape Cod Coliseum was at 225 White's Path in South Yarmouth. The *Cape Cod Chronicle* explained that the venue was "financially beleaguered" in early 1976 and detailed the fall of the Cape Cod Cubs, a local hockey club. *Cape Cod Chronicle*, January 1, 1976, p. 5. Edward Fruean was listed as the owner of the venue. *Lewiston Daily Sun*,

January 28, 1976. McMahon was listed as the owner of the Coliseum. *Cape Cod Chronicle*, September 6, 1979, p. 17.

23 Linda McMahon was the registered agent for the new corporation. The Cape Cod Coliseum was the address for Titan Sports. The company had an ID number of 001003655. Secretary of the Commonwealth of Massachusetts Website, www.sec.state.ma.us.

24 Details of the sale were outlined in an agreement signed by Vincent McMahon Sr., Robert Marella, Phil Zacko, Arnold Skaaland, and Vincent K. McMahon, dated June 5, 1982.

CHAPTER 3

25 Pinkie George and Orville Brown were muscled out by the Heart of America Sports Attractions group. Harry Light was faced with strong competition by Jim Barnett and Johnny Doyle, who sold out to Edward Farhat (a.k.a. the Sheik) around 1964–65.

26 National Wrestling Alliance Membership Roster 1976–77.

27 O'Mahoney was originally scheduled to win the March 2, 1936, match against Dick Shikat. However, Shikat took matters into his own hands and began shooting on his opponent, eventually forcing O'Mahoney to submit.

28 The first $100,000 gate in pro wrestling occurred on May 21, 1952, at Gilmore Baseball Park in Hollywood, California. The show was headlined by Lou Thesz and Baron Michele Leone and drew 25,256 paying $103,277.75.

29 His program featured a string of independent workers, including George Strickland, Chico Garcia, Pancho Villa, Killer Kent, Buddy Kellogg, and Buddy Brown. In the main event, Leon Graham beat Glenn Reinhart. Haft enjoyed his 50th anniversary as a promoter in Columbus in January 1967.

30 *Detroit Free Press*, May 25, 1981, p. 8.

31 More information is offered in *Inside Out: How Corporate America Destroyed Professional Wrestling* by Ole Anderson with Scott Teal (2003).

32 Ibid.

33 GCW syndicated to WLWT (channel 5) in Cincinnati, WKEF (channel 22) in Dayton, WCLQ (channel 61) in Cleveland, and WOAC (channel 67) in Canton.

34 *Cleveland Plain Dealer*, December 4, 1982, p. 71.

35 International Wrestling League (IWL) was an indie promotion based in Georgia run by Jim Wilson and Thunderbolt Patterson.

36 NWA members agreed to reinstate Farhat at the 1982 convention in Puerto Rico "if he still qualified as an active promoter and paid his dues." National Wrestling Alliance meeting minutes from the 1982 Annual Convention in San Juan, Puerto Rico.

37 *Inside Out: How Corporate America Destroyed Professional Wrestling* by Ole Anderson with Scott Teal (2003).

38 MACW changed from channel 29 to channel 4 sometime between November 8 and December 13, 1980.

39 *Buffalo Courier-Express*, unknown date (week of August 30 to September 5, 1981).

40 *Los Angeles Times*, July 4, 1982, p. C1.

CHAPTER 4

41 In 1948, Eaton's son Robert married Marilyn Knight, the daughter of Goodwin Knight, lieutenant governor of California. Goodwin Knight was elected governor in 1953.

42 Deposition of Philip P. Zacko, March 2, 1984, *Bruno Sammartino v. Capitol Wrestling Corporation*, Civil Action No. 82-1979, United States District Court for the Western District of Pennsylvania.

43 Correspondence with Jeff Walton, June 2016.

44 Deposition of Michael LeBell, June 12, 1985, *Titan Sports, Inc., A Massachusetts Corporation v. Mike LeBell*, Case No. CV-85-0282-RMT, United States District Court for the Central District of California.

45 Details of the deal were revealed in *Michael LeBell v. Vincent Kennedy McMahon, Titan Sports, Inc., Capital Wrestling Corporation, and Does 1 to 20, inclusive*, Superior Court of California for the County of Los Angeles, Case No. C 568 506.

46 Correspondence with Jeff Walton, June 2016.

47 Ibid.

48 Deposition of Philip P. Zacko, March 2, 1984, *Bruno Sammartino v. Capitol Wrestling Corporation*, Civil Action No. 82-1979, United States District Court for the Western District of Pennsylvania.

49 National Wrestling Alliance meeting minutes from the 1982 Annual Convention in San Juan, Puerto Rico.

50 Ibid.

51 Letter from James E. Barnett to NWA members dated September 15, 1982. Incidentally, the Braves lost to the St. Louis Cardinals in the National League Championship Series, three games to none.

52 Blanchard was billed as an "associate promoter at the Wrestlethon with Frank Brown." *San Antonio Express*, January 12, 1965, p. 19.

53 Southwest Championship Wrestling Inc. was registered before the Texas Secretary of State on October 15, 1979, by Joseph E. Blanchard. The corporate address was 922 Serenade in San Antonio.

54 *Paris News*, June 29, 1982, p. 14.

55 McGuirk won the world junior heavyweight championship on June 19, 1939, and retained the belt throughout the 1940s. Already blind in one eye, he lost his remaining sight in a car accident on February 7, 1950, in Little Rock, and his career as a pro wrestler ended.

56 Scott's tenure as a booker for McGuirk was relatively brief, lasting from late 1981 until around March/April 1982. McGuirk's promotion also changed its name from Tri-States to Midwest Championship Wrestling.

57 Unknown 1981 article entitled "McGuirk Says He Won't Rehire Five Who Walked Out." Also *Arkansas Gazette*, May 11, 1983, p. 27.

58   *Wrestling Observer Newsletter*, August 10, 1986, p. 1.

59   *Dallas Morning News*, November 1, 1982, p. 36.

60   The show in Santa Rosa was held on June 11, 1979, and featured Murdoch, Mulligan, Little Tokyo, Coconut Willie, Manny Fernandez, and El Mongol — all Amarillo regulars. Each of these grapplers, with the exception of Murdoch, was back in Amarillo for a show at the Sports Arena on June 14. See *Santa Rosa Press Democrat*, June 11, 1979, p. 18.

61   *Albuquerque Journal*, June 12, 1974, p. C1.

62   *Albuquerque Journal*, February 9, 1978, p. F1.

63   Georgia Corporations Division website. Also see *Marietta Journal*, October 1, 1982, p. 19.

CHAPTER 5

64   Muchnick's retirement show drew 19,919 people to the Checkerdome and an $110,000 gate, and both figures were the largest of his nearly four-decade career. *St. Louis Post-Dispatch*, January 5, 1982, p. 17.

65   Muchnick's professionalism and the high standards for his promotion in St. Louis were detailed by his longtime assistant Larry Matysik in *Wrestling at the Chase: The Inside Story of Sam Muchnick and the Legends of Professional Wrestling* (2005).

66   National Wrestling Alliance meeting minutes from the 1982 annual convention in San Juan, Puerto Rico.

67   *Wrestling at the Chase: The Inside Story of Sam Muchnick and The Legends of Professional Wrestling* by Larry Matysik (2005).

68   Race won his first NWA world title on May 24, 1973, with a win over Dory Funk Jr. He also defeated Terry Funk, Dusty Rhodes, Giant Baba (twice), and Tommy Rich for the championship.

69   National Wrestling Alliance meeting minutes from the 1982 annual convention in San Juan, Puerto Rico.

70   The boxer vs. wrestler match occurred on July 1, 1940, in Atlanta, and Dempsey won by KO in the second round.

71   *Orlando Sentinel*, September 22, 1985, p. 6.

72   *Lakeland Ledger*, August 21, 1976, p. 3B.

73   *St. Petersburg Evening Independent*, February 16, 1972, p. 1.

74   Ron and Robert Fuller purchased Gulf Coast Wrestling from the Fields family and renamed their local promotion Southeastern Championship Wrestling (SECW). According to the State of Alabama Corporation Records, Gulf Coast Wrestling Inc. changed to Southeastern Gulf Coast Wrestling Inc. on July 7, 1978. Bob Armstrong was a minority owner in Southeastern with the Fullers, owning 10 percent of the company beginning in 1978. *Dothan Eagle*, May 19, 2012.

75   *The Tennessean*, May 8, 1977, p. 168.

76   Details about this situation were offered in the *Memphis Commercial Appeal*, March 20, 1977.

77 The station paid Owen's production costs in Portland. *Wrestling Observer Newsletter*, April 21, 2003, p. 1.

78 *Deseret News*, August 11, 1979.

79 *Deseret News*, April 9–10, 1982, p. 4B.

80 *Chilliwack Progress*, December 8, 1954, p. 6.

81 Quinn passed away on December 14, 1964, at the age of 58.

82 *Montreal Gazette*, July 23, 1982.

CHAPTER 6

83 An announcement of the deal was made in the *Chicago Tribune*, December 14, 1965, p. C4.

84 *Los Angeles Times*, August 2, 1969, p. B2.

85 Bruiser won his first WWA championship in 1964 and his last in 1985.

86 *Louisville Courier-Journal*, August 26, 1979, p. B3.

87 Memorandum from Mike Levinton to Blair-represented TV stations dated November 4, 1982.

88 Letter from Gunkel to Barnett dated February 4, 1983. The Global Wrestling office was at 5570 Lake Island Drive NW, Atlanta, Georgia, 30327.

89 Letter from Barnett to Gunkel dated February 8, 1983. As noted in the document, carbon copies of the letter were sent to Flair and the NWA board of directors.

90 Letter from Coxe to Mike Levinton of Blair Television dated March 1, 1983.

91 Letter from Barnett to Blanchard dated March 14, 1983.

92 *Wrestling Observer Newsletter*, July 1983, p. 15.

93 The program was featured during the weekend of July 2–3, 1983.

94 *Albuquerque Journal*, July 2, 1983, p. 17.

95 *Mansfield News-Journal*, June 5, 1983, p. 72.

96 There was coverage of the GA–SCW–Global situation in the *Wrestling Observer Newsletter*, July–September 1983.

97 *Augusta Chronicle*, August 14, 1983.

98 *Wrestling at the Chase: The Inside Story of Sam Muchnick and The Legends of Professional Wrestling* by Larry Matysik (2005).

99 *St. Louis Post-Dispatch*, May 22, 1983, p. 74.

100 Ibid.

101 *Globe and Mail*, May 10, 1983, p. 55.

102 National Wrestling Alliance meeting minutes from the 1983 annual convention in Las Vegas, Nevada.

103 Barnett and Anderson's difficulties are detailed in the book *Inside Out: How Corporate America Destroyed Professional Wrestling* by Ole Anderson with Scott Teal (2003).

104 LeBell's resignation was confirmed by NWA president Bob Geigel in a letter to members dated November 22, 1983.

105 National Wrestling Alliance meeting minutes from the 1983 annual convention in Las Vegas, Nevada.

106 Ibid.

107 Ibid.

108 Vincent K. McMahon became the president of the Capitol Wrestling Corporation with the purchase. Notably, the company saw its charter revoked on December 10, 1984. *Michael Le Bell v. Vincent Kennedy McMahon, Titan Sports, Inc. Capital Wrestling Corporation, and Does 1 to 20, inclusive*, Case No. C-568-506, Superior Court of the State of California for the County of Los Angeles.

109 Letter from McMahon to Geigel dated August 31, 1983.

CHAPTER 7

110 The program on WAKR (channel 23) appeared on Saturday afternoons at 1:30.

111 The Akron show was held on February 26, 1983, at the Copley High School Gym. *Akron Beacon Journal*, February 24, 1983, p. 18.

112 As a result of this action, Georgia Championship Wrestling filed suit against Titan Sports. It was filed in the United States District Court Southern District of Ohio Western Division, *Georgia Championship Wrestling, Inc., v. Vincent McMahon, Sr., et al*, case number C-3-84-564.

113 *The Ring's Wrestling* magazine, November 1983, #106, p. 50.

114 *Cincinnati Enquirer*, December 11, 1983, p. 167.

115 An article about Cannon was featured in the *Detroit Free Press*, January 16, 1983, p. 245.

116 *Windsor Star*, March 28, 1987, p. B1.

117 Correspondence with Steve Dini, September 2016.

118 *The Ring's Wrestling* magazine, November 1983, #106, p. 50.

119 *King of the Ring: The Harley Race Story* by Harley Race and Gerry Tritz (2004), p. 107.

120 Linda McMahon interview. *Raw Magazine*, March 2000.

121 Finkel was described as "an announcer and public relations official with Titan Sports Inc." *Syracuse Post Standard*, April 15, 1981.

122 In a 1983 article, promoter Joe Meriggi was quoted as saying, "We signed with Ed Cohen [and the WWF]. He makes the matches and books the shows." *Wilmington News Journal*, July 6, 1983, p. 34. A 1984 article called Cohen a "spokesman" for Titan Sports. *San Bernardino County Sun*, June 24, 1984, p. 55. In March 1983, Cohen appeared as a guest on "Buddy Rogers's Corner," a WWF-TV segment, as the organization's charity coordinator.

123 Ibid.

124 *Wrestling Observer Newsletter*, April 1983, p. 16.

125 Secretary of the Commonwealth of Massachusetts website, www.sec.state.ma.us.

126 Kietzer wrote a letter to the *Wrestling Observer* about the situation. *Wrestling Observer Newsletter*, October 22, 1984, p. 12.

127 "George Scott: WWF's Biggest Booker," by Greg Oliver, November 2001, *Slam! Wrestling* website (slam.canoe.com/wrestling).

128 *Rochester Democrat and Chronicle*, November 19, 1985, p. 25.

129 *Backlund: From All-American Boy to Professional Wrestling's World Champion* by Bob Backlund and Rob Miller (2015).

130 Ibid., p. 443–446.

131 McMahon was reportedly paying KPLR-TV $2,100 per week and five percent of the gross from his live shows in St. Louis. *Wrestling Observer Newsletter*, April 21, 2003, p. 1.

132 *St. Louis Post-Dispatch*, December 30, 1983, p. 17.

133 Ibid.

CHAPTER 8

134 The segment was featured during the weekend of December 31, 1983–January 1, 1984.

135 *Minneapolis CityBusiness*, September 10, 1986, p. 16.

136 Inoki was counted out after being accidentally knocked out. He was originally supposed to beat Hogan in the IWGP final. The date of the bout was June 2, 1983.

137 Hogan detailed his problems with Gagne in his autobiography, *Hollywood Hulk Hogan* by Hulk Hogan (2002), p. 106–107. He also recounted McMahon Jr. discussing future plans for the WWF at his home in Minnesota.

138 *My Life Outside the Ring: A Memoir* by Hulk Hogan, Mark Dagostino (2009), p. 103–104.

139 *Minneapolis CityBusiness*, September 10, 1986, p. 16.

140 *Minneapolis Star Tribune*, May 18, 1984, p. 4D.

141 *Sports Illustrated*, March 25, 1991.

142 *Pittsburgh Post-Gazette*, July 12, 1990, p. 13.

143 *Sports Illustrated*, March 25, 1991.

144 *Wrestling Observer Newsletter*, January 1984, p. 1, 4–5.

145 Ibid., p. 17–18.

146 *The Ring's Wrestling* magazine, November 1983, #106, p. 50.

147 *The King of New Orleans: How the Junkyard Dog Became Professional Wrestling's First Black Superstar* by Greg Klein (2012).

148 The WWF was featured on WNOL (channel 38) in New Orleans and KLRT (channel 16) in Little Rock.

149 Watts talked about this issue in his autobiography, *The Cowboy and the Cross: The Bill Watts Story* by "Cowboy" Bill Watts and Scott Williams (2006), p. 210–212.

150 *Dallas Morning News*, June 26, 1983, p. 2B.

151 *Dallas Morning News*, February 11, 1984, p. 33. Also see *Wrestling Observer Newsletter*, March 1984, p. 1–2 and April 1984, p. 2–5.

152 Famed sportswriter Jerry Izenberg of the *Newark Star-Ledger* stated that McMahon "revolutionized an industry." *Newark Star-Ledger*, May 31, 1984, p. 93.

153 Gagne later said, "I had a fine relationship with McMahon's father." *Minneapolis CityBusiness*, September 10, 1986, p. 16.

CHAPTER 9

154 By the 1980s, blacklisting by promoters was more of an intimidation technique than a legitimate practice. A reporter in 1985 mentioned that an "informal blacklist" of WWF performers had "been bantered about." *Arizona Republic*, April 5, 1985, p. 69.

155 *Wrestling Observer Newsletter*, March 1984, p. 23.

156 *San Francisco Chronicle*, March 21, 1984, p. 66. Also *Wrestling Observer Newsletter*, April 1984, p. 11–12.

157 *Minneapolis Star Tribune*, April 15, 1984, p. 7B.

158 *Minneapolis Star Tribune*, May 18, 1984, p. 60.

159 *Minneapolis CityBusiness*, September 10, 1986, p. 16.

160 *Minneapolis Star Tribune*, April 7, 1984, p. 1A, 5A.

161 *Minneapolis Star Tribune*, June 15, 1985, p. 1A, 9A.

162 Episode of *World Championship Wrestling* on WTBS, aired May 5, 1984.

163 *Inside Out: How Corporate America Destroyed Professional Wrestling* by Ole Anderson with Scott Teal (2003). McMahon reportedly purchased the company for $750,000. *Wrestling Observer Newsletter*, April 21, 2003, p. 3.

164 *Richmond Times-Dispatch*, May 31, 1984.

165 *Richmond Times-Dispatch*, June 7, 1984.

166 *St. Louis Post-Dispatch*, February 10, 1984.

167 In a local newspaper advertisement, the Adams–Garvin feud was billed as "Pro Wrestling's Hottest Rivalry!" *St. Louis Post-Dispatch*, May 11, 1984, p. 25.

168 *Wrestling Observer Newsletter*, May 1984, p. 3, 5.

169 A newspaper advertisement billed the show as "Stars War 1984." *Louisville Courier-Journal*, July 22, 1984, p. C19.

170 *Wrestling Observer Newsletter*, December 1983, p. 1.

CHAPTER 10

171 *The Best of Times* by Jerry Jarrett with Mark James (2011), p. 205–207.

172 *Los Angeles Times*, January 29, 1984, Calendar Section, p. 67.

173 Footage appeared on *Superstars of Wrestling* over the weekend of July 7–8, 1984.

174 Moolah traded the championship with Yukiko Tomoe, Susan Green, and Evelyn Stevens.

175 *Philadelphia Daily News*, August 3, 1984, p. 41.

176 Hulk Hogan made a special appearance on MTV as a guest VJ in the summer of 1984. *Detroit Free Press*, September 27, 1984, p. 35.

177 *Financial Post*, April 5, 1986, p. 13.

178 *Greenwich News*, March 1, 1984, p. 22.

179 *Gettysburg Times*, March 4, 1985, p. 12.

180 *Minneapolis CityBusiness*, September 10, 1986, p. 16.

181 The correspondent was Mick Karch of St. Louis Park, Minnesota. *Wrestling Observer Newsletter*, March 1984, p. 7.

182 *Wrestling Observer Newsletter*, February 4, 1985, p. 7.

183 Details of this deal can be found in *Pain and Passion: The History of Stampede Wrestling* by Heath McCoy (2007) p. 203–204.

184 *Calgary Herald*, September 16, 1984, p. D7.

185 WWF's *World Championship Wrestling* episode broadcast Saturday, July 14, 1984.

186 *Atlanta Constitution*, July 17, 1984, p. 11B.

187 *Palm Beach Post*, October 15, 1984, p. B16.

188 *Philadelphia Daily News*, August 3, 1984, p. 41.

189 *Atlanta Constitution*, July 27, 1984, p. 11P.

CHAPTER 11

190 *Sun-Sentinel*, July 23, 1984, p. B1.

191 *Palm Beach Post*, March 15, 1985, p. 1.

192 The title change occurred on July 23, 1984, in Birmingham.

193 Bruiser sold his interest in the Chicago promotion to Verne Gagne around January 1983. The longtime "front" promoter Bob Luce ran his last show on February 12, 1983, at the International Amphitheatre with all AWA talent. The next show, on April 16, was held at the UIC Pavilion.

194 *Wrestling's Main Event*, December 1984, p. 60.

195 Jarrett mentioned the TV taping in his autobiography, *The Best of Times* by Jerry Jarrett with Mark James (2011), p. 207.

196 Jack Reynolds, who also worked for Eddie Einhorn's IWA in the 1970s, was the first announcer for Pro Wrestling USA in 1984. He was quickly hired by Titan Sports, and Reynolds was a commentator on *All-Star Wrestling*, *Maple Leaf Wrestling*, and *Prime-Time Wrestling* in 1984–85. During the summer of 1985, he was replaced on *Prime-Time Wrestling* (co-hosted by Jesse Ventura) by Gorilla Monsoon. The annual cost of featuring *Pro Wrestling USA* on WPIX was $440,000. *Sports Illustrated*, April 29, 1985, p. 38.

197 *Wrestling Observer Newsletter*, November 12, 1984, p. 7.

198 The syndicated show included promos (interviews) for local live events.

199 *Wrestling Observer Newsletter*, November 12, 1984, p. 23–24.

200 *Wrestling Observer Newsletter*, October 22, 1984, p. 24.

201 *Kansas City Times*, December 12, 1984, p. E1.

202 *Honolulu Star-Bulletin*, February 12, 1985, p. 24.

203 *St. Louis Post-Dispatch*, April 2, 1972, Parade Section, p. 14.

204 *Minneapolis CityBusiness*, September 10, 1986, p. 16.

205 *Baton Rouge State-Times Advocate*, June 12, 1985, p. 20.

CHAPTER 12

206 *Lubbock Avalanche-Journal*, October 26, 1947, p. 7.

207 The WWF show in Dallas on December 28 was staged at the State Fair Coliseum.

Tickets were $13.25, $11.25, and $9.25. *Dallas Morning News*, December 28, 1984, p. 14B, and *Dallas Morning News*, December 29, 1984, p. 2B.

208 *Des Moines Register*, January 21, 1985, p. 22, and *Philadelphia Daily News*, January 30, 1985, p. 74.

209 Schultz was reportedly fired on February 11, 1985, in Los Angeles for trying to "jump" Mr. T. *Wrestling Observer Newsletter*, March 4, 1985, p. 17.

210 *Philadelphia Daily News*, February 22, 1985, p. 101.

211 *Philadelphia Daily News*, December 11, 1984, p. 88.

212 *Fort Lauderdale News*, April 29, 1985, p. 51.

213 *Courier-News*, March 30, 1985, p. 12.

214 *Los Angeles Times*, June 7, 1985, p. E7.

215 *Sports Illustrated*, April 29, 1985, p. 38.

216 *Gettysburg Times*, March 4, 1985, p. 12.

217 *Los Angeles Times*, June 7, 1985, p. E1.

218 *Los Angeles Times*, November 25, 1984, Calendar Section, p. 4.

219 New Orleans received the pay-per-view broadcast via Cox Cable, and 3,000-plus households purchased the WrestleMania broadcast for $10. However, technical problems hampered the showing. *New Orleans Times-Picayune*, April 4, 1985, p. 84.

220 It was reported that Titan Sports spent $16 million in 1984 and brought in only $11 million. Unknown article, reprinted in the *Wrestling Observer Newsletter*, April 15, 1985, p. 4. However, according to papers filed in a trademark infringement case with the U.S. Patent and Trademark Office dated December 18, 2013, the WWF grossed $29,596,974 in 1984. http://tsdr.uspto.gov/caseviewer/pdf?caseId=77626242&docIndex=15&searchprefix=sn#docIndex=15

221 New Japan was responsible for paying "nearly $500,000 as an annual booking contract fee" to the WWF in 1985. *Wrestling Observer Newsletter*, March 4, 1985, p. 13. Inoki's contract with McMahon reportedly ended in September 1985, and he was not interested in renewing. He didn't feel WWF wrestlers fit their style in Japan with the exception of Hulk Hogan and Andre the Giant. *Wrestling Observer Newsletter*, #1, 1985, p. 2.

222 *Sports Illustrated*, April 29, 1985, p. 38.

223 The first WrestleMania grossed "in the $6 million range," including souvenirs and video cassettes. *Wrestling Observer Newsletter*, April 15, 1986, p. 6.

224 *St. Louis Post-Dispatch*, April 2, 1985, p. 5C.

225 *St. Louis Post-Dispatch*, July 1, 1985, p. E1.

226 *Abilene Reporter-News*, May 31, 1985, p. 1A, 12A.

227 *Detroit Free Press*, March 15, 1985, p. 32.

228 *Burlington Free Press*, September 22, 1985, p. 14C.

229 Ibid.

230 *Washington Times*, November 21, 1985, p. 3C.

231 *Arizona Republic*, April 5, 1985, p. 69.

232 *Cleveland Plain Dealer*, November 28, 1985, p. 192.

CHAPTER 13

233 *Orlando Sentinel*, September 22, 1985, p. 6.

234 *Sun-Sentinel*, October 8, 2004, p. 35.

235 *The Trentonian*, February 15, 1985.

236 *Pittsburgh Press*, May 28, 1985, p. D5.

237 *Pittsburgh Press*, June 2, 1985, p. D2.

238 Slaughter was originally supposed to team with Jerry Blackwell, but the latter was prevented from wrestling by the New Jersey State Athletic Commission because of high blood pressure. The show, billed as Star Wars '85, had four no-shows in addition to Blackwell: Terry Funk, Ray Stevens, Stan Lane, and Tommy Rich. Funk was filming a new TV show, Lane had a knee injury, and Rich was double-booked — he headlined a show that same day in Marietta, Georgia. The Meadowlands show drew 18,600 fans.

239 *The Cowboy and the Cross: The Bill Watts Story* by "Cowboy" Bill Watts and Scott Williams (2006), p. 183.

240 *Shreveport Times*, July 23, 1985, p. 4-C.

241 *Tulsa World*, February 8, 1985.

242 *Shreveport Times*, July 23, 1985, p. 1-C.

243 An article in December 1984 referenced Gunkel's attempt to land a major TV outlet like ESPN or WGN. It was said her business partner was Terry Funk. *Atlanta Constitution*, December 3, 1984, p. 1A.

244 *Detroit Free Press*, July 18, 1985.

245 *Indianapolis Star*, April 12, 1985, p. 19.

246 *Los Angeles Times*, June 7, 1985.

247 Blanchard and Behrend were partners in the company Behrend-Blanchard Center State Productions Inc., officially formed in Texas on March 3, 1981.

248 The tour drew about $400,000, but it is unclear how much World Class cleared after expenses. *Wrestling Observer Newsletter*, 1985, #7.

249 Bruiser Brody was reportedly a middleman between Jack Adkisson and Antonio Inoki in this deal. Brody expected to be compensated for his role in bringing the two sides together. Adkisson trained Brody in pro wrestling. *Brody: The Triumph and Tragedy of Wrestling's Rebel* by Larry Matysik and Barbara Goodish (2007).

250 *Wrestling Observer Newsletter*, 1985, #8, p. 3.

251 *Arizona Republic*, April 5, 1985, p. 69.

252 Savage's brother Lanny Poffo also went to the WWF and debuted the same day. The brothers were not acknowledged as such in the WWF.

253 *Portland Oregonian*, May 19, 1985, p. E-18.

254 *Statesman Journal* (Salem, OR), May 23, 1985, p. 14. Reportedly, the May 21 Portland show was the same date as a Piper booking in Los Angeles for the WWF, which he no-showed. It was reported that Piper was told by higher-ups not to appear on the Owen show, but he did anyway. *Wrestling Observer Newsletter*, 1985, #6, p. 6.

255 *Portland Oregonian*, May 19, 1985, p. E-18.

CHAPTER 14

256 *Brody: The Triumph and Tragedy of Wrestling's Rebel* by Larry Matysik and Barbara Goodish (2007).

257 Johnson's comments appeared in Bob Verdi's column in the *Chicago Tribune* and were reprinted in the *Spokane Chronicle*, June 20, 1985, p. D1.

258 *Chicago Tribune*, August 16, 1985. Wolf also called Hogan the "biggest superstar in wrestling today."

259 *Boston Herald*, August 25, 1985, p. 44.

260 *Boston Herald*, August 30, 1985, p. 83.

261 *Hattiesburg American*, September 1, 1985, p. 86.

262 *Wrestling Observer Newsletter*, 1985, #11, p. 1.

263 The date has also been listed by sources as July 8, 1985.

264 *Wrestling Observer Newsletter*, 1985, #7, p. 6.

265 In many cases, even on regular JCP shows, events that featured Flair saw ticket prices increase compared to those without him.

266 Lexington achieved an audience of 8,000 and a record $90,000 gate. *Wrestling Observer Newsletter*, 1985, #9, p. 2–3.

267 Prior to the turn, Flair had been a fan favorite in the Mid-Atlantic region, mostly wrestling heels like Nikita Koloff, Tully Blanchard, and Buddy Landel. On the road, Flair wrestled a number of babyfaces and often performed as a rulebreaker. Among his opponents were Magnum T.A., Dusty Rhodes, Wahoo McDaniel, and Sgt. Slaughter. Because of his popularity, even after turning heel, Flair was cheered in the Mid-Atlantic area.

268 *Richmond Times-Dispatch*, December 3, 1985, p. 19. Crockett's lawsuit against McMahon was settled in early April 1986. *Wrestling Observer Newsletter*, April 15, 1986, p. 4.

269 *Kannapolis Daily Independent*, December 10, 1985. Charlotte was an off-limits city, and the WWF wouldn't return for more than three years.

270 *Baytown Sun*, September 1, 1985, p. 26.

271 *Paris News*, August 23, 1986, p. 9.

272 *Baytown Sun*, September 1, 1985, p. 26.

273 According to one report, the Cotton Bowl extravaganza drew a crowd of 30,241 and a gate of $240,310.50. *Wrestling Observer Newsletter*, 1985, #12, p. 4.

274 The WWF was originally scheduled to run Tulsa on September 22 in a head-to-head situation against Watts but changed the show's date to September 21. *Wrestling Observer Newsletter*, 1985, #10, p. 6. In other cities, where the WWF was established, they went head to head with the local promoter. But since the WWF was just breaking into Tulsa, McMahon didn't want to diminish his chances by going up against Watts.

275 *Portland Oregonian*, October 8, 1985, p. 87.

276 *Wrestling Observer Newsletter*, 1985, #8, p. 4.

277 The two prior near-sellouts occurred on February 14 and March 4, 1985. The May 6, 1985, event, which drew 1,200, did not feature Hulk Hogan.

278 *Ottawa Citizen*, May 17, 1986.

279 The Columbus event was part of the Ohio State Fair on August 13, 1985. An estimated 50,000 fans were in attendance. The crowd was then the largest for a wrestling show in North American history. *Wrestling Observer Newsletter*, 1985, #8 and #9.

280 The final International Wrestling–AWA show took place on July 29, 1985, at the Montreal Forum, and the first IW–WWF program occurred on August 19 in Quebec City.

281 As per the deal he made with Titan Sports, Stu Hart was effectively retired from wrestling. However, once the WWF pulled out of western Canada, the Hart Family was allowed to restart the Stampede promotion, and they did. *Wrestling Observer Newsletter*, 1985, #6, #8, #11, and #12.

282 The ratings for *Saturday Night's Main Event* were called "a bit surprising." *Palm Beach Post*, May 28, 1985, p. 42.

283 *Akron Beacon Journal*, October 4, 1985, p. 39.

284 *Allentown Morning Call*, October 5, 1985, p. 93.

285 By April 1986, Titan had 40 licensed toys and other products. *Financial Post*, April 5, 1986, p. 13.

286 *Biddeford Journal Tribune*, February 12, 1985, and *Financial Post*, April 5, 1986, p. 13.

287 The Wrestling Classic event was part of a campaign known as "Wrestlevision," and Titan originally planned for four additional pay-per-view programs through the summer of 1986. But the "Classic" didn't live up to financial expectations, and the other events were canceled. PPV sales were anywhere from 43,000 to 60,000. *Wrestling Observer Newsletter*, December 30, 1985, p. 3. The second Wrestlevision offering was slated to be held in Bloomington, Minnesota, in January 1986.

288 *Broadcasting Magazine*, January 20, 1986, p. 27.

289 *The Tennessean*, January 20, 1986, p. 29.

290 *Broadcasting Magazine*, January 20, 1986, p. 27.

291 *Financial Post*, April 5, 1986, p. 13.

292 Ibid.

293 *New Orleans Times-Picayune*, August 27, 1985, p. 63.

294 *Alexandria Town Talk*, October 9, 1985, p. 5.

295 *Wrestling Observer Newsletter*, April 28, 1986, p. 1-4.

296 An autopsy revealed that Hernandez died of an acute cocaine overdose. *Wrestling Observer Newsletter*, February 24, 1986, p. 1.

297 *Wrestling Observer Newsletter*, 1985, #7, p. 8 and March 3, 1986, p. 1. WCCW has also been listed as WCWA (World Class Wrestling Association) following Adkisson's split from the NWA.

298 It was believed that many of the departures had to do with Adkisson not giving guaranteed contracts and payoffs like other promoters were doing at the time. *Wrestling Observer Newsletter*, April 28, 1986, p. 2. Subsequently, David Manning became the booker in Dallas. Mantell became the booker for Watts. *The Cowboy and the Cross: The Bill Watts Story* by "Cowboy" Bill Watts and Scott Williams (2006), p. 206.

299 Adkisson started his career working for the Ed McLemore group at the Sportatorium in Dallas in January 1953. This indie operation was at odds with the Houston-based booking outfit for the NWA (Morris Sigel).

300 *Wrestling Observer Newsletter*, August 10, 1986, p. 1.

301 The cases were *Southwest Sports, Inc. v. Mid-South Sports, Inc.*, Dallas County District Court, July 25, 1986, and *Southwest Sports, Inc. v. Byron Robertson, George Gray, John E. Frenkel, Terry Gordy, Michael Seitz, Dale G. Hey and Melissa Hiatt*, Dallas County District Court, July 25, 1986.

302 There were probably a number of reasons for their falling-out. But it was noted that Crockett was disappointed by the turnout for the Crockett Tag Tournament at the Superdome earlier in 1986 and blamed Watts for failing to promote the event. *The Cowboy and the Cross: The Bill Watts Story* by "Cowboy" Bill Watts and Scott Williams (2006), p. 207.

303 In 1986, the Memphis TV show had a CWA logo in the background, and a graphic of "Championship Wrestling" opened the program. Ron Fuller's Southeast promotion was now using the Continental name.

304 *Wrestling Observer Newsletter*, 1985, #9, #10. AWA world champion Rick Martel was supposed to be on the show as well. Bad weather stifled the crowd numbers. This show was syndicated live into to the Dallas area on the same night as a big World Class show in Fort Worth.

CHAPTER 16

305 *Minneapolis CityBusiness*, September 10, 1986, p. 17.

306 Gagne wanted Prince to sing the national anthem. Jennings cost approximately $85,000 for his performance. *Minneapolis Star Tribune*, April 20, 1986, p. 1C, 16C. Melanie Rosales and the TC Jammers also performed on the show.

307 Ibid and *Minneapolis Star Tribune*, April 21, 1986, p. 1A, 5A.

308 *Minneapolis CityBusiness*, September 10, 1986, p. 17.

309 The WWF debuted on CKND-TV in Winnipeg on Saturday, February 15, 1986, at 6:00 p.m. on channels 9 and 12.

310 For years, the AWA promoted monthly shows at Boylan Catholic High School in Rockford. They later regained TV in the city on WQRF-39. The WWF made its debut in Rockford on February 13, 1986.

311 *Chicago Sun-Times*, June 17, 1986.

312 *Wrestling Observer Newsletter*, July 14, 1986, p. 2.

313 *Newport News Daily Press*, October 12, 1986, p. E7.

314 In his autobiography, Race wrote about his loss of more than $500,000 and noted that it was for the Kansas City territory. It is not clear if this amount includes both the Central States (Heart of America Sports Attractions Inc.) and St. Louis (St. Louis Wrestling Club) businesses, or if Race had sold his stake in St. Louis separately. Nevertheless, Race got out of both promotions at about the same time. *King of the Ring: The Harley Race Story* by Harley Race and Gerry Tritz (2004).

315 Geigel was elected to the NWA presidency in August 1985 during the annual convention in Las Vegas. Many online sources incorrectly claim that Crockett was elected president. Geigel was reelected president at the September 1986 convention, also in Vegas.

316 It is believed that Crockett and Geigel split gates evenly in the Central States territory, only after JCP first received a 10 percent booking fee off the top for arranging the talent.

317 *Chicago Tribune*, July 10, 1986, p. E-12.

318 Prior to a six-man tag team match involving Flair, Blanchard, and Arn Anderson, Anderson said they were like the "four horsemen of the apocalypse." The tag stuck and built among fans, and they went with it.

319 *Pittsburgh Press*, July 23, 1986, p. C5.

320 Crockett's *Worldwide Wrestling* was on channel 56 in the L.A. market on Sunday mornings at 11:00. The crowd was estimated at 8,500 to 10,000. *Wrestling Observer Newsletter*, October 27, 1986, p. 8.

321 To promote the venture into Bloomington, JCP had acquired a TV spot on KXLI-41 out of St. Cloud at 10:30 p.m., Sunday nights. This wasn't an optimal station or time. However, beginning on Saturday, October 4, 1986, JCP was featured on KTMA-23 in the Twin Cities at 1:00 p.m. *Minneapolis Star Tribune*, September 28, 1986, p. TV-39.

322 The last cooperative JCP–AWA event took place on June 27, 1986, when Flair appeared in Salt Lake City for AWA's local WrestleRock. Crockett and Gagne butted heads during a spring 1986 meeting where plans to run a Great American Bash show in St. Louis on July 19 were discussed. The parties, which included Bob Geigel and Harley Race, couldn't come to an agreement, and the event was never held.

323 *Chicago Tribune*, September 12, 1986.

324 This information was cited as having originated in the sheet *Wrestling Forum*, by Jon Gallagher. *Wrestling Observer Newsletter*, October 13, 1986, p. 3.

325 *The Cowboy and the Cross: The Bill Watts Story* by "Cowboy" Bill Watts and Scott Williams (2006), p. 223-224.

326 *Paris News*, August 23, 1986, p. 9.

327 *Wrestling Observer Newsletter*, September 2, 1986, p. 1.

328 *Wrestling Observer Newsletter*, April 28, 1986, p. 10.

329 *Honolulu Star-Bulletin*, November 11, 1988, p. 3.

330 *Honolulu Advertiser*, November 28, 1989, p. 39.

331 *Honolulu Star-Bulletin*, July 7, 1986, p. 17.

CHAPTER 17

332 *Globe and Mail*, August 16, 1986, p. C1.

333 *Sports Illustrated*, March 25, 1991. Before McMahon coined the term "sports enter-tainment," he described the WWF as follows: "Pro wrestling is not a sport like the NFL, and it's not theater like Broadway. We can say what it's not, but it's hard to say what it is." *Los Angeles Times*, November 25, 1984, p. S3.

334 *Eau Claire Leader-Telegram*, July 24, 1985, p. B1. Thirty-second commercials went up to $35,000 in 1988. *Channels* magazine, January 1989.

335 *Television/Radio Age*, November 9, 1987, p. 73.

336 *Wrestling Observer Newsletter*, 1985, #11, 1985, p. 8. It was believed that Andre the Giant didn't sign a contract with the WWF at that time.

337 There were actually three different lawsuits between LeBell and McMahon: *Mike LeBell v. Vincent K. McMahon*, Superior Court of California for the County of Los Angeles; *Titan Sports, Inc. v. Mike LeBell*, U.S. District Court for the Central District of California; and *Michael LeBell v. Vincent Kennedy McMahon, Titan Sports, Inc., Capital Wrestling Corporation, and Does 1 to 20, inclusive*, Superior Court of California for the County of Los Angeles.

338 Deposition of Michael LeBell, June 12, 1985, *Titan Sports, Inc., A Massachusetts Corporation v. Mike LeBell*, Case No. CV-85-0282-RMT, United States District Court for the Central District of California.

339 After developing phlebitis, Cannon sold his stake in the Detroit partnership around April 1986. *Windsor Star*, March 28, 1987, p. B1. He sued McMahon for $500,000, filed on March 24, 1987, only a few days before WrestleMania III, held in suburban Detroit. *Cannon Sports, Inc. v. Titan Sports, Inc.*, U.S District Court for the Eastern District of Michigan (Detroit), Case No. 2:87-CV-71100-LPZ. This case was dis-missed with prejudice on May 26, 1988.

340 Gate reports are cited as C$1.1 or $1.2 million. The WWF drew $2 million in gates in one week. *Wrestling Observer Newsletter*, September 9, 1986, p. 3–4.

341 An article stated that Titan Sports had 70 full-time employees on its payroll and "65 wrestlers." *Toronto Star*, August 22, 1986, p. D20.

342 *Championship Wrestling* evolved into the new *Superstars of Wrestling* program and held its last Poughkeepsie TV taping on August 5, 1986. *All-Star Wrestling* became *Wrestling Challenge* and staged its final Brantford TV taping on July 28, 1986.

343 McMahon would stage two TV tapings on consecutive days, the first (*Superstars of Wrestling*) in one location and the second (*Wrestling Challenge*) in another.

344 *Wrestling Observer Newsletter*, August 3, 1987, p. 1.

345 *Asbury Park Press*, May 28, 1987, p. 5.

346 *Asbury Park Press*, May 30, 1987, p. D8. In a follow-up story, the Sheik was quoted as saying, "I usually do not travel with my enemies. I do not like [Duggan]. I do not like his family. I think he probably did it on purpose." A spokesman for the WWF said he was surprised by the fact they were traveling together, and it was explained

that officials went out of their way to put the wrestlers on different flights "to prevent violence." *Asbury Park Press*, June 2, 1987, p. 4.

347 *The Cowboy and the Cross: The Bill Watts Story* by "Cowboy" Bill Watts and Scott Williams (2006), p. 224.

348 *The Cowboy and the Cross: The Bill Watts Story* by "Cowboy" Bill Watts and Scott Williams (2006), p. 227. The deal was reportedly negotiated, and a deal was in place by April 9.

349 *Charlotte Observer*, May 6, 1987, p. 1E.

350 *Wrestling Observer Newsletter*, January 5, 1987, p. 3–4.

351 Ibid.

352 *Wrestling Observer Newsletter*, February 16, 1987, p. 5.

353 JCP wasn't effectively "buying" the Florida territory with the deal. It was a business arrangement that had Crockett running the day-to-day operations and splitting income with the owners of the local office.

CHAPTER 18

354 *Minneapolis CityBusiness*, September 10, 1986, p. 47.

355 *Chicago Sun-Times*, October 3, 1986, p. 90.

356 *Minneapolis CityBusiness*, September 10, 1986, p. 47.

357 *Channels* magazine, January 1989, p. 38–41. According to another interview, Gagne explained, "The ancillary sales have been tremendous. We have a contract with Remco Toys — we started off with six dolls, now we have more than 30. It's doing $10 million to $15 million in sales [of which AWA receives a percentage]." *Minneapolis CityBusiness*, September 10, 1986, p. 47.

358 *Wrestling Observer Newsletter*, March 3, 1986, p. 6, May 12, 1986, p. 10, June 28, 1986, p. 1.

359 *Minneapolis Star Tribune*, March 1, 1987, p. C3.

360 *Wrestling Observer Newsletter*, June 15, 1987, p. 2–3.

361 Idol was managed by Paul E. Dangerly (Paul Heyman). As part of the stipulations, if Idol has been defeated, fans at the Coliseum would've gotten their tickets refunded.

362 Rich reportedly hid underneath the ring for six hours before emerging and attacking Lawler, leading to Idol's victory.

363 Dave Meltzer mentioned the Jarrett–Gagne negotiations as having broken off in November 1987. *Wrestling Observer Newsletter*, November 16, 1987, p. 3. Jarrett posted about his negotiations with Gagne on the Wrestling Classics Message Board on June 29 and July 1, 2002. He also wrote about negotiating with Gagne in his autobiography, *The Best of Times* by Jerry Jarrett with Mark James (2011) p. 227–230.

364 *Grapevine Sun*, December 21, 1986, p. 31.

365 *Wrestling Observer Newsletter*, June 29, 1987, p. 1.

366 *D Magazine*, May 1987.

367 The debut of the revamped show began the weekend of June 6, 1987. Mark

Lowrance replaced Bill Mercer as commentator on the World Class syndicated program. Mercer joined Ken Mantell's Wild West promotion.

368 *D Magazine*, February 1988.

369 *Longview News-Journal*, December 6, 1987, p. 52.

370 Mantell reportedly owned 40 percent of the stock in the Dallas promotion, whereas Kevin and Kerry each had 30. wccwmemories.blogspot.com. Another report stated Kerry and Kevin owned a majority interest in the company, whereas Mantell had 30 percent. *Wrestling Observer Newsletter*, February 15, 1988, p. 6. Mantell, in recent months, had been operating Wild West Wrestling based out of Krum, Texas, and his promotion was gaining stature as an independent group. The Wild West group was absorbed by World Class in 1988.

371 *Portland Oregonian*, July 19, 1987, p. D13.

CHAPTER 19

372 For high-end stations in a top five market, JCP was willing to pay upwards of $8,000 per week for TV time.

373 *Channels* magazine, January 1989.

374 JCP's offices were at 421 Briarbend Drive in Charlotte.

375 According to one source, the Wrestling Network officially debuted on July 1, 1987. *Television/Radio Age*, June 22, 1987, p 63–64.

376 The Dallas office was located at 5001 Spring Valley Road, #920, Dallas, Texas.

377 JCP was selling advertising via barter. It would keep five minutes per show and sell the remaining seven to 10 minutes. Time Sales International was represented by Rick Pack, and the latter reportedly signed an agreement with Crockett on April 8, 1987. Time Sales, which was operated out of Greenwich, Connecticut, was later bought by the Action Media Group. On September 22, 1988, the Wrestling Network became an official federal trademark of the Action Media Group.

378 *Television/Radio Age*, November 23, 1987, p. 20.

379 *Orlando Sentinel*, October 2, 1987, p. 41.

380 Country music was still a part of the tour, with David Allen Coe at the Atlanta show on July 4. That same night, Michael Hayes also delivered a musical performance.

381 It has been reported that Animal and Hawk received $500,000 each and manager Paul Ellering got $275,000.

382 JCP promoted Detroit on the strength of its UWF TV show on WXYZ-7, which was telecast at 12:30 p.m. on Saturday, as well as its WTBS program.

383 *Detroit Free Press*, September 24, 1987, p. 17.

384 At first, Crockett tried to win over cable systems by offering to run Starrcade live at 5:00 p.m. to finish before the Survivor Series started, allowing operators to provide both events to viewers. But Vince McMahon moved his start time from 8:00 to 7:30 to squeeze the life out of that idea. In turn, Crockett decided to keep the 5:00 start

time for his live show, originating from Chicago (4:00 p.m. CST), and run a tape-delayed telecast at closed-circuit venues up and down the East Coast starting at 8:00.

385 The Wrestling Network achieved number four amongst syndicated TV packages during the summer of 1987 but then fell out of the top 15 by early November. The WWF was number three behind *Jeopardy!* and *Wheel of Fortune.*

386 The PPV buy-rate was reportedly 7.0. Some sources claim the Survivor Series achieved around 500,000 buys.

387 Tickets for the CCTV presentations of Starrcade ranged from $10 to $12. A report in the *Philadelphia Daily News* claimed that 65 cities were a part of the CCTV "network." The event was offered at the Philadelphia Civic Center on a 15-by-20-foot screen. *Philadelphia Daily News*, November 20, 1987, p. 81. Starrcade brought in $1.3 million. *Wrestling Observer Newsletter*, January 4, 1988, p. 4.

388 Jim Crockett and Dusty Rhodes reportedly worked out of the Dallas office. Jim Barnett, a former member of the NWA and a big influence on the rise of the WWF, joined JCP and also worked out of the Dallas office in 1987.

389 Interestingly, *UWF Wrestling/Universal Wrestling Federation* and *Power Pro Wrestling* remained in TV guide lineups throughout 1988. The final UWF TV edition was on December 26, 1987.

390 Valiant played baseball at Fishburne Military Academy in Virginia with Vince McMahon Jr. *Pittsburgh Post Gazette*, June 9, 1988, p. 19.

391 *Minneapolis CityBusiness*, September 10, 1986, p. 17.

392 *Wrestling Observer Newsletter*, February 22, 1988, p. 2.

393 RJS Marketing was run by Robert "Bob" Syers out of offices in Ossining, New York. *Broadcasting Magazine*, April 25, 1988, p. 58D. Syers originally worked for Syndicast Services and arranged to keep the AWA syndication package when he formed his own company. *Swimming with Piranhas: Surviving the Politics of Professional Wrestling* by Howard T. Brody (2009) p. 104.

394 *Wrestling Observer Newsletter*, May 16, 1988, p. 2.

395 *D Magazine*, February 1988.

396 *Brody: The Triumph and Tragedy of Wrestling's Rebel* by Larry Matysik and Barbara Goodish (2007).

397 *Wrestling Observer Newsletter*, June 27, 1988, p. 5.

398 It was also mentioned that some "NWA" wrestlers (Midnight Express, Fantastics) were going to be in Oregon "this coming week" for shows in Medford and other locations.

399 Owen and JCP held two other joint promotions in 1989, one on January 11 in Seattle, and the other on January 12 in Portland.

400 *Salem Statesman Journal*, November 23, 1988, p. 9.

401 *Portland Oregonian*, November 24, 1988, p. E2.

402 *Portland Oregonian*, December 3, 1991, p. C1.

403 *Portland Oregonian*, June 4, 1992, p. D3.

404 *Salem Statesman Journal*, December 2, 1988, p. 13.

405 *Kansas City Star*, January 2, 2001, p. A1.

406 Jarrett described the situation with World Class in his autobiography, *The Best of Times* by Jerry Jarrett with Mark James (2011), p. 215–223. Additional details in *Wrestling Observer Newsletter*, November 14, 1988, p. 1.

407 *Wrestling Observer Newsletter*, February 29, 1988, p. 3.

408 *Wrestling Observer Newsletter*, February 8, 1988, p. 1.

409 The Bash was distributed by Request Television, Home Premiere Television, and Turner Network Sales. *Broadcasting Magazine*, April 25, 1988, p. 75.

410 Ibid. Also see *Wrestling Observer Newsletter*, February 29, 1988, p. 7. Regarding the sale of video cassette tapes, see *Television/Radio Age*, May 25, 1987, p. 62.

411 *Charlotte Observer*, May 25, 1988, p. 1A.

412 *Wrestling Observer Newsletter*, April 15, 1985, p. 25, and December 30, 1985, p. 4.

413 *Atlanta Journal-Constitution*, November 3, 1988, p. D2. Also *Broadcasting Magazine*, November 14, 1988, p. 60.

414 *Atlanta Journal-Constitution*, November 3, 1988, p. D2.

415 *Charlotte Observer*, November 3, 1988, p. 1B.

416 *Los Angeles Times*, June 7, 1985.

417 *Financial Post*, April 5, 1986, p. 13.

418 Interview conducted on July 20, 1998, by wrestling historian Greg Oliver for his *Slam! Wrestling* website. http://slam.canoe.com/SlamWrestlingArchive/jul20_santana.html.

419 *New Orleans Times-Picayune*, June 4, 1985, p. D-8.

420 *Portland Oregonian*, October 8, 1985, p. D9.

421 *Channels* magazine, January 1989, p. 39.

422 *Channels* magazine, January 1989, p. 40.

423 Unnamed, undated article, *Wrestling Observer Newsletter*, April 15, 1985, p. 4.

424 *Indianapolis Star*, September 26, 1985, p. 52.

425 *Playboy*, February 2001, p. 64.

426 *Sports Illustrated*, March 25, 1991.

TIM HORNBAKER is the author of eight nonfiction books, including *National Wrestling Alliance: The Untold Story of the Monopoly that Strangled Pro Wrestling* and *Capitol Revolution: The Rise of the McMahon Wrestling Empire*. He lives in Tamarac, Florida, with his wife, Jodi.